NEW YORK'S
JEWISH
JEWS

The Modern Jewish Experience

Paula Hyman and Deborah Dash Moore, *Editors*

NEW YORK'S JEWISH JEWS;

THE ORTHODOX COMMUNITY IN THE INTERWAR YEARS.

Jenna Weissman Joselit

INDIANA UNIVERSITY PRESS
BLOOMINGTON AND INDIANAPOLIS

Manufactured in the United States of America

Library of Congress Cataloging-in-Publication Data

Joselit, Jenna Weissman.
New York's Jewish Jews : The orthodox community in the interwar years
Jenna Weissman Joselit.
p. cm. — (The Modern Jewish experience)
Bibliography: p.
Includes index.
ISBN 0-253-33151-X. — ISBN —0-253-20554-9 (pbk.)
1. Orthodox Judaism—New York (N.Y.) 2. Jews—New York (N.Y.)— Cultural as-
similation. 3. Rabbis—New York (N.Y.)—Office. 4. Women, Jewish—New York
(N.Y.)—Religious life. I. Title. II. Series: Modern Jewish experience
(Bloomington, Ind.)
BM225.N49J67 1990   89-45197
296.8'32'09747109041—dc20   CIP

1 2 3 4 5 94 93 92 91 90

For M & D

The Jews are probably the only people in the world to whom it has ever been proposed that their historic destiny is to be nice. This singular concept has played such an important role in recent Jewish history that it almost characterizes an entire epoch.

—MAURICE SAMUEL, *Jews on Approval* (1932)

Contents

Illustrations precede Chapter 4.

Acknowledgments

A collaborative effort in the best sense of the word, this book would have not been written were it not for the participation of a great number of people. The interest and encouragement of the entire Lookstein family—Mrs. Gertrude Lookstein, Rabbi Haskel Lookstein, and Professor Nathalie L. Friedman—were invaluable, as was the support of the Wurzweiler Foundation, whose past president, Rabbi Max Gruenewald, provided me with the funds necessary to conduct extensive archival research.

Those who shared their memories with me, whether in the context of formal, structured interviews or at other, more informal moments helped considerably to give life to the past. Their ranks included: Edith and Nash Aussenberg, Mrs. Estelle Baumgarten, Rabbi Karpol Bender, Rabbi Jack Bieler, Mr. Hyman Bucher, Professor Bathia Churgin, Nehama and Raphael Courland, Gertrude Herlands Engelberg, and Rabbi Louis Engelberg, Mr. Bernard Fischman, Isaac B. Friedman, Israel Friedman, Judith Gottesman Friedman, Professor Nathalie L. Friedman, Mrs. Elizabeth Isaacs Gilbert, Mrs. Evelyn Greenberg, Rachel Neumark Herlands, Irma and Clarence Horwitz, Mrs. Lillian Jacobs, Rabbi Leo Jung, Alfred Kahn, Professor Gilbert Kahn, Mrs. Samuel Kramer, Mrs. Lillian Leifert, Belda and Marcel Lindenbaum, Mrs. Gertrude Lookstein, Rabbi Haskel Lookstein, Professor Naomi Churgin Miller, Rabbi Moshe Morduchowitz, Debby and Melvin Neumark, Dr. Jeanne Rafsky, Rabbi Shlomo Riskin, Mrs. Selma Roeder, Mr. and Mrs. Julius Sax, Rabbi Herschel Schacter, Rabbi Jacob J. Schacter, Mr. Nathan Salzman, Dr. Marvin Schick, Mrs. Sylvia Shatzman, Rabbi Shubert and Iris Spiro, Mr. Maurice Spanbock, Mrs. Ami Texon, and Mrs. Sadie Wohl.

I have benefited over the years from conversations with my colleagues Jeffrey Gurock, Samuel Heilman, William Helmreich, Barbara Kirshenblatt-Gimblett, Jack Kugelmass, Deborah Dash Moore, and Jonathan Sarna and with my students in YIVO's Max Weinreich Center for Advanced Jewish Studies.

The difficulties in searching for primary materials were eased considerably by the efforts of many individuals. Ruth Abram of the Lower East Side Historic Conservancy and Roberta Gratz of the Eldridge Street Synagogue Restoration Project made available the minutes of the Eldridge Street Synagogue, while Mrs.

Sylvia Kramer graciously lent me a collection of *Jewish Center Bulletins* assembled over a forty-year period by her late husband, Mr. Samuel Kramer; Rabbi Moshe Morduchowitz of the West Side Institutional Synagogue placed at my disposal a number of bound back issues of that synagogue's weekly bulletins and related ephemera. Dr. Noam Shudofsky, administrator of the Ramaz School, was unfailingly helpful in my search for documentary material as was Mr. Robert Leifert, executive director of Congregation Kehilath Jeshurun, who literally unlocked doors to that synagogue's past. Florence Cohen and Ruth Lemberger, of Congregation Kehilath Jeshurun and the Ramaz School respectively, were also quite generous with their time and resources. Mr. Martin Schwarzschild, immediate past president of the Jewish Center, graciously provided me with extant archival material, and Rabbi Jacob J. Schacter, the Center's rabbi, patiently answered my often lengthy questions. Shulamith Berger shared the results of her work on ethnic advertising, while Professor Elmer Offenbacher provided me with the tape of a conversation he had recorded between himself and Rabbi Joseph Lookstein. Professor Mayer Rabinowitz, librarian of the Jewish Theological Seminary, graciously permitted me to quote copiously from Mordecai M. Kaplan's unpublished diaries. Dina Abramowicz and Zachary Baker of the YIVO Library and Marek Web, Fruma Mohrer, and Daniel Soyer of the YIVO Archives facilitated my search through YIVO's treasury of published and unpublished materials. Rabbi Moshe Kolodney of the Agudath Israel Archives opened the files of the Harry Fischel Collection, while the librarians of the Jewish Division of the New York Public Library assisted me in my quest for published matter.

Throughout the numerous years in which this study came into being, my friends—chief among them, my husband—not only listened uncomplainingly as I spun my theories but often, unknowingly, influenced my thinking. For being such a receptive (if captive) audience, I warmly thank them. Finally, this book is dedicated to my parents, Alice and Irving Weissman, whose integrity, fierce intelligence, and passionately held convictions have inspired me more than I can fully say.

Introduction

"Often superaffluent, no longer insecure in the New World or uncertain about their American identity, Orthodox Jews have been freed by secular success to assert triumphantly their Jewish selfhood," noted journalist Natalie Gittelson in the *New York Times Magazine* in 1984, as she documented the resurgence of Orthodox Judaism among contemporary American Jews. In discussing the "rediscovery of Orthodoxy," a phenomenon charted at some length by several periodicals during the 1980s, Gittelson appeared to be somewhat confounded, perhaps even bemused, by the conjunction of latter-day affluence with hoary and antiquated religious practice.[1] Gittelson and her contemporaries were by no means the first to be surprised by the confluence of these two factors. More than fifty years earlier, a great deal of hoopla was made over New York's then-emerging Orthodox population, which, paying fealty to both tradition and modernity, sought to create an indigenously American brand of Orthodoxy. Struck by the amiable coexistence of traditional religious practices with middle-class values, the American public found the notion of a cultured and affluent Orthodoxy as confusing then as they seem to do now.

Increasingly well-to-do and acculturated, the members of this community were determined to temper, and in the process to recast, the prevailing public association of Orthodoxy with backward, unemancipated, and un-Western behavior. Orthodox Judaism "is not synonymous with the unsavoriness of Ghetto Judaism," they insisted, as they sought instead to stress its inherent compatibility with American middle-class social norms.[2] "A synthesis of modern occidental culture and etiquette with ancient Jewish learning and piety," this Americanized Orthodoxy expressed, in religious and behavioral terms, the embourgeoisement of the Eastern European immigrant community.[3]

With its emphasis on "reverence, dignity, cleanliness and harmony,"[4] a determinedly modern Orthodoxy—or what its adherents liked to think of as a "cultivated" or "aesthetic" Orthodoxy—provided a viable and reassuring ritual alternative to both Reform and Conservative Judaism, whose efforts at redefining Jewish ritual appeared suspect to those of a more traditional cast. In a somewhat striking and unusual analogy, Rabbi Leo Jung, one of the more articulate champions of a westernized Orthodoxy, sought to make a case for the inherent viability and adaptability of Orthodoxy by likening the adherents of Conservative Judaism to misguided suffragettes. "Just as the sufragettes [*sic*] erred in taste no less than in judgement as they essayed to become exactly like men, without an appreciation of the fact that difference does not imply inferiority," he declared, "so did the new group of American Jews, who now go by the name of conservative, fail to realize that they could have achieved on the basis of orthodox Judaism that combination of loyalty to *Din Torah* [Jewish law] with modernity of method. . . ."[5]

An improved and vigorously modern Orthodoxy, then, was the answer, not Conservative Judaism and certainly not Reform. Like those movements, the Orthodoxy of the interwar era was fiercely patriotic, lay dominated, oriented toward the here and now, and ethnocentrically American. Where it differed from the other branches was in its approach to the past. Conservators of a traditional religious heritage, the Orthodox sought not so much to remove themselves from the weight of the past as to make it more current, to have it conform to modern-day standards. Once adapted and westernized, "Orthodoxy," insisted one influential synagogue president, "can meet the needs of the day and can meet them even more effectively than the other groupings in Jewish life."[6] The program, if one can call it that, of the cultivated Orthodox entailed no major alterations in liturgy or ritual behavior, nor, for that matter, did it signal any fundamental shifts in religious orientation. What America's Orthodox sought to create was a "healthy Judaism walking hand in hand with a sound Americanism."[7] The task of this volume is to explore just what they meant by that notion.

The children of Eastern European immigrants or, in many instances, immigrants themselves, New York's Orthodox worked hard at building an American Orthodoxy and took the lead in defining its behavioral, cultural, and institutional parameters. With its density of affluent Jews and ease of exposure to Western influences, New York City became the laboratory in which this new American form of religious self-expression was created. Whereas their parents might have been Jews "of the unconscious type," whose piety and religiosity were intimately bound up with the larger cultural ambience of Eastern European Jewish life—a phenomenon Leo Baeck once referred to as "milieufrömmigkeit"—this generation made a deliberate, careful choice in remaining faithful to and promoting Orthodoxy.[8] Because they were as much a cultural generation as a chronological one, their efforts spanned several decades: beginning somewhat tentatively in the 1870s and taking root gradually over the next two decades, an Americanized Orthodoxy came proudly and self-assertively into its own during the 1920s and 1930s.

To be sure, not all of those identified with Orthodoxy in the New World were as welcoming of modernity as the members of New York's Orthodox community. In urban areas west of the Mississippi, not only were there fewer Orthodox Jews, but they remained far more conservative, hesitant in their embrace of modernity. Traveling about the country on a 1929 lecture tour, Mordecai M. Kaplan observed that outside of New York, Orthodox Jews "have no conception whatever of the Jewish problem as one of adjustment . . . Their psychology is entirely that of the small town in the Jewish Pale of twenty-five years ago."[9] Even within the Empire City itself, there were those who steadfastly refused to take "altered circumstances into consideration" and sought to transplant the Eastern European milieu and its key religious institutions into the concrete of New York.[10] Centered in the Agudat ha-Rabbanim, an association of European-trained or "old ghetto type" rabbis, this community attempted to define American Orthodox behavior in European terms. Less sophisticated and less well-off economically, members of this community were rather strong in their collective denunciation of modernization, be it in the form of an English-language sermon or that of coeducation. And yet, the fierceness of their rhetoric lay in inverse relation to their actual strength: in New York they came, increasingly, to be overshadowed, at both the grass-roots and institutional levels, by those more sympathetic to modernity. Parting company with the Agudat ha-Rabbanim by World War I, most of those within the Orthodox camp did not reject Americanization out of hand but sought instead to moderate its influence. "We seek," one such Jew explained, "to deal effectively and happily with the great task of Americanization . . . in such a way that [it] will not mean the alienation from the principles and practices of traditional Judaism."[11]

This book attempts to retrieve the history of those happily Americanizing Orthodox Jews, whose past has been obscured by the rapidly changing nature of American Jewry in the postwar era, and to represent the history of that community as its constituents, the Orthodox by conviction, represented themselves.[12] Throughout, I have tried to be attentive to the subtleties of this experience, invoking the voice, sensibility, and observations of its participants time and again to document and analyze the emergence of what was, in the final analysis, a brand new cultural invention. Recreating selected aspects of New York Orthodox life between 1880 and World War II, this study does not pretend to be comprehensive or all-inclusive; rather than duplicate the efforts of others, I have omitted such topics as the rise of Yeshiva University, the nature of Orthodox rescue efforts during the Holocaust, and the history of the Breuer community, which have been ably treated elsewhere.[13] Rather, the book focuses on what I take to be the representative institutions of New York Orthodoxy—the rabbinate, the synagogue, the modern day school—and certain key issues in the understanding and maintenance of tradition to demonstrate the process by which a self-consciously modern and American Orthodoxy came into being.

The reconstruction of this community's past is made difficult by the absence of a body of literature on Orthodoxy's tenure in the New World. Until recently, America's Orthodox Jews figured little in the historiography of American Jewish religious behavior; it has only been within the last decade that the phenomenon of American Orthodoxy has been seen on its own terms and not as a foil against which to study the evolution of, say, Conservative Judaism or Reconstructionism.[14] In part, the Orthodox themselves created this situation, for when it came to public Jewish affairs they kept a relatively low profile. Orthodox leaders during the interwar years liked to boast that theirs was the largest American Jewish denomination: writing in the *Jewish Forum*, Mizrachi educator Meyer Waxman insisted that, with more than 2500 congregations, the Orthodox comprised "the largest group in American Jewry. . . ."[15] More wishful thinking, a statistical sleight of hand, than a true measure of organizational strength, these numbers masked the fact that the Orthodox kept very much to themselves; as a result, their impact on larger, non-Orthodox trends within the Jewish community remained virtually nil. "You will invariably find that the orthodox Rabbi is, as a rule, reserved for invocations and benedictions and no more," a frustrated Rabbi Joseph Lookstein complained to an audience of his fellow Orthodox rabbis, urging them to take more of an active, participatory role in Jewish communal affairs.[16] Despite his admonition, when it came to civic Jewish affairs, "Orthodoxy," as another clergyman would have it, took "a back seat."[17]

No wonder, then, that students of American Judaism, writing in the years following American Jewry's Tercentenary, were themselves either unfamiliar with or unsympathetic to America's Orthodox, and consigned them to the ghetto. Constructing a sociological model according to which "acculturation and social and economic mobility went hand in hand with the flight from Orthodoxy," some linked Orthodox behavior to the poor and the unacculturated, locking the phenomenon within the context of the immigrant experience.[18] The post–World War II influx of ultra-Orthodox, European, Yiddish-speaking Jews may well have reinforced the identification of Orthodoxy with the "stigma of the ghetto," attesting to the liveliness of that equation.[19] Still other scholars, whose interests lay in exploring the discontinuities rather than the continuities between the New World and the Old, tended to pay little, if any, attention to the efforts of those who persisted in traditional religious behavior. "The fact is," observed historian Benny Kraut in a recent review essay of Nathan Glazer's seminal *American Judaism*, "that the theme of the continuity of religious tradition and some demonstrable ethnic-religious stability just does not fit well in a work that seeks to depict changing or fluctuating Jewish self-perception. . . ."[20] And yet, much to the considerable surprise of those who believed, for one reason or another, that Orthodoxy was destined to wither away with growing acculturation, the denomination, in the words of Marshall Sklare, has "defied the laws of religious gravity."[21]

In some respects, the contemporary resurgence of Orthodoxy to which Sklare alludes is in fact startling, especially to those who had (prematurely) predicted its imminent demise. But when viewed historically, its emergence should seem neither surprising nor unnatural: the apparent "rediscovery of Orthodoxy" could not have taken place had it not been for the efforts of an earlier generation of American Orthodox. Their creation of a complex institutional and religious culture with a network of modernized synagogues and a "galaxy" of progressive Jewish day-schools adumbrated, by several decades, that of today's tightly knit Orthodox communities. Putting it differently, today's "renaissance" of Orthodoxy could not possibly have occurred had not the interwar Orthodox laid the groundwork for and developed the basic infrastructure of a viable and socially acceptable American Orthodoxy.

This volume opens with a portrait of New York's Orthodox Jewry between the wars and continues with an analysis of the modernization of two of that community's most pivotal institutions: the synagogue and the rabbinate. Looking at changes in the architecture, prayer service, and functions of the newly modernized synagogue and, in the chapter that follows, tracing the evolution of an independent American Orthodox rabbinate, this segment of the book documents the extent to which Orthodoxy's core institutions were transformed and Americanized. This analysis, in turn, is succeeded by an examination of the process by which Orthodox women became increasingly more integrated into that community's social structure even as they questioned some of their own gender-related ritual obligations such as kashruth. The chapter that follows traces the efflorescence of the Jewish day-school movement, showing how New York's Orthodox turned from the synagogue to the school in their ongoing efforts to cultivate a distinctive American Orthodoxy. The book concludes with a brief postscript that brings up to date the story of Orthodoxy's encounter with modernity. While each chapter can be taken on its own as a kind of case study of a representative New York Orthodox institution, the book as a whole seeks to demonstrate how Orthodox Jews sought to create their own American Jewish religious culture, one squarely rooted in both the New World and the Old. For, as one Orthodox publication explained: "America, as it supplies its own food and manufacturers, must be the maker of its own traditional Judaism."[22]

NEW YORK'S
JEWISH
JEWS

THE "REASONABLE" ORTHODOX

To many New York Orthodox Jews, December 20, 1924, was a "red-letter day," a day on which "Orthodox Jewry was reborn and revitalized in America."[1] On that evening, in the lush setting of the Hotel Astor, over one hundred affluent and Orthodox New York Jews gathered to raise money for Yeshiva College, America's first combination yeshiva and secular undergraduate institution. Expecting to generate perhaps $100,000 in pledges, the invited guests apparently were so moved by the spirit of the occasion that they donated $1 million toward the school's new campus. Not only did the gathering exceed all of that community's previously held fundraising records but, in the words of the event's chairman, "it showed the world the tremendous potentialities of Orthodox Jewry in America. The smiles of skepticism disappeared. American Jewry had been shown what Orthodox Jewry could do. Most significant of all, Orthodox Jewry had shown itself what it could do."[2]

A self-proclaimed watershed in the collective self-esteem of New York's Orthodox community, the Yeshiva dinner underscored the latter's coming of age. That well-heeled, comfortably American Jews could come together for the purpose of endowing so seemingly oxymoronic an institution as a Yeshiva College bespoke their commitment to an indigenous American Orthodoxy. In its wake, the Hotel Astor dinner unleashed a torrent of delighted commentaries on the freshly proven success of New York Orthodoxy. "Orthodoxy has demonstrated the fact that the observance of the Sabbath, fasting on the Day of Atonement and other hardships are not beyond endurance even in our own luxury-craving Jazz age," boasted an Orthodox Harvard professor, while another commentator was moved to relate that "people no longer feel uncomfortable in the presence of mixed crowds of Jews to be designated Orthodox."[3] As public approbation crowned their communal efforts—even the *New York Times* commented on the campaign—New York's Orthodox felt they were poised dramatically on the edge of a major debut: as a wholly American and modern, socially acceptable enterprise.

1

Hyperbole surrounding the event made it seem as if the formation of a Yeshiva College uptown campus was the sole catalyst for the reawakening of this long dormant Orthodoxy. But in the flush of excitement, commentators grandly overstated the case. Actually, the dinner represented the culmination of several decades of an evolving Orthodoxy rather than its commencement. By the time of the Yeshiva College campaign, Orthodox Jews in New York had, over two decades, successfully created their own environments, in which a "cultured" or "reasonable" Orthodoxy flourished. In such middle-class neighborhoods as the Upper West Side, in Borough Park, Harlem, Yorkville, and Arverne, New York's "alrightniks" created a complex institutional and religious culture. With dozens of modernized synagogues, a modern English-speaking rabbinate, and a network of cultural, educational, and philanthropic institutions that included kosher restaurants, day schools, and summer camps, the Orthodox had established a solid infrastructure that expressed their commitment to tradition. A weekly periodical, the *Jewish Forum*, the voice of "cultured orthodoxy," together with the daily *Hebrew Standard*, "America's Leading Jewish Family Paper," represented its cultural persona. With all these institutions in place, there was every reason to feel, as one eyewitness put it, that "Orthodoxy had not been 'in fashion' *until now*."[4]

If the 1920s and 1930s marked the heyday of New York's Orthodox, its antecedents date back to the closing decades of the nineteenth century, when hundreds of thousands of Eastern European Jews migrated to the Empire City. Though estimates of the community's size are hard to come by, there were enough religiously minded immigrants even at that time to warrant the creation of an infrastructure of ritual institutions: synagogues, ritual baths, kosher butchers, and kosher restaurants. Despite dire and dramatically worded predictions of colossal failure—if you come to America, warned one rabbi whose own tenure in the New World was an inglorious one, "nothing will be left for you to do save dressing in black, wrapping yourself in shrouds and rolling from darkness to abyss"—observant Jews sought to take root in the New World and to build, from the ground on up, a flourishing Orthodox community.[5] By 1900, all of the signal institutions of an American Orthodoxy were in place. A small army of religious specialists—rabbis, *magiddim* (preachers), cantors, *mohelim* (ritual circumcisers), ritual slaughterers, *melamdim* (teachers)—catered to an interested clientele, which in turn read and supported two religiously oriented Yiddish dailies, the *Judisches Tageblatt* and the *Morgen Zhurnal*, as well as a galaxy of synagogues. "Neither is Orthodoxy in New York, or in America, for that matter, a recent importation," remarked one newspaper in 1921 on the seventieth anniversary of the Beth Hamidrash Hagadol, New York's oldest Eastern European Orthodox congregation. The age of this Orthodox synagogue and, by implication, the longevity of New York's Orthodox, "will be news to many a Jew who thinks he knows his New York. . . ."[6]

Admittedly, there were those who knew a different New York, whose optimism about the future of an American Orthodoxy was clouded by doubts. Many contemporary observers during the early years of the twentieth century were quick to lament what appeared to be the "disintegration of the Jews," pointing to the marked decline in synagogue attendance and widespread flouting of the Sabbath.[7] "Sabbath hallowing had become the exception," one pious Jew observed in 1898, "Sabbath desecration the rule."[8] Religious conditions were reportedly so bad, what with lax kashruth standards and the erosion of rabbinical authority, that willy-nilly, the observant Jew was "irresistibly swept away from old religious moorings."[9] Inexorably, or so it seemed, complete secularization accompanied Americanization as the New World dealt a "heavy blow" to the maintenance of traditional Jewish institutions and ritual.[10]

And yet, it was a blow from which religiously minded immigrants gradually recovered. Considerably daunted, possibly even frightened, by the degree of religious anomie characteristic of the immigrant experience, a community of Orthodox stalwarts persisted in the affirmation and maintenance of tradition. "It was time," observed one of this group in 1898, "that the world should be given to understand that there was still some vitality to that remnant of Israel which remains faithful. . . ."[11] No wonder, then, that a distinctly American Orthodox denominational consciousness began to emerge during the closing decades of the nineteenth century.[12] At a time when Reform Judaism had taken hold as the prevailing religious expression of America's Jews, an "orthodox" Judaism appeared as a counterweight. Opposition to Reform helped to shape the internal agenda and public self-consciousness of that emerging community, giving it a focus and a passion that it might otherwise have lacked. In fiercely worded broadsides, America's traditional clergy excoriated Reform, "that veritable Amalek of modern times," for its break with tradition and called on the upholders of tradition to remain steadfast in their commitment and to make known their disapproval of the Reformers.[13] Not politely or passively but aggressively were they instructed to "make a manly stand for the vindication of the dignity of the Torah."[14] One late nineteenth-century rabbi and determined Orthodox crusader, Rev. Meldola De Sola, even went so far as to insist that traditionalists not associate with Reformers. Trafficking with them, he wrote in 1887, was as dangerous as "contact with a man smitten with a deadly contagious disease. . . ."[15]

This division of the religious world into two warring factions—the Reform and the Orthodox—was at once a product of and a response to modernity. For one thing, the very notion of "Orthodoxy" and of "Orthodox Jews"—a distinct community with specific behaviors—was itself a statement of modernity, a concession to the changed reality in which the observant Jew, once in the majority, now found himself. "Those who continued to adhere to tradition when its observance ceased to be the universal characteristic of Jewish society," noted historian Jacob Katz, "were both more self-conscious and less self-confident. Their loyalty to tradition was the result of a conscious decision. . . ."[16]

The name of this new denomination within American Judaism reflected its novelty. Now that the observant were no longer synonymous with but had been reduced to a part, a segment, of Jewish society, traditional adherents cast about for an appropriate designation. For a time, the appellation of "Jewish Jews" held sway. The latter, explained Rev. Dr. J. H. Hertz, the first graduate of the Jewish Theological Seminary, who, following his service as rabbi at the Upper East Side's Orach Chaim synagogue became chief rabbi of Great Britain, are "the plain simple people who do not preserve their religion for Sabbaths or Sundays, but who live it every day and every hour. . . . They do not pick out portions of the Torah and say, 'These we like and others we do not.' Their motto is 'The Torah, nothing but the Torah and the whole Torah.' "[17] Adopting such fighting words as its motto, words that seemed consciously to echo the judicial pretestimony pledge ("the whole truth and nothing but the truth . . . "), New York's embryonic Orthodox community threw down the gauntlet of authenticity. The label "Jewish Jews," however, was soon replaced by the more enduring "Orthodox," a term with which its designees were never altogether comfortable. "There is nothing orthodox about the word Orthodox," one rabbi insisted, as he pointed to the Christian context in which the term was first employed.[18] What's more, the term was not a designation that the Orthodox had purposefully chosen but one imposed on them, or as another rabbi would have it, "inflicted" by the non-Orthodox on loyal Jews.[19] "They, of course, never intended that the word 'orthodox' which means 'right opinion' would be taken in its literal sense," Joseph H. Lookstein wrote in an extended essay on "Orthodox Judaism: The Name and Its Implications," referring to the denomination's detractors. "They intended rather to label that branch of Judaism as static, ancient and unprogressive."[20] And in that effort they succeeded admirably. As far as the outside world was concerned, Orthodoxy was a synonym for the primitive, retrogressive, and un-American aspects of Jewish culture.

Extremely sensitive to the negative connotations of the term and eager to rid it of its "unwelcome associations," the Orthodox continued to look about for more suitable substitutes. Some clergy fancied the use of "traditional" or "observant," while others favored the Germanic "Torah-True." The laity, for its part, saw itself as simply "religious" and divided the world accordingly into two categories: those who were "religious" and those who were not. American Jews who attended an Orthodox synagogue and kept kosher were "religious"; all others, including those within the taxonomically troubling Conservative camp, were not. Despite a continuous search for a more appealing designation, "Orthodox" remained the term by which this community was known. As late as 1952, concerned Orthodox Jews continued to grapple with the onomastic implications of that designation. In an editorial entitled "What's in a Name," the editors of *Jewish Life*, the house publication of the Union of Orthodox Jewish Congregations of America, called upon its readership to wear their Orthodoxy proudly and to invest that term "with such meaning as will win for it unqualified, affirmative response. . . ."[21]

The process of religious declension, then, was not nearly as potent or as unidirectional as it might have seemed at the time. Smaller in number, to be sure, than the unobservant, traditionalists within the Eastern European immigrant community were sufficiently vibrant, culturally, materially, and psychologically, to attempt, in their own way, to come to terms with Jewish life in the New World. For some, this determination to build a New York Orthodox life found expression through the construction of expansive, monumental synagogues. The Eldridge Street Synagogue, or, to give its full name, Kahal Adas Jeshurun Anshe Lubz, built in 1887 in a mix of Moorish, Gothic, and Romanesque styles, was not only the first synagogue expressly built by Eastern European immigrants but also the largest on the Lower East Side. "The building looks quite imposing, standing in the neighborhood it does," reported the *American Israelite*, "and makes even a better impression on stepping into the interior which is distinguished by an elegant simplicity."[22] Its rival, Congregation Sons of Israel Kalvarie, otherwise known as the Pike Street Shuel, played host to the area's most ceremonial and festive occasions. Built in 1903 in a classical style, "the newest of the great synagogues" hugged the corner of Pike and East Broadway.[23] Still other Orthodox Jews, like the congregants of the Beth Hamidrash Hagadol or the First Roumanian-American Congregation, Shaarey Shamoyim, remodeled former churches, transforming them into architectural and public showpieces.

The impulse toward community building also took the form of attempts to impose a European kehillah-like structure on the heavily atomized and fragmented Orthodox community. One such effort, the formation of the Association of American Orthodox Hebrew Congregations, was launched in 1887.[24] Raising $2500 from fifteen Lower East Side synagogues, among them the Eldridge Street Synagogue, Beth Hamidrash Hagadol, and the Hebra Kadisha Anshe Kalvarie, the association hoped to unify New York's smaller Orthodox congregations, which by some accounts numbered in the hundreds, into a consolidated, smooth-functioning whole. Toward that end, the group imported a rabbi, Jacob Joseph, from abroad to serve as New York's chief rabbi. Though that experiment in recreating the European religious milieu ended in failure, as a subsequent chapter records in some detail, it heightened the importance of creating a suitably American institutional framework for Orthodox life. Chastened by failure, Orthodox lay leaders tried a second time to fashion a more avowedly American institutional context for their own Orthodoxy through the creation of the Union of American Jewish Congregations of America, the "OU."

The "Orthodox Congregational Union," a loose confederation of ninety-odd Orthodox synagogues, was established in the spring of 1898. Fifty delegates, lay officials of such established New York congregations as Kehilath Jeshurun, Shearith Israel, Ohab Zedek, Zichron Ephraim, Beth Hamidrash Hagadol, and the Eldridge Street Synagogue, convened with the hopes of establishing themselves as a "representative body."[25] "As scattered fragments," conference proceedings record, "we can do comparatively little . . . " but when unified, they had every reason to hope for a "permanent organization of Orthodox Judaism."[26] Two somewhat vague objectives dominated the proceedings: the first was to "give life to the old faith" by demonstrating its ongoing vitality, and the other, only slightly more concrete, was "to rebuke and repudiate the reformers who have been foisting some strange device upon us, calling that Judaism."[27]

What such high-sounding rhetoric meant in practice was a different matter entirely. Though the UOJCA was hailed by contemporaries as "a stable, dignified organization" that represented the Orthodox perspective, internal squabbling nearly put an end to the organization just shortly after its formation.[28] It was easier to castigate Reform and to issue gloriously charged slogans urging coreligionists to "manfully unfurl the glorious banner of Orthodox Judaism" than to arrive at a consensus on how best to carry out the organization's "mission."[29] The membership could not even agree on the public language of the organization. Determined to "deal effectively and *happily* with the great task of Americaniz[ation]," founding fathers like H. Pereira Mendes and Bernard Drachman insisted on English; it was simply inconceivable that an American Orthodox institution would choose otherwise.[30] But a few extremely vocal lay members angrily demurred. "It would be a fatal blunder to attempt to do business without Yiddish," warned the editors of the *Judisches Tageblatt*. "This is to be a popular movement or it must fall. To appeal to the masses you must communicate with them in the language, dialect or jargon that they may understand. *Yiddish is the language* . . . ."[31] Ultimately, a compromise was reached in which English would serve as the public language of all conferences and published deliberations at the same time that a Yiddish translator would be on hand at all public events to render the proceedings into the people's language.[32]

Having successfully resolved the linguistic issue, the OU attempted to create a climate for the maturation of an American Orthodox Judaism by serving as its advocate. "The special sphere of duty and usefulness of the Union," explained its president, H. Pereira Mendes, in 1913, "is to attempt to guide the hundreds of orthodox congregations . . . towards cultured orthodox ideas so that they can

flourish in their American environment."[33] Toward that end, the Union enrolled local Orthodox congregations as constituent members whose activities it
hoped to oversee and coordinate, thus diffusing "cultured Orthodox ideas." In
its capacity as the congregational arm of the emerging American Orthodox
movement, the OU enthusiastically championed such facets of a modernized
Orthodoxy as a decorous sanctuary service and the use of English-language
sermons and published both small pamphlets and articles on how to go about
laying the groundwork for such innovations. By the late twenties, the OU
turned to the political arena, lobbying for protective legislation in such areas as
Sabbath observance and kashruth. Later still, the UOJCA served literally as the
voice of American Orthodoxy, sponsoring weekly radio broadcasts and the
publication of a monthly magazine, the *Orthodox Union*.[34]

Oftentimes, the OU fell short of realizing its goals. Riddled with financial
problems and confounded by the difficulties inherent in coordinating the efforts
of several hundred fiercely independent synagogues, the organization never
quite lived up to the glory of its rhetoric or, for that matter, its potential. At its
most effective, the organization served as a clearinghouse, a rallying point, for
issues of concern to the modernized Orthodox American Jew. "Presenting
Orthodox Judaism in a light that shall be free of the shadows of the Ghetto," the
OU's function remained largely a symbolic one: as the public address of
America's Orthodox community.[35]

New York's Orthodox most fully articulated and refined their Orthodox
sensibility on the neighborhood level and not in the corridors of the UOJCA.
"Orthodox communities today," noted one observer in 1930, "are in the main
local minded. The natural procedure is along the lines of local activity."[36] The
cultural geography of Orthodox New York was a rich and varied one: from
Brooklyn to Manhattan, Long Island, Queens, and the Bronx, pockets of Orthodox existed alongside their more secular coreligionists; by 1945, a national
registry of over 250 practicing Orthodox rabbis listed close to two dozen
communities throughout the greater metropolitan area where English-speaking,
professionalized Orthodox rabbis served an Orthodox constituency.[37] On the
Grand Concourse and in upper Manhattan, in Far Rockaway and in Jamaica,
Queens, New York's Orthodox Jews lived out their lives within a strongly
flavored Orthodox context. And yet, like so much else associated with New
York Jewish life, the demography of Orthodoxy was a shifting one; every
decade or so a new locus of Orthodox life would appear and supersede an earlier
and formerly flourishing neighborhood. Orthodox Jews moved from one end of
the city to the other, from one side of town to the next, in search of a suitable
and congenial environment.

The Lower East Side was the first Orthodox neighborhood to bear the brunt of larger demographic shifts, or, to put it precisely, the consequence of increased affluence. Until 1905 or thereabouts, New York's Orthodox were concentrated overwhelmingly on the Lower East Side; though Harlem could claim a community of middle-class traditional Jews as early as the late 1890s, downtown remained the nucleus. There was no mistaking the palpably Jewish and ritually attentive ambience of the Lower East Side. Kosher butcher shops and meat wholesalers like Isaac Gellis, whose Essex Street store proclaimed its inventory of "strictly koshar edibles," or S. Ershowsky and Brothers, whose East Houston Street emporium carried the logo "first class kosher," could be found throughout the area, along with dozens of kosher restaurants and catering halls.[38] "Kosher Catering A Specialty," noted the management of the Clinton Hall social hall as it advertised its sterling facilities within the pages of the *Hebrew Standard*; Beethoven Hall, a neighborhood competitor with "elegant club and ball rooms for balls, weddings and banquets" made sure to promote the fact that its kosher kitchen was supervised by one of New York's most revered Orthodox rabbis, Rev. Dr. Philip Klein of Harlem's prestigious congregation Ohab Zedek.[39] The perceived importance of having a ritual stamp of approval tended at times to have a somewhat curious application: one dairy restaurant, in an effort to secure a wider clientele, drew on the popularity of local cantorial personalities by advertising that its kitchen was under the ritual supervision of the "Reverend I. Herlands, formerly cantor of the Henry Street Synagogue."[40] Consumer demand for kosher food was limited neither to meat products nor to public dining spots. Before the advent of Passover, the *Judisches Tageblatt* routinely carried the advertisements of more than thirty Lower East Side matzoh bakers, from the sizable Horowitz Brothers and Margareten factory on East Fourth Street and Meyer London's Bayard Street "Matzos Bakery, Established 1871" to the more modest Finesilver Matzoth Baking Company of 65 Pitt Street, whose tiny Yiddish advertisement insisted that this company was prepared "to sell *the most kosher* matzoh of the highest quality for the lowest price."[41] Jewish bookstores, manufacturers of *tallesim* (prayer shawls) and *seforim* (Jewish books), dozens of ritual baths, and more than a hundred small-sized synagogues helped to define that neighborhood as an unmistakably "Jewish district."[42]

While the Lower East Side remained home to the less acculturated and poorer Orthodox well into the post–World War I period, most middle-class Orthodox Jews had relocated elsewhere decades before, creating a number of Orthodox centers where formerly there had been only one. As early as the turn of the century, demographers and urban policy planners reported numerous instances of Jews moving uptown. Growing prosperity seemed to entail, as a matter of course, a move to the northern parts of the city, particularly Harlem and the Upper East Side. Immigration expert Kate Claghorn noted the presence of large numbers of Russian Jews in Yorkville and Harlem as early as 1901; three years later, the superintendent of the YMHA on 92nd Street and Lexington observed that "numbers of people are moving uptown from the lower sections of the city and we are feeling the effects of the invasion."[43] To Claghorn's mind, so natural and anticipated was the move uptown, which she unhesitatingly identified as a "token of advancement—in assimilation, at any rate," that she coined the often-cited observation that "from Hester Street to Lexington Avenue is a journey of about ten years for any given family."[44] Among those making the move were the newly prosperous Orthodox. Internal records of Jewish institutions record the hegira of their more affluent members northward. The minutes of the Eldridge Street Synagogue, once home to such laymen as Harry Fischel, Abba Baum, Sender Jarmulowsky, and the Cohen Brothers, now residents of Yorkville and Harlem, contain numerous, and at times disgruntled, references to the demographic changes that had beset the congregation. These changes led to talk of opening a branch of the eponymous congregation uptown, and ultimately to a somewhat messy lawsuit as several of downtown's charter members contested the right of those moving uptown to use the synagogue's name and, one suspects, a share of the treasury as well.[45]

From any formal perspective, this northward migration was an individual and not a group phenomenon; and yet, so many socially and economically like-minded Jews moved at the same time and, in many instances, to the same neighborhood that it would not be too farfetched to view it as a collective endeavor. "Many of the people who had come to America in earlier years and who had prospered consequently began to move their residences to the section of the city known as Yorkville. . . . Mr. Fischel," his son-in-law subsequently recorded, "decided to move with the tide."[46] In their exchange of a Lower East Side address for an Upper East Side one, the first generation of affluent Orthodox seemed fully prepared, perhaps even eager, to sacrifice the intensely flavored Jewish ambience of the Lower East Side for the amenities of middle- and upper-middle-class life, even if it meant living in a decidedly non-Jewish neighborhood. "Jews living in that part of town," one Jewish population study of the Upper East Side related," are not as conspicuous as elsewhere. They are living there . . . not as a strongly accentuated separate nationality like, for instance, the Jews on the Lower East Side."[47] The decision to move uptown in search of what Maurice Samuel has called the "spacious life" reflected a powerful desire to leave behind the immigrant neighborhood and its negative connotations and to start afresh.[48] Within a short span of time, its former sons succeeded in dissociating themselves from the Lower East Side and acted as if their earlier home had become "more distant in their past than the Second Temple."[49] At best, the Lower East Side figured in the collective imagination of its now-prosperous erstwhile residents as a somewhat quaint and exotic venue. Following a field trip downtown by the Jewish Center Hebrew School, in which students visited Streit's matzoh factory, the plant of the *Jewish Daily Forward*, and a Montgomery Street *shtiebel* (a small, informal house of worship), the "Center Bulletin" noted that the boys and girls were "thrilled" by the "intensive Jewishness of this picturesque section of the city."[50]

Those who had moved away from the "picturesque" East Side consisted of the newest additions to New York's Jewish middle-class population: "the highest economic class among the Russian Jewry of New York City, the bourgeoisie, the well-to-do and the distinctly Conservative."[51] A generation whose activities and sensibilities were widely chronicled in both poetry and prose, they were known within the immigrant community as the "alrightniks" and, on occasion, even less flatteringly, as a community of "champion Jewish vulgarians."[52] The constituency designated by the term "alrightnik" was a far cry from the so-called typical East Side resident. The latter, according to the astute muckraker Ray Stannard Baker, whose influential book, *The Spiritual Unrest*, poignantly captured the dislocations inherent in the immigrant experience, was a person who "looks very much as he looked when he walked the dirty streets of his native Russian or Austrian village. His black coat, long black beard, his rounded shoulders, the Hebrew curls at his temples, indelibly mark his place in the heterogeneous life of the streets."[53] No such indelible marks distinguished the upwardly mobile resident of the Upper East Side. Clean-shaven and well dressed, he worked hard at being Orthodox and American, as did his family. Though his "grammar creaked," the Orthodox alrightnik, like his more secular cousins, enthusiastically adopted many of the trappings of affluence, outwardly exhibiting the "veneer of modernity."[54] Jewish homes were decorated with the ornate and heavy furniture characteristic of the middle class, their buffet tables bedecked with the requisite cut-glass bowls later made famous by writer Delmore Schwartz. "The dining room," Schwartz wrote in his prose poem "Shenandoah," "contains in vivid signs, Certain clear generals of time and place: look at the cut glass bowls . . . the works of art of these rising Jews."[55] Widely traveled, ardent devotees of the performing arts (it was no coincidence that one of the most financially successful fund-raising devices of the Orthodox synagogue was a night at the opera), these Orthodox alrightniks also maintained summer homes—on the Jersey Shore, in the Catskills, and on Long Island— where they appeared to pay as much attention to the rituals of the sporting life as they did to those of tradition. Some families were so observant of the niceties of tennis, for example, that they expressly forbade those without appropriate tennis attire to appear on the court. Others among them "even rode horseback," a less affluent Orthodox New Yorker recalled with amazement, considering that most of the more senior members of this community were born in Eastern Europe and only a few among them were "thoroughbred Americans," native-born children of Russian immigrant parents.[56] "Years ago," a Harvard psychology professor observed in 1925, "the Orthodox Jew was surely to be identified with the erstwhile denizen of the Russian Pale. He was bound to be either poor or a parvenu. His standard of living was regarded as below par and he was associated with anything but culture." But now, thoroughly grounded in the accoutrements of modern life, "Orthodox Jewry in America is on the way to establishing an aristocracy of its own."[57]

The affluent Orthodox, largely in their thirties and forties, boasted a "splendid laity of lawyers, physicians, journalists, and merchants"; the elite among them were businessmen.[58] Cotton converters, lace merchants, garment manufacturers, building contractors, "real-estate men," and a sprinkling of bankers and lawyers, they had made their money in traditional Jewish occupations. Extremely proud of this recent ascent into affluence, and perhaps even somewhat puzzled by it, the *Hebrew Standard* inaugurated a series in 1916 on representative Orthodox lay leaders to explore the secret of their successes as affluent traditionalists. Running for close to six months, "Jews Who Have Made Their Mark" consisted of interviews with the *"Young and successful and strictly Orthodox"* who had recently come to prominence within the immigrant community, highlighting the whys and wherefores of their mobility and at the same time demonstrating the viability of American Orthodoxy. Profiles of men like Joseph H. Cohen, the lay founder of the Jewish Center, and of influential Kehilath Jeshurun congregants like Samuel Hyman, Joseph Polstein, and the Roggen Brothers, the paper explained, were "an attestation that a strict observance of the Jewish Sabbath is not a deterrent to success. . . ."[59]

Harry Fischel, a Russian-born building contractor whose legendary generosity earned him the sobriquet of the "Russian Jacob Schiff," was perhaps the most representative figure of the Orthodox "aristocracy." Born in Meretz in 1865, Fischel migrated to America in 1885, at the age of twenty, and began his career as a carpenter. He subsequently parlayed his building skills and entrepreneurial imagination into the development of a real-estate empire, first as the owner and builder of dozens of Lower East Side tenements and then, as he prospered, as the builder of luxury apartment houses throughout the city, including a few on Park and Fifth Avenues. As Fischel's financial empire grew, so too did his support of Orthodox institutions: Beth Israel Hospital, Etz Chaim Yeshiva, the Uptown Talmud Torah, and the Central Relief Committee were each the beneficiary of his largesse. Delegations from these and other charitable enterprises were such a regular fixture of Fischel's daily life that he reportedly took them into consideration when building his new home on East 93rd Street. There, we are told, he "erected a handsome and commodious private residence, having in mind the provision of rooms where the directors of the many institutions with which he was affiliated might meet. . . ."[60]

Apparently a keen showman as well as a *"filantrop,"* Fischel could not resist the temptation of capitalizing on his generosity. "His love of display and self-advertisement knows no bounds," related one rather unfriendly contemporary eyewitness. "While he has been identified with an extraordinary number of philanthropic and educational societies and gives quite freely to many a worthy cause, he makes sure that his generosity be cried from the house tops. It is typical of the man that he explains his greed for publicity as a means of stimulating others to emulate his example."[61] Conscious of his success as an affluent Orthodox Jew who, in his own words, "did not exchange his religion for gold," Fischel tended immodestly to view his life as a case study, worthy of emulation.[62] Accordingly, he commissioned his son-in-law, Rabbi Herbert S. Goldstein, to write his biography, a combination fable and cautionary tale. Published in 1928, during Fischel's own lifetime, *Forty Years of Struggle for a Principle* chronicled in considerable detail and in unstintingly flattering terms Fischel's encounter with life in the New World. "The story of Mr. Fischel's manly stand for true Jewish learning, Jewish worship and Jewish life is sure to stimulate others to follow his noble example," wrote Rabbi Joseph Hertz, who, along with dozens of others like Herbert Hoover, then secretary of commerce; Nicholas Murray Butler, president of Columbia University; Felix Warburg; and the editors of the *New York Times* received complimentary copies of the volume.[63]

With the exception of his early years on the Lower East Side, Fischel spent his entire adult American life on Manhattan's Upper East Side. Once a small village "inhabited only by the lonely squatter and his faithful goat," the Upper East Side was radically urbanized by the construction of the Third and Second Avenue Elevateds in 1878 and 1879 respectively, which transformed this sleepy hamlet into an urban, polyglot neighborhood.[64] Like Harlem, its neighbor to the north, the Yorkville area contained a diverse mix of ethnic populations: by 1900, Germans comprised an estimated 26 percent of local residents, the Irish 22 percent, the Italians 19 percent, and the Russian Jews 9 percent.[65] The area was also stratified by social class: Third Avenue served as the great divide, with the poor living east of that thoroughfare and the wealthier element living in the handsome multistory brownstones that lined the side streets between Lexington and Fifth Avenues.

The construction of luxury apartment buildings came late to the Upper East Side, and when it did the area's reputation as the city's preeminent neighborhood blossomed. "Park Avenue is a recent and sudden phenomenon," a former Upper East Sider wrote in 1926. Returning from the war, "we heard for the first time the name Park Avenue as a synonym for wealth. . . ."[66] Ironically enough, the refurbishment of the Upper East Side did not augur well for its local Jewish residents. Though a number of Jewish builders had a hand in developing the neighborhood, many of the newly constructed cooperative apartment houses were openly antisemitic. "Although I was very optimistic when I saw Park Avenue, Madison Avenue . . . putting up new buildings and I was in hopes [sic] that the whole Jewish world was coming here, what do I see?" Jacob H. Rubin, the president of one Yorkville educational institution, asked rhetorically in 1925. "Jews are not wanted here."[67] So disturbed were Fischel and his sons-in-law by the prevailing tenor of the real-estate market that they personally approached a number of influential Jews hoping to put an end to discriminatory practices. "At this time we are endeavoring to learn how many of our friends and acquaintances (both Jews and Gentiles) would be interested in purchasing apartments. . . . If a sufficient number of people respond favorably, I would push this project most energetically," wrote Albert Wald, a young lawyer and later a New York state senator, to a few leading New York Jewish personalities in 1928. Nothing seems to have come of his suggestion.[68]

Thanks to the disproportionate number of Jewish Orthodox elite who resided in its midst well into the 1920s, and to the vitality and cultural eminence of its synagogues like Kehilath Jeshurun or Orach Chaim, the Upper East Side enjoyed a certain celebrity within Jewish New York. "If we had anything," Kehilath Jeshurun's rabbi reflected, "we had *yichus* [pedigree]," referring to the status of his congregants.[69] And yet, that neighborhood failed to take hold as a flourishing and vibrantly Jewish settlement; Harlem, for much of its history, had more than double the number of Jewish residents. From its inception at the turn of the century well into the interwar years, the area remained a quiet and subdued one in which overt signs of Jewishness were discouraged. "There is hardly any sign of Jewish life," remarked an observer of the New York Jewish scene as he profiled Yorkville for a WPA survey, noting the absence of a kosher restaurant or a kosher bakery.[70]

Never very Jewish to begin with, the Upper East Side experienced a sharp drop in Jewish population during the interwar years, leading one stalwart resident to insist that "the neighborhood is played out"; by 1927, for example, Jews on the Upper East Side accounted for a scant 4 percent of Manhattan's total Jewish population.[71] The records of one of the area's leading synagogues, Congregation Kehilath Jeshurun, reflect the diminution in Jewish residents. As early as April 1921, an alarmed membership committee reported that the "synagogue is losing ground" and called on congregants to recruit new members.[72] By then an aging congregation whose average member was well above sixty, the synagogue, with a seating capacity of close to one thousand, could barely attract two hundred worshipers on a regular Sabbath. "The place was so empty," recalled Dr. Jeanne Rafsky, Harry Fischel's granddaughter, "you could count heads."[73] There is, in fact, every reason to suspect that when the young and energetic Joseph H. Lookstein was hired in 1923, it was in the hope that his personality would serve to draw a more youthful element to what had once been the city's premier Orthodox institution.

Launching a number of almost yearly membership drives, "drumming, visiting and interviewing" prospective congregants, and supplementing the drives with an attractive array of social activities, Lookstein sought to turn the tide.[74] By 1947 he proudly informed the synagogue's board that Kehilath Jeshurun had the largest number of members in its history: with 250 membership or family units and 650 units of seat holders, the congregation now served several thousand local residents.[75]

By then, the center of gravity of New York's Orthodox had moved across the park to the Upper West Side, the city's newest Jewish middle-class neighborhood. "Everybody then on the East Side who was anybody moved to these parts," Mordecai M. Kaplan, a resident of the Upper West Side, recalled. "Then it looked as if Central Park West would be the center of the local Jewish aristocracy."[76] With an estimated 39,000 Jewish residents in 1916, its population swelled by over 50,000 by the early twenties. Like so many other uptown neighborhoods, the Upper West Side owed its development to the late nineteenth-century construction of an elevated railway line along Ninth Avenue and the opening, two decades later, of the Interborough Rapid Transit, New York's first subway line; together, they helped to render the northern areas of the city accessible to the middle class. "The dwellers here are not as a rule of the old and historic New York families, or very wealthy as a class but all are people exceedingly well to do," a student of New York social mores observed in 1899. "A fair proportion," he added, "are Hebrews. . . ."[77] It was not until the post–World War I era, though, that the Jewish West Side came into its own, thanks to a combination of interrelated factors. With Harlem in decline by the early twenties, many former residents relocated to the Upper West Side, at the time in the midst of a building boom, as did several of its more prestigious synagogues, which, in the words of one rabbi, "followed the westward drift of our congregants."[78] Ohab Zedek, the former home of stellar cantorial personality Yossele Rosenblatt, took up residence on West 95th Street in 1926, while the Institutional Synagogue, newly renamed the West Side Institutional Synagogue, set down roots in the same year. After renting a series of halls, it purchased a former Methodist church on West 76th Street. When remodeled in 1937, the I.S.'s domed and naturally lit sanctuary provided spacious, sunny accommodations for close to nine hundred worshipers. The postwar construction of well-appointed and spacious apartment houses on Central Park West, West End Avenue, and Riverside Drive, many of them enduring moments of Art Deco architecture, together with the parallel closing of the Upper East Side, rendered the area especially attractive to the growing numbers of the Jewish middle class and gave rise to the area's reputation as a "gilded ghetto." "The Jews of the

well-to-do class," noted Kaplan as early as 1922, "constitute the predominant
element of the population in this West Side section of the city. They are
conspicuous by reason of their vulgarity and flashiness."[79]

The mise-en-scène for *Marjorie Morningstar*, Herman Wouk's highly successful novel of the New York Jewish alrightnik, the Upper West Side sustained an intensely Jewish atmosphere. Within its thirty-block radius, one could
find some twenty synagogues, most of which were Orthodox. "Attending synagogue," wrote Aaron Frankel, a former resident of the area, "can be as comfortably and handily accomplished as the other functions of 86th Street life."[80]
These "other functions" included numerous kosher butchers, kosher bakeries
like Clark-Brody on 90th Street and Amsterdam Avenue, and restaurants like
Steinberg's, a "kosher dairy restaurant" on Broadway and 81st Street; even local
shopkeepers like the grocer and the wine merchant catered to an observant
Jewish clientele, stocking kosher food products and advertising their inventory
of kosher wines and brandies in synagogue bulletins.

The influx of an estimated 15–20,000 refugees from Belgium, Germany, and
Holland intensified the apparent Jewishness of the neighborhood during the
1930s, imparting at the same time a distinctly Mittel Europeaisch flavor to
Broadway and West End Avenue. "Little by little the New York Upper West
Side neighborhood where we lived," recalled Ruth Sapin Hurwitz, "came to
have—or so it seemed—nearly as many German-speaking as 'Jewish-speaking'
residents." ("Jewish on that side of town," she explained parenthetically to her
readers, "is elegant for Yiddish.")[81] Some were drawn to the area because of
relatives with cavernous apartments, which they shared, several family units at a
time, while others were put up in local hotels like the Milburn or the Marseilles
by HIAS and NYANA, two refugee resettlement agencies. Swelling the number
of observant Jews, the refugees in time not only formed the core of support for
what was then an emerging day-school movement but also spawned a number of
overtly Jewish enterprises, most notably kosher catering concerns and kosher
restaurants like Schreiber's, "Good and Strictly Kosher, Famous 25 Years in
Vienna." The gustatory richness of the Upper West Side was enhanced still
further as a number of appetizing stores that specialized in imported items like
halvah, sauerkraut, and "Old World health bread," sprung up alongside candy
shops, whose "tasteful candies made in the finest European manner" catered to
sophisticated European palates.[82] By far the greatest, certainly the most visible,
effect of the refugees' collective presence lay in the changed tenor of life in the
area. "The tempo of life has changed to a slower rhythm," noted one writer for
the WPA in 1941. "People walk slower here, they just stroll in a comfortable
pace as if walking on the boulevards of Berlin or Wienna. And, of course," he
continued, "one hears right and left the guttural sound of German words or
English spoken with decided German accents."[83]

Despite the apparent richness of Jewish life on the Upper West Side, its population dwindled during the fifties as local Jewish residents fled before an influx of lower-income blacks and Hispanics. In a demographic version of musical chairs, the West Side's hegemony as the center of middle-class Jewish life passed to a number of Long Island and Queens suburbs and, interestingly enough, back again to the Upper East Side. "Before long," a West Side resident observed in 1952," our people began moving away into the suburbs . . . wealthier Jews began moving back to the East Side, particularly the avenues where the large apartment buildings are located."[84] To many, it seemed as if the "future of Orthodox Judaism in New York lay in the East."[85]

Thanks to the collective affluence of its residents and the prominence of its rabbis, Manhattan represented the acme of Orthodox life in New York. Proudly likening themselves time and again to aristocrats, its members believed firmly that they "were it."[86] And in a very real sense they were: Manhattan's Orthodox laity set the tone for and defined the representative style of Orthodox social and cultural behavior, while its rabbis gave voice to the formal, institutional standards against which other Orthodox neighborhoods and their clergy measured themselves. Whether in Lawrence, Long Island, or Borough Park, newer enclaves of middle-class Orthodoxy took their cues from Manhattan and imported its notions of appropriate synagogue architecture, sanctuary behavior, and the role of the modern synagogue in constructing their own versions of Orthodox New York life.

But then, Manhattan held no monopoly on a "cultured Orthodoxy." In fact, much of Orthodox Jewish life during the interwar years took place outside of Manhattan Island: Brooklyn's Flatbush, Crown Heights, Bensonhurst, Williamsburg, and Borough Park attracted more than their fair share of the cultured Orthodox and developed in turn their own set of indigenous Orthodox institutions—synagogues, day schools, social clubs. With a far greater range of incomes and social statuses than those likely to be found among the smoothly homogeneous Manhattan Orthodox, the "Orthodox strongholds" of Williamsburg and Borough Park throughout the 1920s and thirties represented two examples of respectable middle-class, "balebatish" (bourgeois) neighborhoods.[87]

Williamsburg was the older of the two communities. Divided by Brooklyn's own Broadway into two separate neighborhoods, each with its own distinct social ecology and milieu, "Old Williamsburg" was a tenement neighborhood that housed, during the early twentieth century, a large immigrant population comparable to that of the Lower East Side. Moving westward into that area of the neighborhood bounded by Lee, Marcy, and Bedford Avenues, one encountered a "very ritzy section" of handsome mansions and brownstone row houses. Home during the late nineteenth century to an affluent German Jewish population to whom goes the distinction of having built Brooklyn's first Reform Temple, on Keap Street, central Williamsburg emerged during the teens and twenties as a solidly middle-class neighborhood; together, the two Williamsburgs contained over one hundred thousand Jews by 1918. A "sunny and very pleasant" place in which to live, the Brooklyn neighborhood attracted upwardly mobile immigrants and their American-born children, who fashioned their own home-grown notion of American Orthodoxy.[88] "It was always a Jewish neighborhood—but real Orthodox," a former resident recalled, an impression confirmed by the statistics of the *Jewish Communal Register*, which, as early as 1918, observed that of the area's forty-nine permanent synagogues, all were Orthodox.[89] The presence of the Young Israel of Brooklyn organization, together with that of the Shomer Hadati, American Mizrachi's youth complement, provided the American-born youth of both genders with a fulcrum for ritual and political involvement; the Yeshiva Torah Vadas, in turn, educated many of the young men at a time when its orientation was both strongly Zionist and educationally progressive. That institution, recalled a former student, was "quite modern for that particular time."[90]

The indigenously American character of this south Brooklyn community was, however, considerably eclipsed by the influx of refugees during the 1930s and a phalanx of Hungarian Hasidim following the war. Intensifying the Jewishness of the area, they claimed it as their own and preferred, as George Kranzler, a sociologist of postwar Williamsburg has observed, "to adjust the standards of the community to their own particular pattern of religious life."[91] For one thing, the use of glatt kosher, a highly stringent form of ritual supervision, replaced the well-nigh universal practice of non-glatt: before the Hasidim arrived in the area, a resident related, "it would not have occurred to me to ask for Glatt Kosher meat. I had not even heard the word until they came."[92] Retaining distinctive Hasidic garb, Williamsburg's newest residents resorted to Yiddish, both on the street and in their schools and numerous *shtieblach*. What's more, this new "Jerusalem of America" had become a hotbed of anti-Zionist sentiment, where earlier Zionism was organically bound up with the neighborhood's Jewish sensibility as "one of the elements of Jewish life." "I remember," Harold Wilkenfeld, a lawyer and Zionist lay leader who lived in Williamsburg from 1920 through 1936, told an interviewer, "going out with boxes to collect for the Jewish National Fund; I recall selling *shekallim* for elections of the Zionist organization and, of course, numerous lectures. I do recall," he added, "many meetings being conducted in protest" at the time of the 1929 Hebron massacre.[93] Putting it all together, the Williamsburg of the postwar era had been radically transformed, and an explicitly Old World, premodern mentality suffused the neighborhood. "It's quite different now," one resident told Kranzler early in the fifties, compactly summarizing the extent of the neighborhood's transformation. "Every second man wears a beard and . . . most of [the children] have a yarmulke and go to a Yeshiva."[94]

Ironically enough, the postwar Hasidification of Williamsburg not only left its distinctive stamp on that community but also saved it from physical deterioration. Sometime during the late thirties and early forties, the neighborhood began to experience a marked decline as the more affluent among the locals began to pull up stakes. The neighborhood, Wilkenfeld explained, "was almost moribund at that time; buildings were boarded up on Bedford Avenue; some of the apartment buildings were closed and tenantless. But, with the influx of the Satmar Chassidim, Williamsburg had a revival."[95] In the interim, the "upper bracket" among Williamsburg residents moved to Crown Heights or to Forest Hills, "there to pioneer future East Sides," while those with lesser means moved to Borough Park, "the next rung in the hierarchy of Jewish neighborhoods."[96]

A vibrant Jewish neighborhood that by 1918 numbered approximately 66,000 Jews, Borough Park was first developed in the early 1900s. At that time, related Isaac Marks, a long-time resident of the area and a former New York City alderman, there were so few Jews that one could barely assemble a *minyan*, a prayer quorum of ten men. In the aftermath of the Great War, however, Borough Park emerged as a popular locale for the "moderately successful Jewish businessman."[97] "The Phenomenal Growth of Borough Park," heralded a 1924 article in the *Jewish Forum* as it described the neighborhood's flourishing Jewish ambience. In this and a companion piece by Joseph Barondess, in which one finds one of the earliest usages of the term "Modern Orthodox," the benefits of living in that area of south Brooklyn, with its tree-lined streets and handsome brick houses, were strongly touted.[98] Reportedly home to the "strongest section of Sabbath observers in the country," Borough Park could also boast a dozen synagogues, ranging from a Young Israel to Temple Beth-El, an Orthodox synagogue (despite its name) with a "gala appearance" whose cantor was the legendary Kwartin; three talmud torahs (afternoon Hebrew schools); the Hebrew Institute of Borough Park, a modern yeshiva; a kosher hospital; and several Zionist organizations.[99] Proud residents tended to think of their neighborhood as an urban village and praised its characteristic "feeling of coziness"; "there is no community that sticks more together than Borough Park," affirmed one of them.[100] As its apparent charms became more widely known, the neighborhood continued to grow, and by 1953, it encompassed an estimated 70,000 Jewish families. Borough Park, remarked one of its postwar boosters, "is far from a ghetto . . . It represents no mere transplantation of foreign ways to the park-like climes of southern Brooklyn. It is totally American in appearance and outlook."[101]

New York Orthodox Jews of the interwar years inhabited a common universe. Despite neighborhood or borough differences in wealth, style, and sophistication—differences of degree, not of kind—growing up Orthodox in New York during this period was very much a uniform experience, one whose participants were conscious of living, culturally if not geographically, within the same narrowly defined world. This was a world whose parameters were defined by a shared interest in promoting kashruth and the Sabbath, whose synagogues boasted modern accoutrements and an English-speaking rabbi, whose children attended summer camps like North Star, Delawaxen, and Delanore, and whose young adults learned the most current social dances at Young Israel forums. Subscribing to the same set of periodicals, dining, on occasion, at the same restaurants, and summering in the same resorts, Orthodox adults also interacted with one another through their participation in the communal politics of the OU and the American Mizrachi party.

More to the point, the Orthodox were bound together by their attitude toward the outside, non-Orthodox world, which intruded hardly at all within their insular, closed Jewish realm. The influx of refugees brought home the horrors of Hitler's Europe even as the feverish fund-raising campaigns of the Mizrachi highlighted the building up of Palestine. But when it came to alternative forms of American Jewish expression, whether that of secular *yidishkeyt* or the non-Orthodox Conservative Judaism, the Orthodox community exhibited a dim awareness and an even more limited curiosity, especially during the closing years of the interwar era. It is striking to find that while the Jewish Center and the Society for the Advancement of Judaism shared a common history as well as a common location—West 86th Street—few, if any, Jewish Center congregants had any idea whatsoever of what "went on" within Reconstructionist circles, nor, for that matter, were they informed about the activities of the seven prominent Conservative synagogues in their West Side neighborhood. It was common knowledge that the Jewish Theological Seminary, or what they dubbed "Schechter's Seminary," was "off limits," but if pressed, many were unable to explain why.[102] What concerned them, held their interest, and served as the stuff of Sabbath table conversation were the politics, social scene, and personalities of Orthodoxy.

Ultimately, though, it was not so much the insularity of the interwar Orthodox as it was their expressive religious culture that unified the community and rendered it distinctive. A brand-new social invention, American Orthodoxy of the 1920s and 1930s sought to blend seamlessly the traditions of the Old World with the challenges and disruptions of the New. Though its adherents liked to think they were continuing in the footsteps of their fathers, any resemblance between the latter's Orthodoxy and their own was a "form of optical illusion."[103] By design as well as default, this was a new

Orthodoxy, as much a response to modernity as Conservative Judaism, Reconstructionism, or secular *yidishkeyt*: the Orthodoxy of the modern era, as Jacob Katz has explained, was a "method of confronting deviant trends and of responding to the very same stimuli which produced those trends."[104] An evolving phenomenon, this new American Orthodoxy was very much a product of the modern urban environment, shaped by the exigencies of acculturation, class, and urbanization. Making middle-class Jews comfortable, at home, within Orthodoxy or, as one of their number put it, "making Jewish Judaism fashionable," lay at the heart of that experience.[105] What animated and sustained that experience was not a lasting preoccupation with Jewish law (*halakha*) or a collective nostalgia for the piety of an earlier, parental generation but rather an ongoing romance with modernity. Instead of shunning modernity, the interwar Orthodox embraced it, deferred to its strictures, and fashioned their institutions in accord with its dictates. Not surprisingly, they interpreted modernity in class terms. The expressive religious culture created by the residents of the Upper West Side or Borough Park reflected the primacy of class, or, more specifically, that of the middle class, against whose canons of what was fashionable, decorous, mannerly, and cultured, they not only evaluated themselves but built their religious institutions. Willingly deferring to external frames of reference, these happily modernized Orthodox Jews defined their Orthodoxy in avowedly bourgeois terms and saw no conflict in doing so. The Orthodoxy fostered by this generation made a strong case for the inherent compatibility of modernity with tradition and as such stands as a case study of the embourgeoisement of ritual.

Those who had made the conscious decision to preserve Orthodoxy were left to their own devices as to its content. Without giving too much thought to the process, they went about effecting a synthesis between their American selves and their Jewish souls. In the absence of a strong, central rabbinic authority, itself in the process of evolution, and with no master plan to guide them, these determined traditionalists had considerable leeway in constructing what they believed to be an authentically Orthodox existence. Inventing the culture as they went along, Orthodox Jews used a mix of intuition, personal memory, and collective imagination to guide their efforts. Mordecai Kaplan recounts a fascinating example of this ad hoc cultural improvisation. In 1917, as a rabbinical candidate being courted by Joseph Cohen, the Jewish Center's president, Kaplan was invited to lunch with the clothing manufacturer at his customary eatery: the Waldorf Astoria dining room. With evident bemusement, the young rabbi, who apparently had no qualms about accepting the invitation to dine in a nonkosher restaurant (fish, undoubtedly, was the bill of fare), relates how Cohen and his fellow guests quietly resorted to the traditional Jewish mealtime rituals.

"The waiters," noted Kaplan, "try to meet [Cohen's] wishes in every way so that neither he nor his guests should feel in the least embarrassed in washing, making the Motzei [blessing over bread] and saying grace after meals."[106]

Whether invoked at the Waldorf or at home, the Orthodoxy fashioned by its well-heeled adherents was neither a very "emphatic" nor an "obtrusive" one.[107] At its core lay a constellation of ritual behaviors that might be termed "official" Orthodoxy. Highly valuing the Sabbath and Jewish holidays, the dietary laws and the act of public synagogue worship, the Orthodox placed a premium on their observance. The celebration of such family-centered Jewish holidays as Passover, whose seder ritual neatly combined a traditional Jewish rite with the middle class's valuation of the family, was also highly esteemed. "We were very Jewish but not strictly Orthodox. . . . everyone was kosher, everyone was religious, not as Orthodox as in this day, but all supposedly religious," observed a leading member of the community as she compared the practices of her prewar generation with those of its postwar successor.[108]

Keeping outwardly distinctive practices to a minimum, Orthodox Jews of this era did not publicly demonstrate or proclaim their Orthodoxy. "It was certainly not a time when you showed your Judaism outside," related one rabbi. "It was a time when you kept your Judaism to yourself."[109] The absence of distinctive dress was a hallmark of that era. Few Orthodox males went about with a *yarmulke* or head covering. At a time when most adult men customarily wore hats, the absence of public *yarmulke*-wearing may well be perceived as a concession to modern sartorial wisdom. But it was more than that: young boys were also not given to wearing them. "There was no such thing as wearing a *kippah* on the street," recalled an Orthodox rabbi's son who came of age during the interwar years.[110] In fact, his father, Joseph Lookstein, one of that generation's preeminent champions of an Americanized Orthodoxy, made quite a point of stressing that the *yarmulke* was to be worn only under certain restricted circumstances. No one graduated the Ramaz School, which Lookstein founded, without learning that the *yarmulke* was an "indoor garment," a phrase that in its own way became a Ramaz School slogan and a signature of Rabbi Lookstein.[111] Although fear of antisemitism may well have influenced the rabbi—Ramaz was located in the heart of German Bund territory—his attitude toward such public displays was widely shared, even in completely homogeneous Jewish neighborhoods. Despite the sharpness of Lookstein's formulation, the practice of keeping one's Orthodoxy under wraps was very much a collective decision, a communal norm.[112]

One sees this reserve in other areas as well, most especially in the limited number of Orthodox Jews who observed the ritual of building and dining in a *succah*, or outdoor structure, during the harvest festival of Succoth. With the exception of Harry Fischel, whose ritual booth was subtly and unobtrusively integrated into the design of his Park Avenue apartment, few Orthodox Jews maintained their own outdoor tabernacles, despite the importance of this ritual commandment. In part, this lapse reflected a concession to an urban environment whose multistory dwellings and limited garden space made it exceedingly difficult to construct these outdoor structures. Even more to the point, it highlighted the very nature of American Orthodoxy during this era: dining in the *succah*, after all, was a highly visible and public act, one that called far too much attention to one's distinctiveness. It was preferable either to dispense with this ritual altogether or to make do with the saying of a perfunctory *kiddush* (blessing over the wine) in the synagogue's *succah* where the structure was virtually hidden from sight, enveloped by the synagogue building per se.

In still other respects, Orthodox Jews were much like everyone else: they enjoyed social dancing and mixed swimming, fancied sleeveless attire during the summer season, and traveled widely. Seeming inconsistencies of the sort documented above—eating out in a nonkosher restaurant while observing the ritual amenities—did not confound them at all; if anything, it served as a measure of their own success in linking the two cultures. How Cohen and his confreres came to develop their characteristic behavior, construct a shared ritual hierarchy, and then implement its practice is virtually impossible to ascertain: neither the lay leader nor, for that matter, his rabbi elaborated on the process by which this modernized Orthodoxy came into being and persisted. What is clear, though, is that ideology played little, if any, role in deciding what to emphasize and what to minimize. To look for guidelines or some overarching interpretive principle that governed behavior, or even to speak in terms of a collective decision to do "x" but not "y," is to attribute to American Orthodoxy a degree of rationality and internal coherence that it simply did not have. "American Jewish Orthodoxy," Trude Weiss-Rosmarin critically observed in 1944, "has as yet not produced an ideology adapted to the American scene and tempo in the manner of, let us say, Samson Raphael Hirsch's *Nineteen Letters*."[113] Not only did Orthodox Jews fail to develop an ideology of American Orthodoxy but, having little need for one, they never drew on preexisting ideological models like Hirsch's *Nineteen Letters* to articulate their position. From time to time, Orthodox clergy like Joseph Lookstein or Leo Jung would invoke the image of Frankfurt Jewry, a model of enlightened Orthodoxy, or the pithy sayings of a sympathetic rabbinical authority like Rav Kook, whose axiom *Yithadash hayashan veyitkadash hahadash*"—contemporize the old and sanctify the new— served as the unofficial motto of the modernizing Orthodox, a legitimation of modernity. But then, these kinds of scriptural testaments were occasional at best and of little moment to the denomination's laymen. Sure of themselves, perhaps even a bit smug, the interwar Orthodox had no need for external legitimation or the imprimatur of a major halakhic authority. Ethnocentric in the extreme, they trusted fully and implicitly in their own efforts and insights.

Throughout, the interwar Orthodox believed themselves to be staunch defenders of the faith, proudly upholding its tenets as they resolutely demonstrated tradition's relevance to modern world. At no time did they believe they were contravening either the spirit or the letter of the law, nor did it ever occur to them that they were circumventing some of its provisions. Whatever they did, and however they did it, qualified in their eyes as normative Orthodox practice, a skillful blend of the ritualistic and the modern. They would have been dismayed to learn that their own brand of Orthodoxy would not, in later years, pass muster as sufficiently authentic Orthodox behavior. But then, when it came to Jewish religious matters, the interwar Orthodox were not a very lettered population. For the most part, the Jewish education of the fathers had stopped either at the elementary-school level or with migration to America—whichever came first; that of the mothers was extremely limited, and that of their sons and daughters, in the days before the advent of the modern yeshiva, was minimal at best. "Their knowledge of Judaism," commented one contemporary, "is limited to the ability to read with ease certain portions of the service that are frequently repeated."[114] Nor were the Orthodox particularly concerned with the theological matters. Very much a this-worldly phenomenon, the religion they championed was almost uniformly concerned with the practical, quotidian realities of adjusting ritual requirements to the freedoms of middle-class life; few appeared to be the least bit concerned with higher existential issues. The successful bourgeois Orthodox Jew, wrote one eyewitness, "is not troubled too much by abstract problems of Judaism." This same observer went on to relate that the middle-class Orthodox Jew lived "an intensely Jewish life without ever giving a thought as to why and wherefore, or making the least attempt to understand its content or spirit. They never open a Jewish book."[115]

In the final analysis, the Orthodoxy developed by its interwar adherents was more of a sensibility, a way of ordering ritual behavior, than a collection of readily distinguishable, externally marked forms of behavior. Concretizing that sensibility through the development of a formal and highly elaborated pattern of association, Orthodox Jews at the time devoted themselves enthusiastically to the cultivation of an Orthodox public persona and denominational consciousness. What mattered to the New York interwar Orthodox was the creation and support of institutions—synagogues, day schools, a rabbinical seminary—that bore an Orthodox imprimatur. And it was within these public institutions that the vision of an indigenous, happily bourgeois Orthodoxy was most fully articulated and the tension between the demands of tradition and the opportunities of middle-class affluent New York life most completely resolved.

With a strong associational consciousness as American Orthodox Jews, the congregants of Kehilath Jeshurun, the Jewish Center, or Borough Park's Beth-El believed that they were not breaking with tradition, as were their more liberal coreligionists, but rather harmonizing it with their own perceived and felt needs as modern American Jews. They held dear the notion that they were both American and traditional; having succeeded, by their own lights, in skillfully integrating the bourgeois experience with a religious sensibility, they felt a keen sense of superiority to those who relinquished one or the other. "To be American and observant, to be like everyone else in their immediate milieu and yet an observant Jew rendered them a cut above the rest," an Orthodox Jew of that era explained.[116] Investing proudly in the construction of a community, they believed that "no one was better."[117]

"BIGGER AND BETTER" ORTHODOX SYNAGOGUES

"A clear, warm day, beautiful skies, an excellent band, sweet-throated choristers and eloquent speakers greeted the vast concourse of Jewish citizens and their elegantly attired dames," reported the *Hebrew Standard* in May 1902 as one of New York's oldest Orthodox congregations, Congregation Kehilath Jeshurun, marked the cornerstone laying of its brand-new building. Luminaries from New York's Jewish establishment, together with a delegation of local politicians, gathered on the platform, with its profusion of flowers and "streamers of bunting," to express their collective congratulations to the Yorkville congregation; at the same time, an all-male choir from the Hebrew Sheltering Guardian society, New York's Jewish orphan asylum, "stirred the hearts of the auditors with the tuneful strains of the old fashioned, yet ever new, Hebrew melodies."[1]

The high point of the day's celebration, however, was not the stirring musicality of the orphaned choir but rather the participation of Jacob Schiff, New York's greatest Jewish philanthropist (and its preeminent Reform Jew), as he wielded the historic trowel and laid the cornerstone of the Orthodox congregation. For some observers, Schiff's presence was even more of an occasion than the cornerstone laying per se. Schiff's participation, the subject of more than one editorial, was hailed as "one of the most pleasing features of the ceremony," an intimation that Schiff had, by his presence, placed his own considerable imprimatur on the activities of New York's Orthodox.[2]

Built at a cost of over $100,000, the Kehilath Jeshurun synagogue was located on East 85th Street between Park and Lexington Avenues. "Undoubtedly one of the finest edifices ever erected by an orthodox congregation in America," gushed the *Hebrew Standard*, the synagogue was a limestone and brick structure built in a mixture of the Romanesque and the Byzantine styles to accommodate over one thousand worshipers. In the vanguard of what would later become a normative building style for New York's Orthodox, the 1902 Kehilath Jeshurun building was a multistoried, "architecturally ambitious" structure with a massive sanctuary (replete with choir loft), a more intimate *beit midrash* (chapel), and a series of vestry or office rooms. Anchored by an external staircase with two symmetrical and imposing flights of steps and displaying a bevy of roseated stained-glass windows up above, the synagogue dominated the New York block of small brownstones and exuded a very strong physical presence.[3] The scale and ornamentality of KJ and the other Orthodox synagogues that were subsequently built during the interwar years—the Jewish Center, Ohab Zedek, Temple Beth-El—rivaled those of the city's Reform and Conservative synagogues and, as such, were a source of considerable pride to New York's Orthodox community; photographs of newly erected Orthodox synagogues were often featured prominently on the front page of Orthodox publications.

Monuments to the bourgeois characteristics of their worshipers, synagogues like Kehilath Jeshurun were built by relatively recent Eastern European immigrants who had made good, "downtown merchants whose bettered circumstances enabled them to live in better style," noted one newspaper.[4] As they moved uptown to the relatively uncharted Upper East Side neighborhood known as Yorkville, some Kehilath Jeshurun members undoubtedly brought with them memories of the Eldridge Street Synagogue, one of the Lower East Side's most handsome and distinguished synagogues, built in 1887, where they had worshiped earlier. Others welcomed the opportunity to construct a modern structure of their own making. Whatever the motivation, the construction of Kehilath Jeshurun reflected an attempt, although one that was never consciously articulated, to create a house of worship that would reflect the "bettered circumstances" of its congregants. "As he moves uptown and puts more expensive furniture in his home," wrote one contemporary observer of the prosperous middle-class immigrant Jew, "he begins a campaign for a bigger and better synagogue. . . ."[5]

In the "bigger and better synagogue" like Kehilath Jeshurun, stained-glass windows were de rigueur, as was the widespread use of velvet. In shades of dark blue or burgundy, velvet covered nearly every available surface: seat cushions, the "invariable two or four red plush chairs on the dais," which were reserved for the rabbis and other pulpit dignitaries, and the ornamental coverings of the Ark and Torah scrolls. Often, velvet was used as the fabric of the *mechitzah*, or partition that divided the men from the women. The overall effect, one congregant related, "was akin to that of a luxe movie theater." Arcaded galleries to seat the female worshiper, elaborate chandeliers, the lavish use of dark woods, marbled floors, and high vaulted ceilings added still further to the lushness of the sanctuary; so too did the presence, during the prewar period, of a doorman at the 85th Street synagogue, who, noted one eyewitness, was resplendent "in a gold band uniform."[6]

"Refined surroundings for Divine worship," the exteriors and interiors of the first generation of monumental Orthodox synagogues were, ironically enough, physical expressions of rebellion, of protest against the dominant form of Orthodox synagogue architecture and of Orthodoxy's characteristic behaviors.[7] At the time Kehilath Jeshurun was built, and for several decades thereafter, Orthodoxy and its institutions were identified in the public mind with what was retrogressive and backward in Jewish life; for many, the most common symbol of the American Orthodox was their "undignified and unsightly little chevrah [immigrant synagogue]."[8] After all, the typical Orthodox synagogue was housed in a kind of makeshift physical plant and presented "a most dour appearance": without buildings of their own, most synagogues were inconspicuously tucked away in a mix of " . . . private dwellings, second story apartments, office buildings and lofts," where male worshipers were crowded in together.[9] Spitoons were commonplace in what critics uncharitably called these "unsanitary synagogues," as was a disturbingly prominent clock, whose persistent ticking distracted worshipers from the business at hand. A "poorly ventilated women's precinct with a capacity of fifteen—but accommodating forty when necessary" housed the infrequent woman congregant, who was separated from her male counterpart by an opaque lace curtain.[10] Throughout, one eyewitness glumly reported, "a subway rush hour" spirit prevailed.[11] Disavowing the typical Orthodox synagogue as "primitive, untutored, undignified and *un-American*," the Kehilath Jeshurun congregant and his like-minded coreligionists created an alternative structure that proclaimed, through its lavish building materials, dramatic space, and abundant use of velvet, that "Orthodoxy does not stand for the milieu of East Broadway."[12]

In its aspirations, no less than in its architecture, Kehilath Jeshurun purported to become a modernized American synagogue, perhaps even "the most modern and beautiful orthodox synagogue in New York," as one advertisement would have it.[13] Having grown in thirty years from a small *chevra* or *landsmanshaft*-type synagogue housed at first in the meeting room of a Yorkville social hall and then later moving to a modest brick building of its own, Kehilath Jeshurun reflected the evolution of the American Orthodox synagogue. Well into the interwar years, most Orthodox synagogues in the New York area were extremely small congregations—"*ansheis*" or "*chevras*"—whose membership, drawn from the same geographical area in Eastern Europe, came together solely to pray or to study Jewish texts. A religious variant of the *landsmanshaft*, or Jewish mutual-aid society, thousands of which dotted the Empire City during the prewar period, these were informal congregations with none of the customary trappings of an American synagogue. "The typical immigrant synagogue," one uptown rabbi related, was "American by geographical location only."[14]

Adumbrating changes in the nature of the American Orthodox synagogue, the 85th Street synagogue marked a real departure, organizationally no less than architecturally, from the prevailing norm. The Orthodox American synagogue was historically an institution defined by and oriented toward the Old World, an institution rooted in geographically derived and communally shared religious customs, or *minhagim*. Now, in a reversal of that sociological tradition, like-minded people of similar religious orientation and fiscal station, but without any other kind of formal social ties, sought one another out within the context of devotion. Membership requirements of the new and more American Orthodox synagogues reflected that shift: no longer was membership contingent on place of birth or kinship ties, as was so commonly the case elsewhere. "Any male Israelite of good and moral character, between the ages of eighteen and sixty, who properly observes the Jewish Sabbath and is not married contrary to the Jewish law, shall be eligible to membership in this congregation," stated the Kehilath Jeshurun by-laws of 1903.[15] Once these two almost generic qualifications were fulfilled, all that stood in the way of full membership in the congregation was one's ability to pay the fees that membership entailed: during the prewar period, these varied from a modest $25 to a steep $250. At the Yorkville congregation in 1903, for example, members were required to pay an initiation fee of $10, annual membership dues of $25, and a $5 yearly tariff toward the upkeep of one's purchased seat, a membership perquisite. At the Jewish Center fifteen years later, the rates were sharply higher: it cost $125 for a family membership.

Whatever the costs of membership, the latter reflected a new notion of communal association. *Landsmanshaft* criteria of belonging, in which members were bound together by geography, memory, and the shared experience of being an immigrant, no longer counted for much; what did were class and common social interests. Traditional social bonds were now supplanted by a more artificial construct, a self-made social contract of confraternity and friendship. The middle-class Orthodox synagogues, observed one critic, are conducted "almost as private clubs or family affairs."[16] The early history of the Jewish Center on Manhattan's Upper West Side is an extreme example of the degree to which common business interests, social ties, and neighborhood propinquity formed the basis for belonging. Though its avowed and manifest purpose was to meet the religious and social needs of the Upper West Side's burgeoning Jewish population in a novel way, through the creation of a synagogue center, its latent purpose was more powerful and compelling still. "Some want a synagogue primarily," its rabbi and founder observed in 1917; "others want mainly a club."[17] Ultimately, the latter triumphed. Touted as a "rich man's club," the Center became a house of worship in which its "typically successful bourgeois type" congregants felt comfortable and at home.[18] In fact, so strongly did friendship and sense of commonality pervade that synagogue that visitors were often made to feel like unwelcome intruders; the prevailing atmosphere, in turn, was often criticized as unduly cliquish.

To be sure, the modernized Orthodox synagogue did not, with one rewriting of the membership statutes, eradicate all traces of its European provenance. In liturgical matters, *minhag* (custom) reigned supreme, reflecting the continued hold of the Old World on the New. Years after most of the European old guard had emigrated to New York, one of their number recalls having been roundly chastised for performing the afternoon, or *Mincha*, prayer service in an inappropriate manner: "in the major key of the German Jews and not the minor key in accord with the Polish *minhag*."[19]

And yet, a proud and overriding sense of their own American Jewishness predominated among the congregants of large modernized Orthodox synagogues like Kehilath Jeshurun or Ohab Zedek. It was that sensibility, their newly affirmed identity as American Jews, that unified and gave focus to the membership. The devaluation of European ties and the attendant highlighting of American social ones boldly differentiated the old-fashioned congregation from its newer analogue, stamping it as an American institution. "Our American-born youth," explained Rabbi Herbert S. Goldstein, "have seen neither the Russian, the Rumanian, Galician, Austrian, Hungarian or German life; they have seen American life. No longer will synagogues be built called the Rumanian Schule, the Bialystoker Chevra, the Chechanover Chevra."[20] Goldstein was right. Once known as "Anshe Jeshurun," the newly constructed 85th Street synagogue was officially designated as "Congregation Kehilath Jeshurun," a far more American and socially inclusive appellation than the traditional-sounding and -meaning "Anshe Jeshurun." (With each of its names speaking to a broad and loosely defined constituency, the synagogue was known variously as the 85th Street Shul, Congregation Kehilath Jeshurun, or "KJ.") Similarly, the name chosen to adorn Goldstein's congregation—the Institutional Synagogue—provided more of a clue to the kinds of activities one would find within its four walls than to the origins of its congregants. The succinctly worded Jewish Center or Borough Park Temple Beth-El, whose Reform-sounding name, one writer assures us, was simply an architectural designation (rather than a ritual one), points to the prevalence of this trend.[21]

Changes of this sort were by no means the sole indices of the Orthodox synagogue's gradual modernization. Internal alterations in the nature of the prayer service followed, almost as a matter of course. Mordecai Kaplan, Kehilath Jeshurun's first English-speaking rabbi, recalled in his diary that "all went well" with his predecessor—"a Yiddish speaking Rav of the old school"—as long as the congregation retained its modest European demeanor. Once the new building was erected, however, congregants were quick to voice displeasure with their *rav*. "They no sooner found themselves in that spacious building," recalled Kaplan, "than their rising next generation began demanding sermons in English. My predecessor who had gradually acquired a knowledge of conversational

English tried his hand at sermonic English and with not too much success."[22] In fact, Kaplan was hired in 1904 to replace his colleague and to set the congregation upon a new and more modern course.

Considerable controversy, however, dogged Kaplan's initial efforts. The presence of a twenty-three-year-old Seminary graduate in the newly consecrated pulpit of Kehilath Jeshurun angered some of Kaplan's more traditional colleagues, who viewed the younger scholar as a symbol of traditional Judaism gone wayward. Determined to make known their views and, they hoped, to force Kaplan's resignation, the Agudat ha-Rabbanim distributed handbills throughout Yorkville denouncing the synagogue, the Seminary, and Kaplan for their joint attempt to modify traditional Jewish ritual behavior.

Apparently, preaching in English was particularly abhorrent to the Agudat, which sought, especially during the pre–World War I era, to limit the impact of such overt and dismaying displays of Americanization. To recently transplanted European Jewish leaders like Jacob David Willowski, the Slutska Rav, a man reputed to be second only to Rabbi Jacob Joseph as a "ranking European Torah personality" in the New World, the English-language sermon posed a grave danger to the future of traditional Judaism. Insisting that it was more acceptable to leave a synagogue than to listen to an English-language sermon, the Slutska Rav (also known as the *Ridbaz*) crusaded energetically for the latter's abolition. "If these practices will not cease," he warned, "there is no hope for the continuance of the Jewish religion. These sermons will open the gates leading our brethren to Reform Judaism."[23]

In what was soon to become a local communal scandal of some note, the Slutska Rav delivered a traditional Yiddish *drasha* at Kehilath Jeshurun's 1904 Rosh Hashanah services, thus preempting Kaplan's English address. Some observers believed that Kaplan, in a gesture of courtesy and hospitality, had willingly deferred to his senior colleague; others, especially the Anglo-Jewish press, believed that the Slutska Rav had forbade Kaplan from preaching in English and, in short order, they made of the incident a cause célèbre. For a few weeks, editorials and letters to the editor flew back and forth within the pages of the Anglo-Jewish press as readers and journalists gave voice to worries over the legitimacy of an English-language sermon in an avowedly Orthodox institution. "I hope that there is no truth in the story," commented the anonymous *Hebrew Standard* columnist known as "Aspaklarya/the Mirror," "that Congregation Kehilath Jeshurun on 85th St. forbade its rabbi to preach in English. . . ." But if there is, he continued, and if Yiddish was preferred over English "on religious grounds, it is a great *Chillul Hashem* [desecration of God's name]."[24] The actions of the Slutska Rav, added the *American Hebrew*, constitute a "blow to honest Orthodoxy," and the paper fiercely criticized the congregation for what it took to be an affront, "an insult to its young preacher," and a "disgrace" to its membership. "The sooner the Slutska Rav gets out of the land, the better for Orthodox Judaism," the *American Hebrew* hotly concluded.[25] At the time Kaplan appeared to have taken the incident in stride. Years later, however, he confessed his considerable displeasure at the affair, relating that when the Slutska Rav was "injected into the situation, I was up in arms. . . .To this day," Kaplan went on to explain, "the Ridbaz lives in my memory as a good deal of a bully and a shrewd business man."[26]

Despite its controversial beginnings, the English-language service would eventually become standard practice in modernized Orthodox synagogues, a sine qua non of its modernity. Still, on the eve of World War I the overwhelming majority of professed Orthodox synagogues, most of them *landsmanshaft-lich* institutions, lacked an English preacher. In a 1918 survey taken of over seven hundred synagogues in the metropolitan area, slightly more than 10 percent featured an English-language sermon or resorted to English in making announcements. Reviewing these statistics, the study's author, none other than Mordecai Kaplan, expressed pessimism for the future of traditional Judaism in America. "One to whom the future of the Jews and of Judaism is an object of concern cannot but view with alarm the condition of the synagogue, as indicated by the cold figures in the statistical columns," Kaplan noted. The figures were part of an elaborately documented chart on the "salient characteristics" of New York's synagogues. The absence of English-language sermons showed just how few congregations had "reckoned with the environment."[27]

If slow to take hold, the use of English was soon standard in those congregations that viewed themselves as modern. Not surprisingly, New York's more affluent Jewish neighborhoods had the highest incidence of English-speaking rabbis. Brooklyn's Borough Park headed the list, followed by the Upper West Side and Harlem; Yorkville came in third.[28] A resident of one of these communities and the congregant of a modernizing Orthodox synagogue once likened the presence of an English-language preacher to that of a "fine piano—it being of no consequence if there is no one in the house who can play it."[29] In this particularly apt turn of phrase, the English preacher, like the piano, that staple of middle-class furnishings, was seen as a symbol of the bourgeois modernity of the Orthodox prayer service. An English-speaking rabbi, recalled Kaplan prior to World War I, was undoubtedly the mark of a "fashionable" congregation, distinguishing it from the less progressive and affluent Orthodox house of worship. Yet even he had to concede that there was more to the growing communal demand for an English-language preacher than the dictates of fashion. "Of course," admitted Kaplan, "there was also something of the religious motive present in their eagerness to secure a man of that type but," he added with his characteristic cynicism, "it was surely secondary to the social [motive]. . . ."[30]

Whether motivated by the dictates of fashion or by purer considerations, there was no question that the English sermon was the modernized Orthodox synagogue's major drawing card and, what's more, was heralded as such. Widely advertised in the Friday religion column of the metropolitan press, the local synagogue newsletter, and on the building's exterior bulletin board, the sermon quickly developed into the chief instrumentality by which to save souls and claim adherents or, at the very least, to draw people to the synagogue. The key dramatic moment, the high point, of the service, the sermon afforded the rabbi the opportunity not only to display his erudition and verbal prowess but, more important still, to strengthen his congregants' affective ties to Orthodox Judaism and to one another. For as one congregant explained, "In the modern synagogue, it is the sermons delivered by the rabbi that afford a means of close contact with his congregation."[31]

In part, the sermon's appeal was therapeutic. "People come to the synagogue burdened with problems. They are frightened by the conditions of life. They are lonely and depressed. They need guidance and moral support. Furthest from their mind is a text and the clever manipulation of it. . . .The task of the Jewish preacher . . . is to rebuke like a Hosea, lament like a Jeremiah and comfort like an Isaiah," explained Joseph H. Lookstein, the greatest Orthodox orator of pre–World War II.[32] Mindful of the emotional and psychological needs of his parishioners, Lookstein transformed the traditional content of the *drasha*, with its "clever manipulation" of sources and wide-ranging appropriation of quotes, into a solidly crafted and emotionally stirring appeal for the relevance of Orthodox Judaism to the modern world. In addresses on "Clothes Make the Man: A Religious Analysis of Fashion," "The Prophetic Tradition," or "Between Washington and Lincoln," Lookstein and his contemporary rabbinic colleagues sought to induce in their listeners a startling array of emotions: optimism, patriotism, civic-mindedness, and, perhaps above all else, a sense of religiosity and spirituality. For that first generation of modernized Orthodox rabbis, the sermon functioned in much the same way as it had for their Reform counterparts in Central Europe close to a century earlier: as a vehicle by which to "improve, edify and to create an atmosphere conducive to 'devotion.' " Or, as Rabbi Leo Jung, somewhat closer to home, put it, the sermon must "stimulate [the] will to Jewishness. . . ."[33]

In addition to its frankly inspirational qualities, the sermon was of considerable educative value. Congregants likened the sermon to a college lecture and were quick to emphasize just how much they learned from it.[34] The preacher's easy familiarity with English dazzled his largely untutored congregants, whose appreciation for the finer points of the English language was heightened in this manner. At times, though, the pyrotechnics of a sermon threatened to overshadow its content. The sermons of Herbert S. Goldstein, a professor of homiletics at RIETS, New York's Orthodox rabbinical seminary, were often criticized for the density of the big words cluttering the narrative. Goldstein's sermons, complained one rabbinic critic, "are often streaked with patches of modern vocabulary which do not harmonize with the rest of the content," while a congregant recalled that Goldstein appeared to have deliberately used arcane and cumbersome words, "the bigger the better," to impress his listeners.[35] At other times, the sermon became an opportunity for its deliverer to display his familiarity with current affairs and thus deteriorated, as a third critic observed, into a "bonton affair for weekly verbosity and unread magazines."[36] And yet, despite the abuses to which it was often subject, the sermon emerged as the most highly touted feature of the Americanized Orthodox service and the one to which most, perhaps even all, congregants paid closest attention.

Getting congregants to listen attentively, and on a regular basis, to a sermon was itself an exercise in modernization. In much the same way that Central European rabbis a generation earlier had struggled to find a representative preaching style, the modernized Orthodox rabbinate of the interwar years took great pains to institutionalize and formulate a homiletical style of its own, an authentic American Orthodox voice. Toward that end, RIETS sponsored courses in homiletics and pedagogy, in which would-be rabbis were instructed in the principles of sermon construction. H. Pereira Mendes, RIETS's first homiletics instructor, championed a brief sermon, teaching his young charges that "you cannot save souls after eighteen minutes of preaching."[37] Lookstein, for his part, looked elsewhere for guidance. Borrowing heavily from the skilled homiletical techniques of Rev. Henry Emerson Fosdick, the preeminent Christian preacher of the day, he unabashedly drew on outside influences in constructing his own preaching style, the canons of which he, like Pereira Mendes, would later teach to RIETS students. The latter, once ordained, were further encouraged to try their hand at sermonizing by studying the contents of sermon manuals published by the Rabbinical Council of America; these manuals contained a collection of the outstanding sermons of a given year.

As the sermon (presumably) induced in its listeners a more reverential, devout, and sacramental sensibility, the highly choreographed and ritualized prayer service of which it was so pivotal a part sustained the mood. Impressed with the mannerliness of the worshipers and the tranquility of the service at Kehilath Jeshurun, one admiring visitor in 1903 wrote to the synagogue's president: "Keeping pace with the symmetric architecture of this grand edifice is the way . . . the Divine Service is conducted in your synagogue."[38] Under the banner of what was commonly known as "decorum," various measures were instituted over a twenty- or thirty-year period to modernize the Orthodox prayer ritual. Decorum embraced a wide spectrum of social behaviors and conventions designed to aestheticize the prayer ritual: a formally choreographed service with ushers to keep disturbing conversation to a minimum, a strictly enacted dress code and the widespread use of English as the public language of the prayer service were among its most common features. However defined, the aestheticizing of the synagogue service represented nothing less than the adaptation of external and essentially secular social rituals to the religious environment of the sanctuary. Matters of style and bourgeois social convention became increasingly reinterpreted—even sacralized—as they were gently and gradually integrated into the modernized Orthodox prayer service. Ends in themselves, the aesthetic improvements of the traditional prayer service were not accompanied by corresponding liturgical changes, nor did they signify any fundamental reorientation in religious policy, as had been the case with both Conservative and Reform Jews. Rather, the objective throughout, as one congregant put it, was "to practice complete decorum, the same as in reformed temples, *without deviating one iota from our Orthodox traditions.*"[39] Claiming decorum as their own, American Orthodox Jews sought to remove from it any taint of Reform or unduly modernized Judaism and redefined the concept, rendering it socially neutral and thus acceptable. Theirs was to be a Judaism of restrained and controlled modernity, one in which the applied physical attributes of decorum were ultimately to become an organic, integral, and established *behavioral* norm; the kind of corresponding ideological implications that marked those more liberal in orientation were conspicuously missing.

In the process, upwardly mobile immigrants of the kind likely to worship at Kehilath Jeshurun or the Jewish Center replaced traditional Jewish notions of etiquette with those drawn from the larger social context and applied Western standards of behavior to their own conduct and institutions. With their newly acquired "taste for the beautiful and the decorous," they found their synagogues wanting.[40] Cramped and undistinguished quarters, the use of Yiddish, a kinetic prayer style, jumbled and disorderly proceedings, and informal spirit were now anathematized. "Orthodox Judaism," lamented H. Pereira Mendes, "has suffered too long from an indecorum which . . . has no place in American Jewish life."[41] When evaluated and defined in terms of occidental standards of behavior, everything about the typical Orthodox immigrant synagogue, from its "unbearable din" to its "disheartening spectacle of disorder," was the subject of opprobrium and the object of improvement.

Reading contemporary critiques of the immigrant, or "downtown," synagogue (of which there were many), one is struck by the frequency with which commentators call attention to, and lament, what was to their minds the excessively busy, even frenetic, character of the prayer service. Written during the period before World War I, these accounts, although overstated and overblown at times, provide a firsthand, internal view of what was then characteristic synagogue practice among New York's Orthodox. In what is the fullest and most detailed indictment of the downtown synagogue, a report written by Elias

Solomon, who, coincidently enough, would later assume the post of English-speaking minister at the 85th Street synagogue during the World War I years, the spontaneous and seemingly unrestrained nature of the service drew the most ire. A young rabbinical student at the Jewish Theological Seminary when he composed his critique, Solomon found the immigrant prayer service "shocking to a refined person" such as himself. As the none-too-sympathetic *American Israelite* categorically observed, "our downtown brethren have not the slightest notion of what is the meaning of decorum in the House of God."[42] In the absence of a uniform prayer book, Solomon observed, each worshiper prayed noisily aloud, at his own pace, and with great physical activity. "The customary habit of congregants of swaying the body to and fro, backwards and forwards," was a particular distraction and a "great source of annoyance."[43] Much to Solomon's further annoyance, an English-language rabbi was nowhere in evidence; instead, the primary religious specialist, assuming there was one, was the cantor, who, it seemed, contributed to the overall disorder by his excessive vocalizing, or, in Solomon's words, "vocal gymnastics."[44] Given to performing lengthy musical renditions of the prayers more for his own sake than for the sake of heaven, the cantor unduly prolonged the service, leaving the worshipers bored and inattentive. "It had all been very boring, or most of it," recalled one young worshiper brought to the synagogue by his devout father, "the unintelligible reading of the Law, the hurried prayers, [my] father constantly finding the place in a book whose Hebrew was meaningless and whose English translations . . . sounded crooked, stilted, redundant and uninspired."[45]

Frequent interruptions of an avowedly commercial nature contributed still further to the chaos of the divine service. Making public donations at the time of the Torah reading or during the auctioning of communal honors, a practice known colloquially as *shnuddering*, was not only common to virtually all premodern Orthodox synagogues but was the bugaboo of those intent on modernizing the service. *Shnuddering* was a major source of revenue; congregants bid for any number of causes ranging from charity to the acquisition of a chandelier, the upkeep of the synagogue, or the purchase of a gift for a retiring employee. Rejecting the notion that these practices were sacred, time-honored Jewish traditions, possibly even *mitzvas* (ritual commandments or obligations), its critics found them instead to be "excrescences . . . barnacles that impede the smooth sailing of the ritual service."[46] There was simply no room in the sanctuary for unseemly money-making schemes, no matter how laudable their intent, insisted those with decorum on their minds, as they fought determinedly to rid the service of its commercialism.

Given the intrusion of overtly material matters into the service and the absence of any controlling ritual presence, it was no wonder that the prayer service was anything but orderly. Congregants walked about the sanctuary while saying their prayers, exited en masse during the chanting of the memorial service, and, at the conclusion of the Sabbath morning service, fled the sanctuary so energetically that, accordingly to one observer, "pandemonium reigns."[47] When not perambulating around the room, worshipers chatted noisily with their neighbors, freely trading insults and exchanging gossip and business tips. Synagogue minutes amply document the frequency with which members of the typical *landsmanshaft* "shul" indulged in the hurling of insults or in the creation of disturbances. The Eldridge Street Synagogue minutes on at least a dozen occasions during the pre–World War I period record the activities of members whose rambunctious conduct upset the orderliness of the service. In 1915, one member was fined the hefty sum of one dollar because he had "created a disturbance in the shul during the period of the prayers, maligned the officers as well as other members of the shul . . . and us[ed] such base language."[48] Under these circumstances, it was not the least bit surprising that worshipers appeared to be more engaged by public mundane conversation than with private matters of the heart.

For many self-consciously upwardly mobile immigrants who liked to see themselves as "people of aesthetic tastes," the indecorous and informal downtown synagogue served as an uncomfortable reminder of their immigrant origins. Where decorousness and civility, proper comportment and manners, reflected acculturation, its absence, in turn, seemed to reflect a stubborn and unseemly retention of un-Americanized and immigrant behavior. Time and again during the closing decades of the nineteenth century and the opening ones of the twentieth, immigrants and their children were taught that manners and civility were the attributes of an American. Popular culture as well as the central agencies of assimilation like the public school and the press hardly distinguished between bourgeois behavior and Americanization, making the two synonymous and intertwined.[49] Immigrants were told repeatedly that to be an American was to engage in middle-class forms of behavior, that rationality and order characterized the best American enterprises, and that cleanliness was not just of physical benefit but a social value as well. The confluence of bourgeois behavior with Americanization, then, provides the larger social context for understanding Orthodoxy's pronounced emphasis on decorum. In light of the prevailing critique of manners, the litany of defects associated with the immigrant synagogue falls squarely into place: just as immigrants as a whole were pointedly enjoined to change their personal behavior to conform to that of Western norms, so too were their religious and social institutions expected to change were they to take root in the New World.[50]

In making over the Orthodox synagogue in this newly found and highly cherished image of urbanity, New York's Orthodox were driven not only by their attraction for what was modern and Western but by something more compelling still: a fundamental and unswerving belief that the typically undecorous service threatened the future of an American Orthodoxy. What was at stake was not simply a matter of style and taste but its implications. As the champions of a "clean, decorous service" understood matters, the "disheartening features" of the downtown Orthodox synagogue single-handedly alienated the younger generation of American Jews and, consequently, threatened the future of Judaism in the New World.[51] "If the parents of our youth had made it their set purpose *to drive* their children away from the Jewish synagogue," fiercely noted Rabbi Jung in 1926, "they could have employed no better method for that end than the management and conduct prevalent in the average shul."[52] Decorum, then, was the vehicle by which those of the modernized Orthodox persuasion sought to halt the erosion of commitment among their young. Hoping to appeal to the younger, American-born generation on their own terms, Orthodox Jewry used the well-appointed, orderly service as their drawing card. The synagogue service, explained Rabbi Joseph H. Lookstein, perhaps one of the most ardent exponents of a well-regulated and articulated prayer service, "is a medium for furthering and advancing the interests and welfare of Judaism. If the worshiper, in many cases estranged from Orthodox Judaism, is impressed by the beauty and inspiration of the orthodox service, he becomes amenable to the other teachings and ideals of Traditional Judaism."[53]

The equation of the future of Orthodox Judaism with decorousness was not lost on the young. In fact, a contingent of college-age, largely native-born New Yorkers from traditional homes responded to the pressures of modernity by creating the "Young Israel" synagogue movement on the eve of World War I. Through their espousal of a "modern and attractive" synagogue service and the elevation of decorum into their "cardinal principle," Young Israel members underscored the importance that youth placed on decorum and order and thus challenged the notion that Orthodoxy was old-fashioned, a religion whose appeal was limited exclusively to the elderly and unacculturated.[54] Anticipating developments in New York's more established synagogues, the Young Israel movement created a network of affiliated synagogues throughout the metropolitan area where decorum was the order of the day.[55] "It was a very lively service," recalled one early Young Israel of Williamsburg worshiper. "I took to it very quickly." The Young Israel, he went on to explain, "was an iconoclastic institution . . . there were several principles which were almost revolutionary as compared to the synagogues of the day." Among them: A waist-high *mechitzah*, "the active participation of women in congregational singing, . . . the wearing of small *tallesim* and the rule against *shnuddering*."[56] With over several thousand members by the 1940s, the Young Israel succeeded in cultivating a natural constituency for "cultured Orthodoxy."

In its adaptation of what was essentially a middle-class interpretation and performance of traditional religious ritual, modernized Orthodoxy, whether in the form of a Young Israel or a more established uptown synagogue, created a new system of expressive religious behaviors and, with it, a new set of ritual norms. Individual synagogues varied in their degree of fealty to this new display of decorousness, with some far more assiduous in its cultivation than others. And yet, one can clearly point to the emergence during the interwar years of a distinctive American Orthodox prayer style and prayer service. A 180-degree turn in personality from the service in the typical downtown synagogue, the modern Orthodox service of the interwar years was performed amidst lavish surroundings; where its predecessor was noisy and cacophonous, "you could hear a pin drop from beginning until the end" in the westernized Orthodox sanctuary.[57] All characteristic tendencies toward noise and disorder were tamed as worshipers were admonished "to sing in key and in tempo and not go on their own vocal way, outsinging their neighbors."[58] They were also instructed when to approach the rabbi or synagogue officials and how to receive an honor; when to solicit funds and when to converse. The provision of a uniform prayer book capped the process of standardization. Not only were congregants expected to conform to the same social norms and behave in a like manner; they were also obliged to worship in concert. The Hebrew Publishing Company prayer book with an English translation by Rev. I. Singer was generally the text of choice. "Its conformance to strict tradition and its clear and limpid English," an enthusiast observed, "have combined to make it *the* version of all others."[59]

Adherence to a strictly enforced dress code, an absolute "essential," helped further to standardize the synagogue milieu; appropriate attire consisted of jackets and ties, a black silk *yarmulke* in some synagogues (a black felt hat in others), and a small, narrow silk prayer shawl for the men; head coverings for the women; and top hats and striped pants for synagogue officials. The latter, one eyewitness related, were given to wearing Prince Albert suits, "called rather irreverently, *Prinz Yankels*, and high hats," some of which belonged to the synagogue itself. "It's up to the incumbent to fit into the hat," this congregant explained, "and many a son has had difficulty recognizing his father on the dais solemnly disguised in one of those toppers."[60] In fact, many synagogues began the practice, soon to become widespread, of keeping on hand *yarmulkes* and *tallesim* for the male worshiper who arrived without such ritual trappings, and flimsy lace doilies for the married female worshiper sans hat. "If you attended a formal party," explained Rabbi Lookstein of this practice, "you would be asked to wear formal clothes. If you were a soldier in the army, you would have to dress in accordance with the regulation of uniform. The Taleth," he concluded, "is the formal garment for worship in an orthodox synagogue, or a uniform if you will. . . ."[61] Carrying this principle a bit further, some synagogues banished to the rear of the sanctuary those who failed to conform to its sartorial norms. At the Jewish Center, where the wearing of hats was customary, the synagogue bulletin carried the following admonition: "Visitors who arrive without hats and others who for any reason have to wear skullcaps, will be seated in the rear rows."[62]

Conducted along rational lines, the service manifested a new-found concern with time and routine; Sabbath morning services began, more or less promptly, at 9:00 A.M., concluded at noon, and featured a sermon at approximately 11:15. In fact, so conscious of time were the rabbis of the modernized congregations that they set strict limits on the length of their sermons: thirty minutes in one congregation, forty in another. "You could set your watch by the rabbi's sermon," more than one congregant proudly related as they extolled the oratorical restraint of their rabbi.[63]

Bound by time, worshipers were also bound by social convention. Upon entering the synagogue, the male worshiper would hang his coat in the coatroom (no unsightly coat piles to clutter the sanctuary) and collect his prayer paraphernalia—prayer shawl, prayer book, and black silk headgear—from specially designed receptacles located either at the entrance to or the rear of the sanctuary; in other instances, niches in front of each worshiper's seat contained prayer book and Bible. Donning ritual attire, regular synagogue attendees would proceed directly to their accustomed seats while newcomers would be escorted by an usher or the sexton to vacant quarters. Ushers, often "trustees for the men and young boys for the ladies," were stationed at strategic intervals throughout the sanctuary and played a crucial role in the implementation of order.[64] Wardens of propriety, they were on the alert for any infraction, be it improper dress or improper conduct. Their very presence, it was hoped, discouraged conversation and the characteristic urge to move about at the same time that it "added dignity" to the service.[65]

Meanwhile, the prayer service itself was redesigned to the point where there was almost nothing spontaneous or improvised about it. A set piece, reenacted and refined week after week, the Sabbath service was staged according to strict and unaltering guidelines. Almost every contingency of the modernized prayer service was attended to in advance, be it the allotment of communal honors or the cantor's designated repertory. In the interests of uniformity, many prayers, like the "Mourner's *Kaddish*," were now said in unison, with the rabbi or cantor in the role of conductor; individual worship (often discernibly loud) was strongly discouraged lest it promote cacophony. The theatricality and undue vocalizing of the cantor also came in for more than its fair share of criticism. A guest at the dedication exercises of the Eldridge Street Synagogue, initially well disposed toward the cantor, whose "sympathetic voice and pleasing delivery" he admired, quickly changed his mind upon observing the cantor "mark time with a lead pencil after drawing his tallith over his right shoulder."[66] In much the same spirit, the proceedings of a rabbinical association meeting record the wry proposal that all "prima donna cantors, especially those who lengthen the services, be hung." The more sober suggestion, however, that the cantor be limited "to a time schedule" carried the day.[67]

Many synagogues sought some kind of accommodation between the cantor's interest in performing and the congregation's patience. Congregational singing, the middle ground, quickly caught on as the preferred solution. An increasingly popular form of prayer in which congregants participated actively, albeit under strictly defined circumstances, in the prayer ritual, congregational singing was a way not only of reining in the vocal excess of the cantor but, more to the point, of developing an interactive and engaged audience. In many synagogues, the cantor and rabbi would meet together with a few of the more musically inclined congregants to teach them the latest tune so as to ensure, through their presence, a promise of musical participation. So determined was the Kehilath Jeshurun to make participatory song viable that in 1930 it granted two weeks' leave to its cantor so that he might "study Congregational Singing."[68] Frequent English interpolations and a pronounced predilection for responsive readings were additional manifestations of the newly enhanced service. "From personal experience," observed Lookstein, "I have seen the welcome thrill on the faces of worshipers when, for example, during a Yizkor service an English psalm or prayer is read. I am convinced," he added, "that a slight concession in this regard might keep within the folds of orthodoxy a multitude who might otherwise desert us."[69]

The elimination of *shnuddering* was yet another concession to modernity. Despite the fiscal toll the decision exacted of congregations accustomed to generating a considerable portion of their income from that practice, commercialism was ultimately disallowed, although in this instance the process of change was exceedingly slow. Given the financial benefits of *shnuddering* and, one suspects too, the strong emotional sentiment for the practice, it was not so easily discontinued. At Kehilath Jeshurun, for example, it took close to forty years (!) before the administration completely abolished the public sale of honors. Reluctant to let go entirely of such a time-honored practice, the board throughout this forty-year period proposed a number of alternative measures to control some of its more flagrant abuses: *shnuddering*, it was suggested, should be permitted only at the discretion of the president or limited solely to "*simchas*" (happy occasions, celebrations of milestones).[70] When each solution turned out to be unworkable, a new variation was instituted. Finally, in 1943, the congregation took "the bold step" of eliminating the practice altogether, arguing that it "imparted an unsavory commercial character to one of the most sacred parts of the service."[71]

The conclusion of the sacred service was as orderly and ordered as that which preceded it and was a far cry from the stampede of hungry worshipers depicted in critique after critique of the premodern Orthodox sanctuary. Worshipers waited in their seats until the final salutation and then exited quietly. Sometimes, as at the Jewish Center, services culminated in a formal handshaking ceremony, in which congregants queued up at the rear of the sanctuary to shake their rabbi's hand and to exchange polite conversation; this practice evolved into as integral a part of that synagogue's official ritual as, say, the chanting of "Adon Olam," the traditional prayer marking the end of the service. One former Center congregant remembers how her mother would question her every Sabbath as to whether or not she had shaken the rabbi's hand, as if the Sabbath were incomplete or improperly observed without having done so.[72]

The transformation of the Orthodox prayer service into a highly orchestrated, well-run, and decorous affair did not happen overnight. A gradual and cumulative process in which change and stasis were mixed together, the aestheticizing of the service took a number of years before being fully implemented. In some instances, the initiative for ritual change came from the laity, who would, from time to time, publicly complain that the "service in the Sanctuary is not *yet* as decorous as one would like."[73] In other cases, a more Americanized clergy would be the first to advocate the introduction of new sanctuary behaviors. Whatever the impetus, each manifestation of decorum received wholehearted and complete ritual legitimation by the clergy of the modernized synagogue. Using gingerly phrased language to avoid any possible association with Reform, the rabbinic proponents of modernized Orthodoxy, men like Lookstein or Jung, called the proposed ritual changes "procedures," "innovations," or, more traditionally perhaps, "*takanoth*" (ritual enactments). Through their careful avoidance of the word "reform," they anchored these changes within Jewish law and invoked the *Shulkan Arukh* and other halakhic sources in support of their position. "American Jews," insisted Lookstein, "must be made to understand that decorum and dignity . . . *are provisions* of the Shulkan Arukh," as he attempted to prove that modernized Orthodoxy contravened neither the spirit nor the letter of the *halakha* in its insistence on decorum and order.[74]

Despite the use of euphemisms and corresponding efforts at textual legitimation, not every manifestation of decorum was initially well received; friction and intrasynagogue dissent were often the companions of change, especially on the part of the more Europeanized old guard, which found it difficult to adjust to some of the innovations. Overcoming their resistance impeded the process of ritual reform, slowing it down. "I must admit," confessed Harry Fischel, a representative of the old guard, on the occasion of his fortieth anniversary of membership in Kehilath Jeshurun, "that at the beginning [English prayer] was a great hardship to me and probably to a few more of the old school." But seeing that it drew younger members, he continued, "not only did I decide to put up with it, but I even gave my entire approval."[75] Fischel was not always so obliging; in fact, he and his like-minded coreligionists were often quick to brand a proposed change as "Reform" and thus block its introduction. When, as early as 1906, young Kaplan suggested ways to improve sanctuary behavior, his suggestions were dismissed as too "Reform" in content. But then, continue the minutes,

> after deliberating on all matters . . . we [the Board] have come to the conclusion that not in any way, shape or manner . . . [do the following] involve any reform measures . . . but we recognize the fact that there should be more decorum in our service, that speaking during the reading of the Torah should not be countenanced, but forbidden; that the Sexton should not be permitted while making "Mi shbeirach" [prayer for one's welfare] to inquire the names of members or attendants at worship; . . . that during the sermon no person should be permitted to enter the Synagogue or leave the same, except in case of great necessity. . . ."[76]

Neither frivolities nor "gimmicks," the uniform prayer book, well-ordered service, and dress code were essential to the process of rendering Orthodoxy fresh and were viewed by many as an indication of its successful accommodation to America.[77] "We have incorporated several new features in our service," Lookstein wrote of his use of English interpolations and congregational singing, "in order to make them more interesting and more intelligible . . . Come and see for yourself how thoroughly *at home* you will be made to feel."[78] Ultimately, making Americanized Jews feel at home within the Orthodox sanctuary lay at the heart of the campaign to westernize and modernize the prayer ritual. The accommodation and integration of "aesthetic touches that appeal to the modern Jew" was designed, above all, to prove unequivocally that Orthodoxy could hold its own in America. For, as Max Etra, Kehilath Jeshurun's president, explained in 1945, "Orthodoxy can meet the needs of the day and can meet them even more effectively than the other groupings in Jewish life. . . ."[79]

Underlying this practical, applied exercise in manners, one can discern the making of an ideology: an aesthetic of religious expression. For the interwar generation, decorous behavior functioned as a kind of ultimate value like truth or goodness; what was well mannered and orderly was of a higher order. The incorporation and canonization of a middle-class style of prayer and comportment into the traditional prayer service was therefore a statement, however faintly limned, of purpose and of orientation; the insistence that matters of style were an essential part of the Americanized Orthodox prayer service reflected an attempt to establish a community with shared ritual objects, gestures, and, above all else, social behaviors.

At times, perhaps, the interwar Americanized Orthodox synagogue went too far in its advocacy of decorum, sacrificing fervor to order and dignity. And over the years, what had once been fresh, spirited, and possibly even "revolutionary" had hardened, as innovations often do, into formal ritualism and had even become the butt of humor. "It's okay to come to KJ without a *yarmulke*," a contemporary joke had it, "but God forbid you arrive without a tie." Zealous in the service of the decorous, interwar Orthodox Jewry might well have overstated its commitment to modernity, which it equated wholeheartedly and unstintingly with manners and proper comportment.

Interestingly enough, that equation no longer holds: subsequent generations of Orthodox Jews do not quite share their predecessors' enthusiasm for a well-regulated and choreographed prayer service. Orthodox Jews who had come of age during the late fifties and early sixties found the traditional modern Orthodox service unduly formalized, stilted, and dry; its rules and regulations, English interpolations, and proudly enforced dress code were widely seen as obstacles to, rather than agents of, religious expression. Rejecting decorum as both an ideology and a form of behavior, this "post-decorous" generation has welcomed a different, more relaxed atmosphere within the sanctuary.[80] And yet, despite the current devaluation of decorum, the efforts of that pioneering first generation of modernized, Americanized Jews resulted in an enduring social phenomenon: an American, religious "community of manners."[81]

The notion of a community of manners was an inclusive one designed to embrace the entire family, not just the adult male and female worshipers. Children, to be sure, were not welcome in the orderly sanctuary except for those over a certain age (immediately pre–bar mitzvah) or those endowed with quiet temperaments. Ample room, however, was made for them in "junior congregation," a parallel Sabbath-morning youth service conducted by and for youngsters, where they were "initiated into the accepted synagogue procedures." Saturday-afternoon youth clubs, known variously as "*onegs*" or "groups," and the weekly Talmud Torah, or afternoon Hebrew school, catered to them as well.[82] All kinds of social clubs—sports, folk dancing, boy and girl scout troops—rounded out the picture. Far from being incidental to or apart from the Americanized Orthodox synagogue, children were central to its sense of itself as a modern, family institution. Cultivated by the modern RIETS rabbi as an expression of both his personal and institutional commitment to modernity, children and their parents were encouraged to avail themselves of the increasingly numerous recreational and educational services provided by the synagogue and to make of "their shul" a second home; it was only the sanctuary (like the fancy living room) that remained off limits for youngsters.

In its appeal to the children, the Americanized Orthodox synagogue of the interwar years reflected a new sensibility. This formerly all-male preserve was reconstituted, in typically middle-class American fashion, as a family enterprise, an institution in which "all the members of the family would feel at home."[83] With a complement of social activities that spanned the needs and interests of a diverse population, the synagogue maintained and cultivated a "healthy social spirit" and sought avidly to transform itself into the hub of Jewish associational life. "From the chess room and library of rare books favored by the grandfather to the kindergarten used by the grandchild," the text of one promotional brochure explained," the Center reaches out to every member of the family."[84] So seriously, in fact, did the synagogue personnel of the period believe that the synagogue ought to be a second home that they urged members to celebrate personal family events—a *bris*, a bar mitzvah reception, or even a wedding—at that address. Toward that end, the Jewish Center designated a special house committee to oversee arrangements for these celebratory rites of passage. "The service, the decorations, the artistic setting and all the numberless details that go with the necessary arrangements for such formal occasions," trumpeted the brochure, "are now in the hands of the Jewish Center. Henceforth members need only give the date—and the Center will do the rest."[85]

In their cultivation of the middle-class family, many synagogues even went so far as to integrate the commemoration of Mother's and Father's Day with the traditional Sabbath service, "taking advantage," as one observer put it, "of days of national significance and endowing them with religious meaning."[86] On the Sabbaths preceding these two holidays, special prayers would be recited in the sanctuary and a celebratory collation feting parents held following the service. Such observances, one participant recalled, served to emphasize "the family character of these occasions."[87]

Once such secular institutions as Mother's and Father's Day were comfortable accommodated within the precincts of the Orthodox sanctuary, it was no wonder that congregants of the modernized synagogue sought out opportunities for expressing their patriotic sensibility, yet another hallmark of their highly valued middle-class orientation. Appropriating Thanksgiving Day, the synagogue made the holiday an integral feature of its calendar, one widely regarded by its celebrants as "an opportunity for the integration of Judaism and Americanism."[88] A new cultural invention, the synagogue's Thanksgiving ceremony, described as a "service of unusual charm and impressiveness," featured the recitation of specially chosen prayers, the reading of a proclamation, and the delivery of a speech by a guest lecturer, usually a non-Jewish American of some note.[89] While some among the (more youthful) celebrants found the proceedings a bit ponderous, "dull as dishwater," there was little mistaking the importance attached to the occasion. It was, after all, "a ceremonial kind of thing."[90]

The Jewish Center, together with its northern neighbor, the Institutional Synagogue, represented the fullest expression of the family centered-synagogue. Both had multistoried buildings completely "given over to the varied needs of our organization."[91] The Center's ten stories contained a gymnasium, reading room cum library, swimming pool, and auditorium, while the I.S.'s building housed facilities "to interest every member of the family, old and young," including game rooms, an open-air nursery, basketball and handball courts, and a dining room.[92] Synagogues that lacked such appointments renovated their existing, if limited, facilities to accommodate as best they could the need for expanded social fare. "The large Board of Directors' Room," reported the *Kehilath Jeshurun Bulletin* in 1932, "is being redecorated and remodeled along Colonial lines as a room to be used for social functions."[93]

By far the most concrete expression of the synagogue's interest in and concern for its youth was the afternoon talmud torah, more popularly known as "Hebrew school." "We owe it to our membership," Lookstein related, "to provide religious education for their children." The absence of such a facility, he went on to say, is a "serious handicap."[94] Meeting twice a week in the afternoons and on Sunday mornings, the supplementary school sought to instill in its young charges of both sexes a keen awareness of their Jewishness as well as the necessary ritual and social skills with which to express it. "*Do you want* to give your child a feeling of self respect? To build up your child's character? To insure the future of Jewish life in America and elsewhere? To surround him with worthwhile select companions and friends? To make him aware of the romance of his people? *Give your child a Jewish education!*" advertised the Institutional Synagogue.[95] In much the same grand spirit, the rabbi of the Jewish Center had this to say about the objectives of his Hebrew school: "To give the child a proper Jewish training, to acquaint him fully with all the sources of Jewish knowledge and to create in him a love for the religious and social practices peculiar to his race."[96]

An overly ambitious undertaking, especially when one considers the limited hours actually spent in the classroom, the afternoon Hebrew school encompassed an eclectic curriculum: religious practice, Jewish history, Jewish music, the prayer book, Bible, Hebrew language, current events, and, above all else perhaps, preparation for the bar mitzvah. Though it often deteriorated into little more than a "Bar Mitzvah preparatory school," the supplementary Hebrew school remained, until recently, the regnant form of Jewish education for middle-class American Jews.[97] Inasmuch as the Hebrew-school experience provides the larger context in which to understand the emergence of the Jewish day-school movement, further discussion will be postponed until a later chapter.

The most popular manifestation of the newly Americanized Orthodox synagogue, however, was neither its youth activities nor its afternoon Hebrew school but rather its sisterhood and men's club; no avowedly modern synagogue was without them. Concrete symbols of the coming of age of the institution, these two voluntary associations made possible an active social life under the umbrella of the synagogue and, in the words of one sisterhood president, lessened "the anonymity . . . so much a part of New York City urban life."[98] Within the socially acceptable parameters of the synagogue, these two adult clubs not only provided an ongoing, institutional context for "good fellowship and dignified enjoyment," but at the same time nurtured and reinforced the notion of the synagogue as a second home and its members as part of the synagogue *family*. "A congregation without a sisterhood," Lookstein explained, "is like a home without a mother. It is the Sisterhood that brings in a spirit of hospitality, friendship, sociability and warmth into a congregation."[99] "Sociability," the Men's Club of KJ explained in a small pamphlet on that topic, "is the very life and essence of the group. It is the mortar and cement by which the membership is fused into a fellowship . . . caus[ing] them to experience a sense of kinship."[100]

Sources of fellowship, the adult clubs were also a medium of cultural enhancement, a surrogate college. Under their aegis, adult members took classes in Bible, Hebrew, and Jewish literature even as they attended lectures on Jewish history, current affairs, English literature, and Zionism. "Intelligent Americans and Jews," explained the KJ Men's Club, "require regular and wholesome intellectual stimulation."[101] Cultural forays to the theater and the opera were yet another facet of the men's club and the sisterhood programming, as were regularly sponsored theme-Sabbath and holiday services, among them a popular "father-son" Sunday-morning prayer service followed by a basketball game. For the women, the sisterhood's classes in Bible, Jewish history, and kosher cooking had practical value as well as providing them, as chapter 4 documents, with much-needed Jewish educational and ritual skills.

Key components in the modern synagogue's makeup, the men's club and sisterhood enjoyed a strong fiduciary relationship with their parent institute, supplementing its income and absorbing the cost of such extras as a public-address system, scholarship funds for the afternoon Hebrew school, bar mitzvah gifts, an American flag. The origins of that relationship are unclear, probably a matter of spontaneous generation; in the long run, though, the sisterhood and men's club grew to be a staple and much-counted-upon source of revenue for the synagogue. Meanwhile, concern for the fiscal well-being of the synagogue tended to endow the avowedly social orientation of the men's club and sisterhood with a higher purpose and, in a way, legitimated these social ventures as an outlet for "dignified charity" or, better still, as a venue for the pursuit of "sacred hobbies."[102]

Though the Orthodox rabbinate encouraged the proliferation of such extradevotional activities within the synagogue, it stopped short of completely embracing what would, in the post–World War II period, emerge as the "synagogue-center." A more expansive elaboration of the social programs first developed at the Jewish Center and the Institutional Synagogue, the synagogue-center represented the notion that "social togetherness rather than religious worship" lay at the heart of the modern synagogue.[103] "A multi-faceted entity serving the social, cultural and spiritual needs of the community," the center purposefully minimized the sacred, preferring to highlight the convivial, in an adumbration of what would be seen, a generation later, as an expression of ethnicity.[104] Providing second-generation Jews and their children with a socially acceptable public context in which to spend their leisure time—taking classes, swimming, engaging in all manner of sports—the synagogue-center was enthusiastically promoted by the postwar Conservative movement; the latter, in turn, was rewarded for its reinvention of the synagogue's function by becoming the fastest-growing American Jewish denomination.

Though an apparent success, the center concept was not without its critics. Conservative and Orthodox leaders alike feared that the social component of the center overwhelmed the sacred, rendering the synagogue little more than a social and catering facility. "Whereas the hope of the Synagogue Center was to Synagogize . . . the family, the effect has been the secularization . . . of the Synagogue," complained Israel Goldstein, a leading New York City Conservative rabbi. "If the Synagogue Center has had the effect of easing the distinction between the sacred and the secular, it has been at the expense of the sacred."[105] Denouncing those who would prefer a "Palestinian folk song" to the Prophets, the Orthodox Lookstein argued that, in its modernized format, the center failed to bring Jews closer to their ancestral heritage, instead distancing them from tradition. "A well planned and efficiently directed study group in the congregation," he insisted, "will do infinitely more good than all the prattling about Jewish culture, all the 'horahs,' and all the mockery of the imitation 'Oneg Shabbat,'" a pointed reference to the common practice of substituting a late Friday-evening forum for the traditional *Kabbalath Shabbat* service. "The Chevra Shas and Mishnayas," he concluded, referring to the study circles of the centuries-old synagogue, "were valid once . . . their validity remains."[106]

In fact, traditional activities of the Orthodox synagogue like the *chevra shas* or the traditional third meal of the Sabbath, the *shalah sheudas*, were by no means abandoned by the bustling Orthodox congregation; though admittedly drawing a different and numerically smaller clientele than a father-son basketball game, they remained a part of the Orthodox synagogue's purview. Interestingly enough, however, even these avowedly traditional pursuits were dressed in a kind of bourgeois nomenclature. A 1923 Jewish Center report on the synagogue's extracurricular activities put down the continuing popularity of the Saturday afternoon "Third Meal" to the "Rabbi's custom of using the . . . leisure time at the *tea-table* in discussing Jewish law," thus subtly linking such bourgeois conceits as leisure and the ritual of afternoon tea to a time-honored Jewish activity.[107]

It was not easy to seek a balance between the *chevra shas* and the swimming pool, and the tension between these two poles goes far in explaining the restraint with which many Orthodox rabbis greeted the center's development. Lookstein's antagonism toward the center, doubtedless fueled by its ongoing success within the Conservative camp, reached full expression during the postwar period: on at least one occasion, in his annual report to the membership in 1944, he devoted considerable attention to that phenomenon. Despite KJ's plethora of social activities, explained its rabbi somewhat hotly, the congregation never aspired to being a synagogue-center. "Our building does not echo with the bouncing balls, the crackle of billiards and the thud of bowling." To some, perhaps, the absence of club rooms, gymnasiums, and swimming pools "represents a serious deficiency," Lookstein observed. But as far as he and his synagogue were concerned, "we are triumphantly and gloriously a House of God . . . a place of religious communion."[108]

As the modernized Orthodox house of worship grew into an institution larger than the sum of its individual parts and, concomitantly, as its membership grew to the point where not everyone knew everyone else personally, it became increasingly necessary to have some kind of apparatus to tie together its disparate functions and to provide an institutional center. Toward that end, more and more Orthodox synagogues of the interwar years, like their counterparts in Reform and Conservative circles, embraced the new medium of the "shul bulletin." No more than five or six pages in length, weekly or bi-weekly newsletters like the *KJ Bulletin* and the *Institutional Review* kept congregants abreast of forthcoming events, informing them of deaths, births, marriages, and bar mitzvahs within the congregational family and serving as a kind of printed pulpit for the rabbi, who would resort to the "Rabbi's Page" or the "Rabbi's Column" to editorialize on current affairs.

The bulletin also provided a steady diet of ritual information. It not only published the time of Sabbath candle lighting and synagogue services but summarized and compactly outlined the highlights of an upcoming holiday or fast. A column known as "Judaism in Practice," published on the eve of, say, the High Holidays, distilled information from the more traditional Jewish codebook, or *Shulkan Arukh*, and in well-edited paragraphs on such aspects of the holiday as "Observance in the Home," "Greetings," the "Memorial Light," and "Wearing White Garments," anticipated, and answered, the ritual questions an observant congregant might ask of his or her rabbi.[109] Redirecting the traditional encounter between *rav* and layperson, the creation of a "Judaism in Practice" or a comparable column in the synagogue bulletin served as a modernized, highly structured substitute for the traditional responsum.

The tone of the shul bulletin varied from institution to institution. Some bulletins, reflecting the more austere personality of their editor (usually the incumbent rabbi), were limited to spare and brief announcements. Others introduced a palpable note of small town-ness to the proceedings through the publication of recipes or a weekly gossip column. "Getting Personal," a densely packed feature of the *Institutional Review,* breezily recorded the comings and goings of its members, touting their personal accomplishments or return to good health. A few representative entries: "For Whom the Wedding Bell Tolls. . . .Mazel Tov to Mr. and Mrs. Henry Kaufman upon the marriage of their daughter. . . .Ditto to Mr. and Mrs. Harry Mirken upon the engagement of their daughter. . . .Bob Kirsh, son of Mr. and Mrs. Alex Kirsh rolled his right foot into a cast right after a roller-skating fall. . . . We have a new Marco Polo, Max M. Horowitz flew 15,000 miles during the short period that he has been away from the Synagogue."[110]

Regardless of its specific style, the synagogue bulletin was a useful, handy, and increasingly popular vehicle of communication, which served to weld together the membership into a community of worshipers or, nominally, a community of readers. A hallmark of the modernized, Americanized synagogue, the bulletin affirmed even as it gave voice to the congregation's perception of internal homogeneity and sense of solidarity. "For the membership at large," reported one student of the new phenomenon, "a bulletin is the weekly bond between themselves and the synagogue; and for the rabbi," he added, "a means of contact with his members."[111]

The growing interwar synagogue required not only a symbolic center like the weekly bulletin but also an actual one, a highly elaborate machinery to coordinate and oversee the daily press of activity. In many houses of worship, the rabbi superintended the day-to-day operation of his institution—overseeing the budget, planning activities, raising funds—becoming, often to his regret, a kind of professional manager or, as Arthur Hertzberg has written, "an institutional executive."[112] "I wish the congregation could be free of financial worry," exclaimed one rabbi besieged by the chores of fund raising, so that the "rabbi . . . could then do the kind of work that [he] should be doing." It's good, he added, that I do some teaching; otherwise, "I would have become a real *am haaretz* [ignoramus]."[113] But then, as the synagogue's chief executive officer, the rabbi had at his disposal a growing executive staff to run what was quickly emerging as an institution with all of the earmarks of a business: hefty operating budgets, deficits, accounts receivable. By the mid-1940s, a synagogue staff routinely comprised no fewer than five or six employees: in addition to the rabbi and the cantor, the key religious specialists, the prototypical Orthodox congregation of this period housed an assistant rabbi, an executive director who often doubled as the educational director, and the impressive-sounding ritual director, a fancified euphemism for the *shamas*, or sexton. In theory, management was to function as a team, with each member responsible for a different, if interlocking, set of responsibilities. Thus, according to KJ's directives, the sexton was to arrive fifteen minutes before the start of every synagogue service, welcome strangers and furnish them with prayer books and prayer shawls, serve as the congregation's cantor in his absence, register all donations proffered during the Yahrzeit service, and have "more economy with the lights."[114] Then as now, that theory of synagogue administration did not quite conform to practice, and friction between the rabbi, *shamas*, and executive director became a commonplace of synagogue affairs. "I don't know what I would have done if Miss . . . had not gotten married," one rabbi wrote of his apparently less than estimable head administrator. "For all we know, Judaism may be saved because [she] found a husband."[115]

The (married or unmarried) executive director notwithstanding, control of the synagogue was vested in and closely monitored by its officers—president, first vice-president, second vice-president, treasurer, financial secretary, recording secretary—and its board of trustees. Exclusively male in composition, the officers and the board were made up of the moneyed interests of the congregation, who were expected to transfer the skills that had won them considerable financial success in the outside world to the more intimate confines of the sanctuary. "We have the greatest cloakmaker in the world here," observed a Jewish Center congregant of his fellow worshipers and trustees. "We have the greatest collarmaker in the world here. We have the greatest banker, etc., etc."[116] Admittedly, inclusion on the board of trustees carried with it the fiduciary responsibility, the sacred trust, of seeing that the synagogue's finances were in good shape and policy matters smoothly implemented. But to some observers, its more important function by far was its confirmation of *kavod*, or status, on those designated as trustees. "To be a trustee [of the Jewish Center]," its former rabbi, no friend of the board, recalled in 1919, "simply means to have the 'privilege' of paying $1000 annually as membership dues instead of the $200–250 that the members pay. . . .When it was found that the running expenses of the Center could not be met with only twelve trustees," Kaplan added sarcastically, "they voted to add six more."[117] Unquestionably elitist, the board's composition reflected the middle-class community's valuation of financial success and material security. It also made sense within the overwhelmingly bourgeois ambience of the interwar Orthodox synagogue: who better to oversee and control the synagogue's affairs than those equipped with well-demonstrated business and managerial talents?

Running a synagogue made for quite a lively political culture. Like the astute businessmen they prided themselves on being, synagogue trustees were enamored of meetings: trustees' meetings, officers' meetings, special meetings, general meetings—hardly a week went by without one sort of official gathering or another. In much the same spirit, the modernized Orthodox congregation avidly took to the formation of numerous committees, in what was perhaps the sole manifestation of a democratic ethos. Religious services, cemetery, house, finance, reception, education, and membership committees, and even a "Committee on Mi Sheberachs," later to be renamed the Ritual Committee, were among the most common endeavors.[118] In part, the profusion of committees reflected the impact of professionalization and specialization on the local synagogue. As much a sign of the business orientation of the lay leadership as a holdover from the progressive era during which the synagogue came of age, the phenomenon testified to the belief that every problem, no matter how small, benefited from concentrated and considered treatment.

The synagogue's fondness for this method of administration was perhaps even more a legacy of its premodern, *landsmanshaft* antecedents. Though quick to shake off other facets of the *landsmanshaft* experience—the use of Yiddish, the system of *shnuddering*, the absence of decorum—the more modernized institution wholly absorbed its predecessor's penchant for committees. The *landsmanshaft* synagogue had almost as many committees as it did members and discovered in the creation of a committee a useful tool for problem solving and communal harmony. Unflaggingly, a succession of committees makes its way across the minutes of those associations.[119] The Eldridge Street Synagogue, for example, boasted a Burial Plot Committee, a Finance Committee, a Seat Committee, a Mortgage Committee, and an ominous-sounding "Investigations" Committee, whose mandate was to recommend "respectable persons" for membership. The synagogue's lay administration also encompassed the Committee to Repair the Gable and the Roof, the Committee to Repair the Sefer Torah's Errors, the Committee to Rent an Electrician, and the Committee to Auction a Cantor. Even the most humble of tasks called for the creation of a committee. Faced with the chore of correcting some defective plumbing, the synagogue authorized the formation of a committee. "Yitzhok Goldman," the minutes record, "reports as the Committee for the Pipes."[120]

Thanks to the energetic, intrusive involvement of the laity in the affairs of the interwar synagogue, the basis for much of the institutional culture of the contemporary American Orthodox synagogue first emerged during that period. "The synagogue, remodeled and renovated," observed Lookstein in 1946, on the eve of his synagogue's extensive architectural alterations, "will be our gift to the next generation even as the present structure was the past generation's gift to us."[121] Much the same can be said of a host of administrative and fund-raising procedures, still in force today, that were first adopted or invented by the shul presidents and treasurers of the interwar years. As an index of the growing professionalization of the synagogue's administration, one can point, perhaps most vividly, to the machinery of fund raising. The emcumbrances of today— annual dinner dances, souvenir dinner programs, "ads," the erection of memorial plaques, the "calling of names" during the Yom Kippur appeal, the discreet pledge cards collected during services—each of these strategies first emerged during this period.[122]

In the premodern synagogue not much thought was given to rationalizing the congregation's finances. Concern with the financial well-being of the synagogue animated many a board and membership meeting, but few thought in terms of a systematic approach to fiscal health. Whatever the congregation happened to take in from its customary sources of income—membership dues, the sale of seats, donations, and *shnuddering*—would have to, and usually did, suffice.[123] Growth in the synagogue's programs and consequently in the size of its budget necessitated, however, a far different approach, one made all the more pressing once *shnuddering* fell into disfavor. The premodern synagogue's most continuous source of income, *shnuddering* was also a relatively effortless way to raise money, as its opponents were soon to discover. In more than one congregation, its abolition entailed a considerable drop in revenue: at KJ, for example, synagogue income fell by $3000, leaving the congregation temporarily insolvent.[124]

Seeking an alternative source of income was not easy, but the resourceful laity tried a variety of approaches, some of which have become, in their own way, as much a part of the modernized synagogue as *shnuddering* had been for its predecessor. Increased income, one synagogue president suggested, could be "derived from a more intensive campaign to rent seats for the High Holidays and to induce more people to use the Synagogue for weddings," while others touted the benefits of endowing a memorial plaque.[125] "A permanent monument in the House of God," the memorial tablet, its architects explained, not only served as "an everlasting tribute to the memory of a departed soul" but also provided "an opportunity to advance the work and interests of the Synagogue."[126] "In the case of a cemetery plot, the money is sunk into the ground or into a costly family tombstone," explained one donor of his decision to endow an entire suite of memorial plaques. "In the case of a Memorial Tablet there is the added satisfaction of knowing that one's contribution goes toward the upkeep of the House of God."[127] As a fundraising device, the memorial tablet enjoyed great success, both within and without the Orthodox movement: adorning the walls of the sanctuary or *beit midrash*, these sturdy bronze "monuments" ultimately became as much a part of the ritual architecture of the modernized American synagogue as the Ark or Eternal Light. Other, perhaps more imaginative and worldly, lay leaders turned to the theater as their fiscal salvation and sought to reduce the deficit by hosting a theater party. As

Lookstein in 1929 explained to a somewhat skeptical audience: A congregation would purchase a block of tickets to a Broadway show for four or five dollars a seat and sell most of them for seven dollars and the balance at six dollars, thus earning a neat profit on the sale.[128] When all was said and done, however, the preferred method for generating additional income—then, as now—was simply to raise membership dues.

Modernized Orthodox Jewry of the interwar years attached inordinately high importance to its synagogue. Transforming it from a humble and occasional institution into a veritable "beehive of activity," the core of their associational and public lives, this generation fashioned the synagogue into the preeminent American Jewish institution.[129] Whether motivated by religious concerns or by more quotidian ones, the pronounced emphasis placed on the orderliness of the prayer service, a well-run youth program, and a successful fund-raising drive reflected the degree to which "the shul" had become the focal point of the American Orthodox Jew's ceremonial and ritual life. Public prayer had always been a highly valued component of traditional Jewish observance. But New York's Orthodox brought what appears to have been a new and different meaning to that act, investing it with a stature that it did not have in premodern times or, for that matter, in Europe. Emphasizing the importance of a modernized, decorous service with an English sermon at its core, the interwar Orthodox defined the synagogue service per se as the linchpin of their personal commitment to Orthodoxy; subsequent generations, by way of contrast, would invoke a different standard or agenda—say, Jewish education or more stringent ritual observance. In fact, for the Orthodox Jew of the interwar years, the public affirmation and expression of one's ties to Orthodoxy escalated in importance and for some, perhaps, even superseded private ritual observance in the home.

The subsequent transformation of the synagogue into a family-oriented institution further accelerated this trend, reinforcing the preeminence and centrality of the synagogue. Within its four ambits, middle-class, proudly American Orthodox Jews expressed their Jewish selves even as they attested to and affirmed the possibility of synthesis between modern America and traditional Jewry. Reflecting on the history of American Orthodoxy since World War I, Lookstein proudly maintained that "traditional Judaism successfully adapted itself to America and became 'American traditional Judaism.' " The vehicle of and venue for Orthodoxy's successful modernization, continued Lookstein, was the Orthodox house of worship. "In the synagogue, in the service . . . in the language of the sermon . . . , we have demonstrated in traditional Judaism that we are capable of adaptation to the new world."[130] No wonder, then, that the modernized and revitalized Orthodox synagogue became, and for at least two generations remained, the cornerstone of that community's commitment to American Orthodoxy.

"AN UTTERLY NOVEL PHENOMENON"

The Modern Rabbi

In the spring of 1919, amidst considerable public interest, five young men were graduated as rabbis from the Rabbi Isaac Elchanan Theological Seminary (RIETS), New York's most staunchly Orthodox rabbinical school. "An historical event," trumpeted the *Jewish Forum*, noting that "from this day on, orthodoxy has found itself."[1] Until recently, the weekly explained, Orthodox American Jewry had been disorganized, inchoate, and spiritually flaccid, for "what did not exist was an American Orthodox rabbi." But with the emergence of an entire class of Orthodox rabbis, "not only an Orthodox rabbi in the full meaning of the term but an American rabbi as well," Orthodoxy, it seemed, had now come into its own.[2] These five RIETS graduates, to be sure, were not America's first Orthodox rabbis. In existence since the turn of the century, the school had graduated dozens of rabbis in its more than twenty-year history. What's more, a handful of traditionalist rabbis, proud possessors of a European *smicha* (rabbinical ordination) in one hand and a Ph.D. in the other, could be found scattered throughout the eastern seaboard ministering to Orthodox congregations. For at least two decades, clergymen like Bernard Drachman, Henry Schneeberger, and Henry Pereira Mendes had sought, each in his own way, to exemplify the harmony between authentic Jewish practice and modernity.[3]

For all that though, there was something palpably new in the graduation of these five young men, the "first fruits" of a newly reorganized and consciously Americanized Orthodox rabbinical school.[4] Under the tutelage of Bernard Revel, who had assumed leadership of the small and undistinguished institution in 1915, the rabbinical school determinedly pursued a course of study that not only made room for secular studies but, even more to the point, firmly declared itself a training school for Orthodox rabbis, an identity that it had previously eschewed. Established in 1896 as a typical European yeshiva, RIETS made no provision for training young men as professional rabbis. The latter, one of its supporters related, was little more than an "incidental function," implicit in the process of talmudic study.[5] "Proficiency in Talmud and related fields," writes one historian, "*could* lead to ordination," but, he adds, "the distinction between vocation and avocation was not emphasized or even clearly delineated."[6] If, by dint of acquiring sufficient knowledge, a student wished to receive ordination, he appeared before each one of three leading European rabbis, who tested the candidate's textual expertise to see if he passed muster. The informal, highly personalized process of certification made it clear that the application of rabbinic knowledge was by no means the school's desired objective; study for its own sake, for the purpose of producing learned talmudic scholars, and not professional rabbis, lay at the core of the pre-Revel Yitzchak Elchanan Theological Seminary. In fact, one veteran alumnus remembered, though with a certain amount of hyperbole, that when he was growing up in the years prior to World War I, the Orthodox community in New York frowned upon the notion of a professional Orthodox rabbinate and considered it a "terrible crime . . . to establish a yeshiva for the purpose of training rabbis. . . ."[7]

With Revel at the helm, however, RIETS steered a different course as the institution increasingly assumed many of the features associated with a modern seminary. Revel himself symbolized RIETS's new orientation.[8] Born in Lithuania in 1881, Revel was a youthful prodigy whose expertise in Talmud earned him a coveted *smicha* from Rabbi Isaac Elchanan Spector, after whom, appropriately enough, the New York rabbinical seminary was named. Arriving in America in 1906, he briefly studied law at Temple University before earning advanced degrees in Semitics and comparative literature. Equally at home within the folios of the Talmud and of contemporary literary exegesis, Revel institutionalized his own unique brand of synthesis at RIETS.[9]

Moving into new and expanded quarters, the rabbinical school, newly named the Rabbinical College of America, made it clear that its primary purpose was to rear a generation of modern, English-speaking Orthodox rabbis. "The new rabbinical College," explained Harry Fischel, a prime mover in its reshaping, "holds forth as its object, 'Orthodox Judaism and Americanism,' that is; its aim shall be to educate and produce Orthodox rabbis who will be able to deliver sermons in English, so that they may appeal to the hearts of the younger generation and, at the same time, who will be thoroughly qualified to occupy positions with congregations demanding conformity with the strict requirements of Orthodox Judaism."[10] Toward that end, Revel significantly expanded the course of instruction in both Judaic and secular studies, supplementing the traditional Talmud curriculum with courses in Jewish history, theology, philosophy, literature, and Hebrew grammar and assembling a modern, scientifically trained faculty in the liberal arts. Increasingly, English and Hebrew replaced Yiddish as the prevailing language of instruction in secular and religious studies respectively. "With time," explained H. Pereira Mendes, the first professor of pedagogy and homiletics at the revitalized institution, "I believe the Rabbinical

College will become more American, gradually lessening the use of Yiddish and having all instruction . . . only in pure Hebrew and English."[11]

In most respects, Revel proceeded with "daring and rapidity" in effecting these changes.[12] But he also had his cautious streak and, in one area—that of homiletics, later the hallmark of the English-speaking westernized Orthodox rabbinate—moved rather tentatively. Some two years after becoming the school's president, Revel posted a notice on the school bulletin board advising rabbinical students to spend more time on Talmud and less on the study of "sermonics and Midrash." This "innocent notice," however, caused quite a furor among the more senior rabbinical students, who viewed the pronouncement, among other things, as "a gross evasion of the practical aspects of the Rabbinate." Following a student protest (this in 1917!), Revel apparently retracted his earlier statement and forthwith established a homiletics department—or so the story has it.[13] And the story does not end there. Revel, newly persuaded of the merits of practical training for the rabbinate, moved resolutely to expand instruction in that area. "But Dr. Revel's interest in Homiletics once roused, was not so easily satisfied," an eyewitness recalled, noting that the school's president enlarged the number of required courses in the homiletics department and years later introduced a course in "practical Rabbinics."[14]

Revel's appointment and his subsequent success in training dozens of American-born boys for the Orthodox rabbinate marked a turning point, a watershed in the institutional fortunes of American Orthodox Jewry. Moving energetically—even, some would say, aggressively—RIETS's new president sought to produce an indigenous Orthodox rabbinate and thus reduce American Orthodox Jewry's dependence on Europe on the one hand and on the Jewish Theological Seminary on the other. Revel effected a quiet revolution in the social history of America's Orthodox rabbinate, for at the time of his appointment, no self-consciously Orthodox rabbinical seminary existed in New York or elsewhere in the United States. Hitherto New York's Orthodox rabbi received his ordination from one of several sources: the typical European yeshiva like Volozhin or Slobodka, Hildesheimer's more neo-Orthodox rabbinical seminary in Germany, or New York's Jewish Theological Seminary. Dr. Philip Hillel Klein and Bernard Drachman, rabbi and associate rabbi respectively of the influential Harlem Ohab Zedek, for example, held degrees from the Hildesheimer and Breslau Seminaries, while Rabbi Leo Jung of the Jewish Center was the product of Hildesheimer's and Cambridge University. Closer to home, the Jewish Theological Seminary provided many of the clergy for New York's Orthodox synagogues well into the 1920s. At Kehilath Jeshurun, New York's premier Orthodox synagogue, it was not until 1923 that a RIETS graduate held the post of English-speaking rabbi; earlier, each of its English-speaking clergy—from Mordecai Kaplan on through Elias Solomon—was a Seminary graduate.

Before the 1930s, the boundaries between the Jewish Theological Seminary and RIETS were fluid and, to some observers, even indistinguishable.[15] Founded in 1886 by a number of New York Orthodox clergymen (among others), the Seminary directed its attention to New York's immigrant Jewish communities in an attempt to Americanize their traditional religious observances and, at the same time, to present an alternative to the regnant Reform movement. Mordecai Kaplan, himself a product of the Lower East Side and one of the earliest rabbinic students at the Seminary, recalled that when it came to substantive theological or religious issues, little distinguished the views of the Seminary from those of its Lower East Side constituents. The Seminary's brand of Jewishness, he confided in his diary, differed from the immigrants' only in matters of style—in being "uptownish, that is, being university bred and rendered in good English."[16] Other clergy agreed. Although they looked to the same constituency, the two schools, insisted H. Pereira Mendes, were not rivals but complementary institutions: where the Seminary trained rabbis, RIETS, as he saw it, educated an Orthodox laity. The two, he explained in an article in the popular *Jewish Forum*, "work in harmony, each helping the other."[17]

But Revel and his supporters did not see things quite that way, especially after Solomon Schechter assumed office as the Seminary's chancellor in 1902. Instead, they sought to make RIETS the only legitimate training ground for America's Orthodox rabbinate. As one rabbinic colleague observed at the time, "Revel is very determined and aggressive in his purpose to outdo the Seminary. . . . The entire movement resembles on a small scale that of the Jesuits who have saved Catholicism from imminent dissolution."[18] Not surprisingly, New York's Orthodox community saw in Revel's actions a kind of declaration of independence from the Seminary and, perhaps even more to the point, from its traditional reliance on the European yeshiva. With a modern RIETS, American Orthodox Jews were no longer "spiritual parasites, dependent upon Europe and European leaders for guidance and inspiration."[19]

Implicit in Revel's reorganization of the Rabbi Yitzhak Elchanan Theological Seminary, known in abbreviated fashion simply as "Yitzhak Elchanan," was a reformulation of the American Orthodox rabbi's mandate and responsibilities. RIETS's new curriculum depended on a fresh and, for America, virtually unprecedented conception of the Orthodox rabbinate: one in which pastoral and social roles expanded at the expense of judicial and theological ones. Increasingly, the latter were on their way to becoming "vestigial" functions.[20] "In the modern congregations of America," observed Israel Friedlander, "there is little demand for the exercise of such functions."[21] Although a comparable western-oriented traditional rabbinate existed in central and western Europe as early as the mid-nineteenth century, no such parallel obtained in the New World.[22] It was almost as if, in America, a cultured Orthodox rabbi was an oxymoron, a contradiction in terms. "A modern minister at the head of such a congregation," one observer colorfully declared, referring to a typical Orthodox synagogue, "would have about the same effect as a handsome new cut velvet collar on an old threadbare coat."[23] Occasionally, Revel and his supporters would invoke the European model—the institutional success of Samson Raphael Hirsch was a particular favorite—to legitimate their own social invention, but such historical parallels were essentially unnecessary, for "something was stirring in American Jewish life," as one observer put it, that necessitated the creation of a modernized Orthodox rabbi.[24]

Interestingly enough, those fashioning the concept of the new modernized Orthodox rabbi also drew upon popular American notions of the modern Jewish clergyman. In fact, when it came to behavior, little distinguished the earliest generation of modern Orthodox rabbis from its more liberal counterparts. In matters of dress, speech, function, and self-perception, the pre–World War II Orthodox rabbi was noticeably similar to his Conservative colleague; matters of belief and theology differentiated the two, not the performance of their functions. Officiating at a funeral with another Orthodox colleague, Kaplan observed that a "graduate of Yeshiva that acquires that way of speaking," referring to a polished and syntactically correct English, "can easily pass as a Conservative rabbi."[25] High praise indeed!

While the RIETS administration may have been reticent about its reconstruction of the Orthodox rabbinate, the student body was not. With a self-consciousness almost without parallel in the history of America's Orthodox Jewish community, rabbinical students at RIETS prior to World War II took eagerly to this new vision of the Orthodox rabbinate and viewed themselves unabashedly as "religious pioneers."[26] Buoyantly optimistic and energized by the knowledge that they were, as Jung himself recalled, "an utterly novel phenomenon," they set out to change the very nature of the American Orthodox rabbinate and, in turn, as one Conservative rabbi grudgingly put it, "to de-ghettoize orthodoxy."[27] Abandoning careers in law and medicine, they looked upon the emerging Orthodox rabbinate as an exciting career opportunity, one in which they were likely not only to do well financially but to affect lives. "Do the Jewish people need another lawyer?" Herbert Goldstein asked himself as he was poised to enroll in law school. "I also thought to myself," he recalled, " . . . will the Jewish people need another English-speaking Orthodox rabbi—especially for the young people? My answer to myself was 'yes.' "[28]

Not unexpectedly, Goldstein himself wrote one of the earliest and fullest extant descriptions of the "English-speaking Orthodox rabbi." A Jewish Theological Seminary graduate who supplemented his Seminary ordination with a *smicha* from Rabbi Sholom Elchanan Jaffe, the dean of the Yiddish-speaking rabbinate in the early 1900s, Goldstein symbolized the "new type, the American type" of Orthodox rabbi. Cutting a dapper figure in his frock coat and top hat and eager to display a large, if not always correctly employed, vocabulary, Goldstein attempted, first at KJ and then later at his own Institutional Synagogue in Harlem, to make Orthodoxy appealing to young native-born Americans. An exceptionally popular rabbi, Goldstein possessed a sharp, almost uncanny, ability to understand the needs of American-born youth and to balance their affinity for things American with the requirements of tradition. "Young America," he observed, referring to the second-generation American Jew, "desire[s] to break down these Ghetto walls. They desire to live as their neighbors . . . as Americans. It is evident," he explained, perhaps alluding to himself, "that only those who themselves have gone through this kind of youth and social life can be in sympathy with this type of young man and woman and meet him or her (!) on their own level."[29] Under such circumstances, Goldstein purposely delimited the sphere of influence of the European *rav*, "the old style, ghetto type," and restricted it to purely legal and theoretical matters. Hailing the European rabbis as "physical storehouses of the Jewish law," he deferred to them on halakhic issues. "I fully recognize that in regard to questions of Halakha, of Jewish law, we must look to our older rabbis." But as far as the future of Orthodox Judaism was concerned, that he entrusted to those native-born American Jews who, like himself, were products of an American Jewish ministry. Unless young men who are "both *genuinely Jewish and genuinely American* occupy American pulpits," he warned, "*Orthodox Judaism can have little hope of survival.*"[30]

The ideal type of Orthodox rabbi, as prescribed by Goldstein and developed by RIETS, was someone like the Harlem rabbi, who could keep in step with young America: aware of cultural trends outside of his study, the model American Orthodox rabbi ought to be conversant with the works of Aristotle, Bacon, and Bergson, able to speak the language of youth, and, most noticeably, sympathetic to athletics. An Orthodox rabbi for well over fifty years, Louis Engelberg attributed his early success to his ability to "play a good game of basketball."[31] For Goldstein, too, knowledge of and affection for American sports, in his case baseball, contributed tangibly to his success. An avid New York Giants fan, Goldstein heartily endorsed physical activities at his Institutional Synagogue and often liked to invoke sports lingo or references. Noticing a contingent of youngsters about to leave services before their scheduled end, he would gently rebuke them by saying, "Would you leave a baseball game before the last out?"[32] Ultimately, the strength and appeal of the modern Orthodox rabbi lay in his ability and inclination to engage his congregants. Often the "family chaplain," he, like his rabbinical colleagues elsewhere, was called upon to tend actively and personally to the emotional needs of his congregants, as an integral participant in family ritual dramas.[33] "A pastoral psychiatrist," the Orthodox rabbi of the interwar years was expected to be available for circumcisions, funerals, weddings, bar mitzvahs, and comparable expressions of the rites of passage.[34] Today, it is almost a commonplace, a given of rabbinic life, that the American rabbi of any denomination is evaluated by the degree to which he excels in his pastoral duties. But when seen historically, the relative "newness" of this conception becomes apparent. Beginning in the interwar years, Orthodox rabbis added an entirely new dimension to their spheres of activity, and with it, a new identity.

Despite the excitement over RIETS's reorganization and the inherent potential of an indigenous American Orthodox rabbinate, not everyone in New York's Orthodox community viewed the process with delight or even equanimity. Particularly strong criticism of the institution's legitimacy emanated from the small but vociferous right-wing element of New York's Orthodox: the European-trained and -oriented rabbinical community. Throughout the Revel era, unflagging criticism from the right, the loyal opposition, dogged the rabbinical seminary, as it does to this day. Brandishing denunciatory leaflets and threatening to issue bans of excommunication, this body loudly and clearly made its opposition known. Organized as early as 1902 as the Agudat ha-Rabbanim, its members saw themselves not only as the watchdogs of traditional behavior in the New World but also as heirs apparent to the European *rav* and his prerogatives. The more traditional, Agudat-affiliated *men* did not take too well to the new American rabbi, whom they saw as an encroacher on and serious violator of their own religious sensibilities and authority. For one thing, they did not believe that the RIETS-trained rabbi possessed sufficient learning to qualify as a "rav" in the traditional sense of the word. A poor and inauthentic version of an Orthodox rabbi, the RIETS rabbi "was not," in their estimation, "sufficiently learned talmudically. He was too modern and tended to veer from tradition. He was a social worker and not a rav."[35] For another thing, the Agudat members possessed an altogether different conception of the rabbi's functions. For the Agudat, Europe, not America, remained their frame of reference; accordingly, they defined the rabbi's responsibilities from a traditional European perspective.[36] Pastoral, or what has come to be called practical, rabbinics interested them not at all; what did was the rendering of halakhic decisions and the ongoing study of the Talmud. Their interest in communal affairs extended as far as kashruth supervision; the last "was their primary preoccupation," noted one Americanized Orthodox rabbi somewhat facetiously.[37] Not for them the counseling sessions, weekly sermons, basketball games, ecumenical and intra-denominational symposia, the women's sisterhood, or adult education that took up most of the modern rabbi's daily calendar. Such seemingly secular activities fell under the banner of frivolousness, *narishkeyt*, and contravened the sacred, sacerdotal nature of their roles. Quick to disapprove of a RIETS education, they also frowned on the signal attributes of the modernized Orthodox service, like ushers and decorum, reserving particular scorn for the English-language sermon, as we have seen. To their way of thinking, the modernized Orthodox synagogue service was *"tref"* (unkosher) and its officiant a *"shaigetz"* (non-Jew).[38]

No wonder, then, that the traditional European *rav* was often at considerable remove from his constituents. "The gravest problem of the orthodox rabbi," wrote Rabbi Moses Z. Margolies, one of their number, "was his isolation. . . .he stood alone."[39] At best, congregants regarded the European *rav* with an admixture of awe and distance; as one observer put it, they listened to him with what might be called a "sacramental attitude . . . what he says is a sort of liturgy with them and they are perfectly satisfied. . . ."[40] All too commonly, however, the traditional *rav* was so out of touch with the needs and sensibilities of his congregants that he remained, for most, little more than a "functionary . . . a very humble, quiescent, apologetic official," bereft of moral authority.[41]

In painting such a dispirited and gloomy picture of the traditional European *rav* in America, Rabbi Margolies probably had in mind the failed career of Rabbi Jacob Joseph, whose tragic and unfulfilled life in the New World graphically illustrated the chasm between traditional notions of the European rabbinate and a less than welcoming America. Brought to the New World in 1887 from Vilna, where he had served as a communal preacher and *dayan*, or judge, Rabbi Jacob Joseph was designated New York's chief rabbi by a loose confederation of Orthodox laity acting entirely on their own behalf. The self-styled Association of American Orthodox Hebrew Congregations hired the European *rav* to weld New York's disparate Orthodox immigrant congregations, then estimated at over one hundred, into an organized community structurally akin to the European *kehillah*, and, by so doing, to raise the level of Orthodox practice.[42] Like his European counterparts, the Vilna preacher was also to supervise what was then, and continues to be, New York's fragmented, intensely competitive, and often unscrupulous wholesale meat and poultry business.

An eagerly anticipated development, Rabbi Jacob Joseph's career was riddled, almost from the start, with manifold problems. Within less than a year, repeated challenges to the rabbi's moral authority undermined the entire enterprise. Contentious butchers refused to accept his supervision; his sponsors, frustrated by the butchers' lack of cooperation, failed to stand behind their chief rabbi, and the entire scheme collapsed, as Irving Howe has colorfully observed, "under the weight of the *plumbe*" (a lead seal used to stamp kosher meat).[43] New York's abortive attempt at creating a chief rabbi ultimately foundered on the voluntaristic nature of American Jewish life. Ill conceived from start to finish, the notion that somehow the European system of rabbinical organization and, with it, the "old style, ghetto type" rabbi could be successfully transplanted to the New World proved to be a chimera. The personality and skills of Rabbi Jacob Joseph, a gentle and sweet man temperamentally ill suited to the position of New York's chief rabbi, hastened the project's dissolution. Unable to speak English and with no apparent comprehension of the peculiarities of New York Jewish life, the city's first and last chief rabbi died a broken man, materially and spiritually impoverished.

Ironically enough, his death in 1902 provided New York's Orthodox community with the opportunity to demonstrate its respect and affection for Rabbi Jacob Joseph. A crowd estimated at anywhere from 25,000 to 50,000, New York's largest funeral to date, turned out to assuage its collective guilt at the unfortunate fate of New York's chief rabbi—in death, if not in life, the object of considerable esteem and respect.

Unlike Rabbi Jacob Joseph whom he succeeded (unofficially) as the dean of the Orthodox rabbinate, Rabbi Moses Z. Margolies (known acronymically as the Ramaz) enjoyed a successful and enduring career as the "uncrowned head of New York's orthodox Jewry."[44] An unusual combination of a traditional East European *rav* and an acute and sensitive observer of American social mores, Margolies served both as president of the Agudat ha-Rabbanim and, for some thirty years, as the Yiddish-speaking *rav* of Kehilath Jeshurun. A gentle, effective spokesman for American Orthodoxy, the Ramaz succeeded, where so many of his colleagues did not, in keeping himself open—and acceptable—to both the right-wing and the more self-consciously modernizing Orthodox communities.

With his gentle countenance and flowing white beard, "the Ramaz looked like Moses except that he wore gold-rimmed spectacles," one family member recalled.[45] Called to Boston in 1889 from Slobodka, he served as the rabbi of the Baldwin Place Synagogue, "the headquarters of orthodox Judaism" in the North End, Boston's immigrant Jewish neighborhood.[46] Like most European rabbis newly transplanted to America, the Ramaz spent much of his time supervising local kosher butchers and, according to one family account, so antagonized them by his ritual strictness that he had "many enemies among them." Determined to teach the Ramaz a lesson, a band of disgruntled butchers allegedly banded together to poison the meat at his daughter's wedding supper, sickening some 2000 guests, including the bride.[47] With the exception, though, of Boston's kosher butchers, most Boston immigrant Jews venerated the Russian-born and -trained rabbi: when one young man announced his forthcoming marriage to the Ramaz's daughter, "it was as if there had suddenly been conferred on my family . . . the award of the Legion d'Honneur. From that moment, they were set apart, revered, envied."[48]

Despite his formidable reputation, the Ramaz was a simple and unaffected man who frowned on displays of pretentiousness and whose home was always open to visitors. "Everyone came to his apartment . . . for help, for advice, for spiritual guidance and for relief in ritualistic dilemmas. About the last, the Ramaz was almost unique in tolerance, sympathy and humor."[49] Whether answering *shaylahs*, or ritual questions, with regard to the kashruth of a chicken, the permissibility of using an elevator on the Sabbath, or the construction of a *mechitzah*, Ramaz invariably took the more liberal and charitable view and ruled in favor of his congregants, "seeking always to make the Torah the law of life for the Jew."[50]

After several years of service, during which the Baldwin Place rabbi was held in such esteem that his photograph reportedly hung in the living rooms of many immigrant Jewish households, he left to take up the post of rabbi at New York's Kehilath Jeshurun. His congregants, disturbed by his departure, decided nonetheless to pay him an "architectural tribute," and when the time came to rebuild the Baldwin Street Synagogue, they did so, it is said, "in exact, if scaled-down imitation of the Ramaz's [new] synagogue."[51]

Margolies's installment at KJ early in 1906 as the more senior *rav* to Mordecai Kaplan's modern English-speaking "minister" was instigated by an alliance of the older, more traditional members of the congregation with the Agudat ha-Rabbanim, who found Kaplan's new style of practical rabbinics and his Seminary background incongruous with the proclaimed Orthodoxy of one of New York's most prestigious Orthodox congregations. "The effect of a Rav," Kaplan was to recall years later, "was filled by the late Moses Z. Margolies, who preached in Yiddish and only occasionally but who gave the congregation the illusion that it was maintaining the East European type of rabbinate."[52] Silencing, by his presence, would-be critics of KJ's proud Americanized Orthodox constituency and practices, Margolies set in motion a working relationship between the Old World rabbi and his American colleague that would eventually be emulated elsewhere. Years later, the European *rav* of a suburban midwestern community wrote to Eliezer Silver, Agudat president during the twenties, complaining that a Yeshiva graduate had recently moved into town and threatened his rabbinic turf. The alarmed rabbi, it seems, wrote to the Agudat leader in the hope that he would use his good office to help ensure that the younger rabbi would be "submissive to his authority [that is, that of the older European *rav*] . . . just like the relationship between New York's Rabbi Margolies and his assistant."[53]

However paradigmatic the relationship may have seemed to outsiders, it did not always work out that well within KJ. Not one to brook interference or to take well to criticism, Kaplan chafed under the Ramaz's hegemony; what's more, the congregation's inability "to entrust its spiritual destiny into the hands of a Seminary graduate" so disturbed the young Kaplan that he soon quit its pulpit.[54] His successors, Herbert S. Goldstein and Elias Solomon, similarly remained only a few years in that junior position before striking out on their own. The relationship of superordinate to subordinate worked best, and for the longest period of time—some thirteen years—when Joseph H. Lookstein assumed the pulpit as assistant rabbi in 1923.

Despite a considerable gap in years and markedly different training, the older *rav* and his junior assistant Lookstein developed an intensely close relationship, more like that of mentor to pupil than superordinate to subordinate. That Lookstein married the Ramaz's granddaughter, Gertrude Schlang, shortly after assuming his position served only to deepen what had already emerged as a unique and almost symbiotic relationship. Throughout his apprenticeship to the Ramaz, Lookstein learned firsthand the internal workings of the synagogue as well as the art of dealing with people. The Ramaz, in turn, welcomed Lookstein's new-fangled notions of decorum and, by publicly sanctioning them, helped to ensure their implementation. "I obtained the approval of Rabbi Margolies to introduce certain features into the service, like the announcement of pages, interpolations to explain certain prayers, readings in unison and responsive readings. He understood my motives," Lookstein reflected.[55] Thanks to this successful partnership, Lookstein was hired as the congregation's senior rabbi after the Ramaz's death, in 1936, at the age of eighty-five. He was to serve in that capacity for over half a century, until his own death in 1978.

To many observers, Lookstein emerged as the representative "new type, American type" of Orthodox rabbi of whom Goldstein, his slightly older colleague, so avidly spoke. Lookstein himself often liked to refer to the novelty of his position. "Here, then," he observed of his career in the rabbinate, "was a symbol of what American Judaism could achieve—an orthodox rabbi trained in a traditional Yeshiva . . . and commanding at the same time the language and culture of the modern day and comprehending the spirit and mood of America."[56] Born in Russia in 1902 of what he often boasted of as Hasidic ancestry, Lookstein came to New York at the age of ten. Even as a youngster, he displayed considerable rhetorical skill and, for a spell, was known as the Lower East Side's "boy orator."[57] Growing up first in that downtown neighborhood and then in Brownsville under severely straitened circumstances, Lookstein's decision to become a modern Orthodox rabbi grew organically from several factors: familial tradition (Lookstein was descended from twelve generations of rabbis), his verbal and social skills, and a naturally pious and religious sensibility. These qualities combined with the opportunities and challenges inherent in the new rabbinate "to attract" him. "I wanted," he would write years later, "to be a modern version of the rabbi of old."[58]

Bringing to bear an acute sociological understanding of both the rabbinate as a profession and the needs of his affluent, rapidly acculturating congregation, Lookstein distinguished himself as a congregational rabbi, a "pulpit rav." Having graduated from City College with a master's degree in sociology, Lookstein systematized and ordered the business of being a rabbi. With a piercing, almost ritually obsessive, penchant for detail and a keen scientific awareness, he maintained records on virtually every aspect of synagogue life, from its financial well-being to his sermons. Following the conclusion of the Sabbath, KJ's rabbi would dutifully record his impressions of the day's events on little index cards that included such categories as the weather, the number of worshipers (broken down by gender), the topic of his sermon, and how it was received. He would then review this material with his staff, using the "data" to evaluate and refine synagogue life. A practitioner par excellence of practical rabbinics, a subject he later taught to subsequent generations of rabbinical candidates at RIETS, Lookstein also devised a set of membership applications and marriage records that, reflecting his training as a sociologist, contained financial, residential, and demographic information on prospective members and married couples respectively, something of a novelty for the characteristically disordered Orthodox congregation.

His attention to detail extended beyond the documentary to the physical plant of his synagogue as well. Determined to have his synagogue stand as a peer with the Park Avenue Synagogue and Temple Emanu-El, or, as he himself put it, "the appearance, the conduct and the dignity should be what prevails in a Temple," Lookstein personally inspected the building from top to bottom, making sure that the bathrooms were clean, the brass finishings of the sanctuary polished, and its prayer books untattered and regularly dusted.[59] A passionate devotee of the notion that "God is in the details," Lookstein concretized that principle throughout his synagogue in a consistent and well thought out attempt to remove, both physically and conceptually, the negative associations many, if not most, Americanized Jews had of the Orthodox synagogue. "Strong on exteriors," Lookstein lent elegance, sophistication, and worldliness—qualities especially valued by the determinedly bourgeois Jews of his community—to the Orthodox synagogue where none of these qualities had previously existed.[60]

Lookstein's understanding of and sensitivity to the Upper East Side alrightniks that made up the congregation, no less than his administrative and managerial skills, was grounded in his sociological imagination—in his grasp of the reality of New York Jewish life during the interwar years and beyond. Harboring no illusions about the ritual knowledge or behavior of his congregants, Lookstein met them on their own terms, seeking gently and subtly to transform them, at least associationally, into Orthodox Jews.[61] "Rabbis, it is true," he explained to a convention of his colleagues, "should strive for and should be judged by their scholarship, their at-homeness, in the sea of the Talmud, their capacity to manipulate the folios of our rich and undying culture. But, unfortunately," he went on to say, "their usefulness is determined in our day by the ability to conduct an interesting and decorous service."[62] Accordingly, Lookstein devoted himself to that task, seeking to make regular Sabbath worshipers and, by extension, committed congregants of local residents. In retrospect, Lookstein deliberately limited his influence to the circumscribed ritual sphere of the sanctuary and Sabbath service. Lowering his sights, he had minimal expectations when it came to the ritual practice of his congregants and did not hold them to a high level of observance—for which, in later years, he was considerably criticized by more "aggressively Orthodox" clergy and laymen. Lookstein never thundered from the pulpit, delivering fiery *musar*-like addresses about the importance of performing one ritual or another. Taking his congregants "as far as they would go," Lookstein preferred "subtly and unobtrusively" to get them to observe kashruth more diligently or to maintain the Sabbath, and he appealed to them, on occasion, on an individual but never a communal level.[63]

From time to time, the KJ rabbi was troubled that his congregants were not as punctilious in their observance as he might have liked. And yet, ritual laxity was no bar to friendship or, in more of a striking departure from the norm, from membership in his congregation. The constitution of KJ mandated that a prospective member had to be a full-fledged Sabbath observer. Lookstein, with Margolies's imprimatur, overturned that time-honored principle. Proudly, he related in an interview shortly before his death that he had "opened up the membership" by discarding that proviso. "Our job," he explained, "is to take non-Sabbath observers and to make them Sabbath observers."[64] For Lookstein, hard at work during a period in which Orthodoxy was overladen with many negative connotations, it was enough to get affluent, Americanized Jews to attend an Orthodox prayer service and to support Orthodox institutions. It was their self-awareness and reflexivity as Orthodox Jews, not their ritual behavior, that mattered.

Reverential, orderly and ordered, contemplative and dignified, Lookstein's highly choreographed and ritualized service appealed to Upper East Side Jews, bringing them into the sanctuary. The high point of the service, however, was Lookstein's sermon. A celebrated "master of the language" with a keen ear for the evocative phrase, the verbally skilled rabbi used his scrupulously timed forty-minute address to good advantage.[65] "As relevant as the Saturday morning news," Lookstein liked to say of his sermons, which skillfully blended a *midrash* and a few phrases from the portion of the week with news items culled from the *New York Times* in what appears to have been an enormously successful attempt to "make traditional Judaism relevant."[66] Lookstein's sermonizing, remembered another congregant worshipfully, "was just like a college lecture."[67]

Of a piece, Lookstein's efforts were designed to engage the middle-class Jew ritually, culturally, and above all, associationally with cultured Orthodoxy, or traditional Judaism, a term Lookstein preferred to the sharper-sounding and more confining "Orthodox." Transforming the synagogue into the nucleus of a community, Lookstein considerably expanded the base of social and cultural interaction for those who were Orthodox in orientation and spoke often of his congregants as members of the "KJ Family." No mere rhetorical flourish, that phrase conveyed the sense of an extended kinship network of Jews who gathered at the synagogue for religious as well as purely recreational purposes. In later years, with the formation of the Ramaz School, Lookstein's community building expanded to include an elementary and high school as well.

Much as Lookstein transformed the formerly moribund Orthodox synagogue into an active social center, he transformed the Orthodox rabbi from an aloof, distant, if revered, personality into a socially accessible one. Affable, witty, a "chevra man," Lookstein placed himself directly at the center of his congregation.[68] Together with his wife, Gertrude, he sustained the powerful illusion of the KJ fictive family by holding numerous get-togethers at his own residence, events that were called "at homes."[69] The Looksteins freely socialized with their congregants—both within and without the synagogue—sharing their interests in the opera and theater, European travel, fine food, and beautifully designed clothes. "Palsy-walsy" with his congregants, Lookstein personalized the character of the rabbi and, in the process, redefined the nature of the Orthodox congregation's internal dynamic.[70] This is not, however, to suggest that Lookstein and his congregants were intimates or that all conventions of respect and distance between rabbi and congregant were abrogated, for that was by no means the case. Despite his affability and openness, Lookstein was seldom called by his first name. And yet, in creating social and personal bonds between himself and his congregants—whom he saw unequivocally as "his people"—Lookstein established a new and unprecedented "protocol" between rabbi and layman, one in which a strong sense of interconnectedness was repeatedly and variously expressed.[71]

"A master builder," Lookstein sought to make room for himself and his Orthodox colleagues in circles outside of the synagogue where, historically, Orthodox rabbis were noticeably absent, "the least heard and the least felt."[72] For him, Orthodoxy posed no barrier to participation in interdenominational causes like the Synagogue Council, the New York Board of Rabbis, or the Jewish Welfare Board's chaplaincy program, and he served several of these organizations actively, in some instances even as their president. "We have to become more definitely and articulately part of the community," he admonished his rabbinic colleagues, many of whom frowned on communal cooperation with those less observant than they. Determined to recast Orthodoxy's image, Lookstein urged his Orthodox counterparts not only to publish and to appear on radio or speaking programs but to participate in organized communal ventures like Federation and Hadassah. "We must not allow ourselves to be relegated to the sphere of kosher supervision alone," he declared.[73]

Through it all, whether chairing an interdenominational symposium, officiating at a funeral, or reviewing his ministerial performance, Lookstein sought to render Orthodox Jewish life compatible with middle-class America, making it "so palatable."[74] An architect of the modernized Orthodox experience in the New World, Lookstein reconstructed both the image and the reality of the American Orthodox rabbi.

A more restrained but equally emblematic and influential modern Orthodox New York rabbi—for some the very "epitome of orthodoxy"—was Leo Jung, the spiritual leader of the Jewish Center from 1922 until his recent death in 1987.[75] Unlike Lookstein, Jung was not schooled at RIETS but received his training abroad. And yet, throughout his lifetime, he cultivated strong ties with that institution, even going so far as to seek its presidency following Revel's death. Proud of his association with the school, Jung liked to boast that it was he who "turned the community away from the Seminary toward RIETS" and thus "made a revolution" in American Jewish life.[76] A Cambridge graduate with a cultivated continental accent and a dapper appearance, Jung was born in Moravia in 1892, spent his early teens in London, and received ordination from the Hildesheimer Seminary in 1920. Later that year, he emigrated to the United States, where he assumed a pulpit in Cleveland before moving on permanently to the Jewish Center in 1922.

Far more of a scholar than his colleague across the park, Jung consistently sought to provide a philosophical underpinning to Orthodox life, or what he preferred to call, in the German tradition, "Torah-true" Judaism. In his sermons, many of which were subsequently published, his numerous scholarly articles, and his guidebooks to traditional Orthodox life, he put forth a rationale for Orthodox Judaism, linking it to high ethical values, aestheticism, and American patriotism. At a time when few English materials on Orthodox Judaism existed, Jung's texts, "the only things around," provided a measure of intellectual coherence to American Orthodoxy.[77] "There was an almost complete lack of available information about the Jewish solution of modern problems," Jung recalled. "Traditional Judaism was found unrepresented and that vacuum gave rise to all sorts of unjustified views."[78] In his *Essentials of Judaism* and his multivolume *Jewish Library*, with its essays on the role of women and Judaism in a changing world, among many other topics, Jung sought to lay out clearly, concisely, and intelligently Orthodoxy's relevance to modern urban America.

Far more Eurocentric than most of his fervently American colleagues, in both his philosophic outlook and his cultural approach to Judaism, Jung frequently drew parallels between the established Orthodoxy of Europe and that which he hoped to fashion in New York. Sensitive to the continuities between the cul-

tured Orthodoxy of Central Europe and that of New York's emerging Orthodox, Jung had the former consciously shape the latter, especially at the Center,
his home base for over sixty years. A proven success in the Old World, a
cultured Orthodoxy, he believed, was eminently capable of withstanding the
challenges of modernity, provided its practitioners were themselves suitably
equipped. One must distinguish, he explained in his *What is Orthodox Judaism?*
between "Orthodoxy as a system of life and the present panorama of Orthodox
Jews in America." Orthodoxy's perceived weaknesses and "disabilities," he
went on to explain, "are due not to Orthodoxy but to the Orthodox Jew," by
which he meant the pious immigrant.[79] "Orthodoxy," he would insist repeatedly, "is not to be identified with Ghetto conditions"—or what he described as
"a combination of Eastern European culinary habits, considerable superstition,
and disorganized, unharmonious, often unintelligent, presentation."[80] Through
the institutionalization of "a most cultured form of Jewishness" at the Jewish
Center in New York (and elsewhere throughout the nation), Jung sought to
render the prevailing stereotypes obsolete. In that connection, he liked to repeat
the story of an encounter he had had, early in his career, with a non-Orthodox
Jew who had flatly accused him of being a hypocrite. "You look, speak and act
like a gentleman," Jung was told. "Your education must have been deep and
wide; you couldn't possibly be Orthodox."[81]

Jung's intellectual mien, courtly European manners, and gentle personality, qualities that turned on its head the prevailing stereotype of the Orthodox rabbi, endeared him to his well-heeled congregants, who found in their
rabbi a personal embodiment of that which they highly valued in their own
lives. "Here was a young Rabbi, Ph.D., bearded, English-speaking, a Cambridge graduate with dynamic interests in matters normally associated with
Yiddish speaking sages!"[82] Complementing and at times enhancing his congregants' own middle-class sensibility, Jung laid great stress on the amenities—aesthetics, decorum, manners—and ritually sanctioned them in his
addresses and sermons. "Rabbi Jung," wrote one of his admirers, "was
among the foremost who helped with the transportation from the lower East
to the upper West, and dressed yiddishkeit with aristocratic clothes."[83]
Like his bourgeois congregants, he too possessed a decidedly snobby streak,
not only manifesting a real coolness toward Lower East Side and other
nonaesthetic Orthodox Jews but, conversely, overstating the merits of his
own congregants. Unabashedly, Jung hailed his congregants as "a new type
of Jew and Jewess," and, on other occasions, as aristocrats, "heirs to the
tradition of the European Jewish aristocracy which sat at the table of
princes and honored the princes by honoring Jewish law."[84] Not surprisingly, Center congregants cottoned to that notion and made it their very
own. In the course of being interviewed, Jewish Center members repeatedly

expressed the notion that during the interwar years, theirs was the "aristoc-racy" of New York Jewry.

Towering intellectually, if not physically, over the captains of industry that made up his congregation, Jung freely displayed his erudition as he constructed densely worded and abstruse sermons or biweekly addresses in the synagogue bulletin. Center congregants listened in rapt attention, "never ever bored" by the Germanic rabbi as he spoke on such themes as "Inward Pioneering," "The Birth of the Jewish Family," "How to Keep Steady in a Crisis," "Between Washington and Lincoln."[85] Rarely exhortatory, Jung's sermons tended to stress the ethical component of Orthodox Judaism and its inherent compatibility with modern America far more than its ritualistic aspects. "I began to pay attention," Herman Wouk would later write of his first encounter with Rabbi Jung, "and then the ideas surprised me: religious ideas, articulated in the light of secular wisdom I had learned, and some secular wisdom that I hadn't learned."[86] In one respect, however, the Center rabbi departed from what was rapidly becoming a rabbinic norm: he publicly encouraged ritual observance. Adherence to the family-purity laws was one ritual whose performance he publicly and firmly advocated, as chapter 4 will disclose.

Like Lookstein and his other rabbinic colleagues, Jung was a great believer in the notion of an extended community and referred often and lovingly to the "Center family." Center congregants themselves took to heart Jung's sense of community, so much so that extrasynagogal social events were incomplete without the rabbi's presence; his contribution of a few sweet and well-chosen words to the celebrants became an indispensable part of the festivities. Through study circles, dinner dances, theater parties, afternoon teas, a regular *shalah sheudas*, and his much-touted decorous prayer service, Jung sought to make the Center into the centerpiece of Orthodox community. "The Center's pattern of Living Judaism," its rabbi related proudly, "has become internationally famous. Committees or individuals have come from all over . . . to learn from its inspir-ing services as well as from its methods."[87] By the same token, "a modern rabbi," Jung wrote of himself, "must be not only a scholar and speaker, but a peacemaker between parents and children, a marriage counsellor and . . . an ambassador of interdenominational goodwill."[88]

As involved outside his 86th Street congregation as he was within it, Jung did not simply pay lip service to the notion of an "ambassador of goodwill." With his ongoing knowledge and awareness of conditions in Europe during the thirties and forties, the German-born clergyman became a central figure in the resettlement of Europe's refugees. Enlisting the support of his merchant con-gregants, he obtained hundreds of affidavits for those seeking admission. A member of the Joint Distribution Committee's executive committee for several decades, Jung regularly visited Central and Eastern Europe, securing kosher food and financial support for indigenous Orthodox institutions. Closer to home, he personally tended to the financial needs of dozens of impoverished rabbis through the creation of the Rabbonim Aid Society, the favored charity of Center women.

Considered thoughtful, gentle, and, in later life, even saintly, Jung represented yet another model American Orthodox rabbi. Though strikingly different in personal style from, say, Lookstein, he too sought to render Orthodoxy at home in America. "If thirty Leo Jungs had been effectively placed all over the United States at the time he began his ministry," commented one of his congregants fondly, "I believe American Jewry today would be largely orthodox in outlook. . . ."[89]

By the 1940s, as the number of RIETS graduates had climbed to over one hundred, securing the seminary's legitimacy, there was no question that New York's Orthodox pulpits would be occupied exclusively by "RIETS Men." "By that time," observed one of the earliest RIETS graduates, "it became evident that an American-trained orthodox rabbi was not just a phenomenon but a fact, potent and promising."[90] But until the English-speaking, American-trained Orthodox rabbi had become a normative presence in Orthodox congregations, his candidacy for the pulpit often led to an intramural fight and the intrusion of "shul politics." Interest in hiring a young English-speaking rabbi tended frequently to divide a congregation into two camps, that of the older, more Europeanized element and the newer, more American contingent. "This tendency to look upon the congregation as consisting of two classes of members, those of the 'old guard' and those of the 'young guard,'" wrote Kaplan of his own experiences as KJ's first English-speaking clergyman, "has been in vogue ever since they began to feel the need of an English-speaking rabbi."[91] Much the same was true of Lookstein's appointment, close to twenty years later. Even at that time, Lookstein recalled, speaking in the third person, "this new phenomenon was not fully grasped. The older members were still a little suspicious; the young ones a little apprehensive. The young rabbi was appointed, not elected, for a period of six months. It was only after the lapse of that *Trial Period* that he was elected as assistant to the Rabbi Margolies."[92]

Once hired, the English-speaking, proudly modern rabbi had to translate what he had learned in the classroom into practice, and in that context, his relationship with his congregants, or *balebatim*, as they were more commonly known, was pivotal. In fact, it might be fair to say that in the fashioning of the American Orthodox rabbi, his relationship with his congregants influenced him as much as, if not more than, the formal education he had received at RIETS. A brand-new social invention, the English-speaking, modernized Orthodox rabbi had to build his own career and, by extension, his congregation from the ground up.

Unsure of himself—and of them—and with few apparent models on which to rely, the interwar Orthodox rabbi came of age during a very real, intense, and often hotly contested period of trial and error. "I began my novitiate very tremulously," recalled Lookstein. "My first steps in the rabbinate were hesitant and unsteady. I had to learn everything. . . ."[93]

Given the novelty of his position and often his youth as well, the interwar RIETS rabbi tended to welcome advice from some of his more seasoned congregants, who, in the time-honored tradition of laymen everywhere, were eager to dispense it. But then, they too were unsure of themselves, uncertain as to the limits and possibilities of their own role and the extent of their relationship with the highly educated, polished rabbi whose secular educational attainments were unequivocally superior to their own. After all, despite their material accomplishments, few interwar congregants held college degrees and consequently, as one rabbi observed, "gloried in both [their rabbi's] rhetoric and college accent."[94] A modern English-speaking rabbi was a source of status to many congregants, a symbol of their modernity and progressive orientation, and therefore an innovation they were not inclined to challenge. For some congregants of the modernized Orthodox synagogue, engaging a modern rabbi "would raise the congregation to the level of the fashionable ones which boast of English-speaking modern rabbis."[95]

Status aside, congregants of the interwar Orthodox synagogue liked to generate ideas of their own as to the functions of their rabbi and expressed those ideas within the context of lay-dominated synagogue committees. Through the medium of the Ritual Committee, the Decorum Committee, the Social Committee, and a myriad of other associations that came to characterize the modern synagogue, the laity exercised its own system of checks and balances on the power and authority of the rabbi. In many instances, their own expectations had a great deal to do with the shaping of the rabbi's role. For some, it was sufficient that their rabbi be "good for women with nerves," speak English well, and deliver a rousing sermon. For others, he needed only to look dignified.

The object of all this attention, meanwhile, had to define the limits of his relationship with his congregants: was he their peer, on a first-name basis with some or possibly all of his congregants? What was his role—counselor, confessor, social director? How far did his authority extend? Rejecting out of hand the age-old notion of the rabbi as a "spiritual recluse," a man removed from day-to-day contact with his constituents, the modern rabbi had to create, from scratch, an alternative identity.[96] The intense, frequently scrappy, and mutually dependent relationship that emerged from this give-and-take between congregant and rabbi ultimately reflected the newness of the modern rabbinate.

Not all modernized rabbis took well to the laity's penchant for self-expression and roundly criticized it, and them. Some Jews, recounted one severely chastened rabbi, "take to the synagogue activities as a duck to water . . . they use the synagogue as a medium for the instincts of intrigue and politics." Pawns in some intramural feud, rabbis, he concluded, "are used as the tools for the realization of their purposes."[97] Other clergy, then as now, accepted criticism as their due, especially in such apparently minor, if symbolic, issues as the sermon and dress. "In the early days of my ministry," recalled Lookstein, "my sermons never exceeded twenty minutes in length. . . .I thought that my congregants would appreciate such brevity. But apparently they did not. One evening a delegation called on me and asked me to extend my preaching time to at least thirty minutes," because, they insisted, "it was impossible to develop a theme in less than half an hour."[98] Some congregants were also quite free with their sartorial wisdom. Upon assuming the KJ pulpit, Lookstein was advised by one of his congregants (later to be his own father-in-law) on what to wear: "striped trousers and the cutaway coat that the well-dressed rabbi wore in those days." Left to his own imagination when it came to purchasing an overcoat, Lookstein, it seems, committed quite a sartorial gaffe. "I strutted into the synagogue on Friday night wearing proudly my Pitkin Avenue creation—a belted gray Wrumbo coat—and I noticed," he recalled, "that the worshippers were looking at me strangely. After services several of the 'elders' came over to say 'gut Shabbos' and most gently and sensitively told me that my outer garment was not becoming to a rabbi. . . ." Properly admonished, Lookstein exchanged his Pitkin Avenue purchase for a more conservative and suitable garment. "Before long," he recalled proudly, "I heard that the young people, especially the girls, regarded me as the best dressed rabbi they ever had."[99]

Given the newness of the situation and the absence of precedents, most laymen tended to defer to their rabbis, especially when it came to theological or doctrinal matters, in which the rabbi had few, if any, peers. "There are certain decisions in Jewish life which cannot be determined by majority vote of the Board of Trustees or of the membership of the congregation," maintained one long-standing synagogue president, singling out religious matters as a case in point.[100] In one celebrated instance, however—that of Mordecai Kaplan and his Jewish Center congregants—such an arrangement between rabbi and laity did not prevail. Ultimately, considerable disagreement over doctrinal issues led to a rupture that prompted the rabbi's resignation both from the immediate site of his problems and from traditional Judaism altogether. The outline of the story is familiar to most students of New York synagogue history; thanks, however, to the availability of Kaplan's diaries, it is now possible to reconstruct the imbroglio from Kaplan's perspective.

"I find myself at the beginning of a new spiritual exercise which holds out great promise," noted Kaplan in his diary in April 1915, as he and several young West Side Jews formed plans to establish a "Jewish communal centre."[101]

Several years in the making, the Jewish Center, as it became known, was a unique development in Jewish communal affairs, the first synagogue-center. The latter, Kaplan explained, is not "merely a house of worship or a rich men's club," but rather an institutional expression of "Jewishness."[102] Adumbrating by more than a decade the concepts set forth in his pathbreaking 1935 volume, *Judaism as a Civilization*, the Center contained a sanctuary, a day school for children, a gymnasium, and other features designed to show how Judaism "could be lived as a civilization, not religion."[103]

Somewhat disillusioned by what he perceived to be his own failure while junior rabbi at KJ, Kaplan had also come to doubt the efficacy and viability of Orthodox Judaism, doubts he confided to his diary repeatedly between 1914 and 1921 and to a few of his colleagues in the Jewish Center undertaking. Meeting with garment manufacturer Joseph H. Cohen, later the Center's first president and Kaplan's nemesis, Kaplan claims to have expressly revealed his philosophical qualms about revelation and other doctrinal matters so that "they would have no reason to say afterwards that I had misled them."[104] But apparently Kaplan was not nearly as direct on this, or on many other points, as he believed himself to be: from the outset, his relationship with Cohen and several other Center board members foundered on the issue of Kaplan's doctrinal purity. Repeatedly, Cohen sought to get Kaplan to agree that "the Shulkhan Aruch be the last court of appeal in religious matters," only to have the young rabbi evade the issue by calling for the exercise of his own discretion.[105]

"I am really surprised at myself that I have held on to the Center so long," confided Kaplan to his diary in the summer of 1919.[106] Frustrated by continuous debates with Cohen, the slowness with which it took to finance and build the multistory "synagogue with accessories," and his fierce and unshakable dislike for the "typical bourgeois Jews" that made up his congregation, Kaplan despaired of making much headway with his notion of the "reconstructed synagogue."[107] The young rabbi's dissatisfaction soon became a matter of public record when, in the spring of 1921, he challenged the synagogue board by insisting that he and he alone determine the educational content of the Center day-school, the first of its kind in America. The board, allegedly under Cohen's powerful "spell," refused Kaplan such leeway; "to safeguard the orthodoxy of instruction," they insisted on establishing a Committee on Education, which, together with Kaplan, would develop and oversee educational policy.[108] Disheartened by this turn of events, Kaplan began increasingly to voice concern over his suitability as the Center rabbi. "Unless the board comes round to my way of thinking," Kaplan noted in his diary, "I am simply wasting my time and my energy for a lot of people who are spiritually and Jewishly beyond redemption. . . ."[109]

Ultimately, Kaplan agreed to the board's demand that matters of non-Orthodox belief like biblical criticism would not be taught in the Center school. At the same time, however, he sought to make it clear to his congregants that he was not prepared "to surrender an iota" of his views and "would not pussy foot concerning them either."[110] "I will uphold the Shulkhan Aruch as the code to be practiced in the synagogue," he informed his congregants, "but I am not Ortho-dox and do not want to be bound to upholding Orthodoxy in the Center."[111] While this might have resolved the issue to Kaplan's satisfaction, it did little to comfort Cohen and his followers, who urged Kaplan's resignation. After a heated Board meeting with "much yelling," the board voted to retain Kaplan provided he abide by a number of compromise measures. (Curiously enough, Kaplan's diary fails to mention what they were.) Writing about his decision to stay on, Kaplan explained that he accepted this arrangement not because he believed it to be a workable one but because of his own pride. "I want to resign from the Center but I don't want anybody to make me do it."[112]

He was soon to change his mind. Shortly after the compromise was effected, Kaplan was presented with a "set of resolutions" designed to end the continuous tension between the Center rabbi and its lay leaders. Among the provisions to which Kaplan was to assent was that "the underlying religious principles of the Jewish Center were conceived in the spirit of Orthodox Judaism," and "in letter as well as in spirit, every activity of the Jewish Center shall be carried on in accordance with the principles of Orthodox Judaism."[113] For some unexplained reason, perhaps out of politi-cal naïveté, Kaplan was taken aback by the content of the resolutions and painfully noted at the time that "they came as a shock to me." Nevertheless, still eager to occupy the Center pulpit and at the same time to retain his own personal and ideological integrity, Kaplan proposed an "amendment" to the resolutions that would allow him to "teach and preach in accordance with the dictates of his conscience."[114] Not unexpectedly, this amendment was rejected out of hand.

Kaplan then swallowed his pride and remained at the Center in the hope that both time and his own notions of American Judaism would prevail. The Cen-ter's president, however, had had enough of Kaplan by then and sought actively to encourage his departure. Barely civil to the young rabbi, Cohen, some con-gregants recall, virtually "excommunicated" Kaplan, holding him at arm's length and forbidding him to sit on the pulpit; as Kaplan himself recalled, Cohen was "after my scalp."[115] Throughout the fall of 1921, Kaplan's failure to resolve the matter to his satisfaction gnawed at him, weakening his resolve to remain at the Center; interestingly enough, however, Kaplan refrained from writing in his diary during what must have been an extremely turbulent period. An unchrac-teristically terse entry a few months later, in January 1922, records that Kaplan resigned from the Center, together with thirty-five of its congregants (some of whom were relatives), and organized the Society for the Advancement of Judaism a day later.[116]

Fresh and spirited, the interwar generation of Orthodox rabbis manifested a real sense of purpose as its members set about articulating a new identity and role for themselves in the American Jewish community. "Orthodox Judaism is becoming more assertive, better disciplined," one of its clergy observed, referring to a growing sense of professionalism among his colleagues.[117] "Having sloughed off their foreign mannerisms, having changed the vernacular from Yiddish to English ... and having learned the lessons of organization and of publicity," wrote one Conservative rabbi of his Orthodox colleagues, "they are marching ahead with menacing strides."[118] Perhaps the clearest indication of the new spirit was the formation, in 1935, of the Rabbinical Council of America, an organization that sought to represent America's westernized Orthodox rabbinate. An amalgam of two organizations, the Yeshiva Rabbinical Association, formed in 1928 as the RIETS alumni association, and the Rabbinical Council of the Union of UOJCA, the clerical arm of that Orthodox umbrella organization, the Rabbinical Council of America (known popularly as the RCA) attempted to standardize and formalize normative Orthodox rabbinic practice even as it brought together clergy with a similar orientation. Breaking with established precedent, it declared itself the voice of the American Orthodox rabbinate.[119]

As a clear and unmistakable alternative to the more European and conservative Agudat ha-Rabbanim, the RCA found itself repeatedly in competition with the older organization. The latter, not surprisingly, viewed the RCA as a johnny-come-lately and one, moreover, whose rabbinic credentials and standards were far inferior to its own. Despite occasional admonitions from the Agudat and even a few attempts by RCA members to seek "a closer bond" with the older organization, to play Hillel to its Shammai, institutional boundaries between the two groups calcified.[120]

Credentials figured predominantly on the RCA's agenda and crystallized differences between the two rabbinic associations. Given its partial antecedents as the Yeshiva Rabbinical Association, the Rabbinical Council unhesitatingly accepted all RIETS graduates as members; the Agudat, in contrast, maintained far more stringent membership requirements. Where the RCA held that a RIETS student who had graduated with the ordination of *yoreh yoreh* (pertaining to matters of ritual and ceremonial law) possessed the requisite authority of an Orthodox rabbi, the older rabbinic body insisted that only those with more advanced credentials of *yadin yadin* (pertaining to matters of Jewish civil law) could be so designated. In formally rejecting the Agudat's standards and setting forth its own, the RCA challenged not only the hegemony of the older organization but, even more to the point, its authority. The intramural friction that resulted lasted for several years, often sapping the energy of the younger organization and thwarting its potential. Repeatedly throughout the latter part of the 1930s and continuing well into the postwar period, the RCA was forced to defend itself against angry charges, made by the older group, that its members were upstarts, illegitimate defenders of the faith, or that "American orthodoxy has compromised its principles because of . . . the English-speaking rabbi."[121]

At times, challenges to its membership requirements arose even from within the RCA itself.[122] Swallowing the critique of the older rabbinate that their rabbinic background was not what it ought to be, some RCA members sought to have the RCA restructure its membership requirements to accord with those of the Agudat, a notion that was ultimately defeated. At yet other moments, questions arose about the flexibility of the RCA's membership requirements: should RIETS graduates who were no longer practicing rabbis be allowed to remain as RCA members? And what of Orthodox rabbis who officiated in congregations where mixed seating prevailed? Should they be expelled from the organization and their status as Orthodox rabbis revoked? In the first instance, the RCA decided firmly that those who formally left the rabbinate were ineligible for membership. But deciding the fate of the practicing Orthodox rabbi whose congregation "deviated" from Orthodox practice was not as easy, nor was the RCA position as unambiguous. For months, the RCA Membership Committee "grappled with this agonizing problem" and concluded eventually that, given the "commanding urgency of the current situation," formal expulsion of the offending rabbi was not the answer.[123] Instead, the RCA proposed that before assuming the pulpit in a mixed-pew congregation, the rabbi should receive clearance from the RCA; as for the Orthodox rabbi already ensconced in such a congregation, the RCA eventually ruled, in 1948, that he did not qualify for membership. It then diluted the impact of this harsh decision by declaring that, when warranted, exceptions could be made.

A clear case of institutional growing pains, this kind of persistent internal wrangling over credentials was mandated, in part, by the RCA's need, common to all new organizations, to define itself in opposition to preexisting institutions, in this case the Agudat. It also reflected, more fundamentally, the novelty of the Orthodox rabbinate as a whole. An evolving phenomenon, the modern Orthodox rabbinate of the interwar years had not yet fully come to terms with its own persona or completely refined its thinking on matters of authority, practice, or philosophy. The continual and often heated discussions over membership requirements captured on a large institutional scale the kinds of pressures and self-scrutiny that rabbis were undergoing on the local level and marked, if painfully, the coming of age of the proudly modern Orthodox rabbinate.

The overriding importance of establishing itself as a self-sufficient rabbinic body, capable in its own right of rendering judicial and moral decisions, was by far the most potent motivation behind the ceaseless debates over membership standards. Where once the nascent Americanized Orthodox rabbinate had deferred tacitly to the Agudat, conceding its superior grasp of halakhic matters, it was now eager to claim that authority for its own. The establishment of a Halakha Commission and a Committee on Rabbinical Practice betokened the RCA's determination to become the regnant religious authority among New York's Orthodox. But in the absence of a strong rabbinic figure capable of holding his own with the old rabbinic guard, such intentions were not fully realized until after the war. It was not until 1953, when Rabbi Joseph Soloveitchik formally assumed the chairmanship of the Halakha Commission, that the Americanized Orthodox rabbinate possessed such a champion.

Scion of a distinguished rabbinic family of talmudic scholars, Joseph Soloveitchik emigrated to the United States in 1932 following his graduation from the University of Berlin with a Ph.D. in philosophy.[124] Settling in Boston, like so many of his predecessors, he founded the Maimonides School, New England's first Jewish day-school, and devoted himself to its development. With the death in 1941 of his father, Rabbi Moses Soloveitchik, the young Boston rabbi assumed his father's position as head of the RIETS talmudic department, a position he would later hold for over four decades. A masterly, if intimidating, teacher, and a profound and original thinker, Joseph Soloveitchik trained several generations of Orthodox rabbis for whom he articulated and refined a coherent ideology of Orthodox thought and practice. "The ultimate spiritual guide and legal mentor" for the Americanized Orthodox community and with few, if any, peers, Soloveitchik eventually became known as "the Rav," *the* rabbi, a testament to the august regard in which he was held by his constituents and to his unchallenged position as this generation's preeminent spokesman for the more modern Orthodox position.[125]

Even before the Rav lent his considerable imprimatur to the moral and halakhic authority of the English-speaking rabbinate, the RCA sought to develop a cohesive policy on matters of ritual observance and to institutionalize normative American Orthodox behavior. But what was that? Hundreds of queries on a staggering array of issues poured into the office of the RCA during the interwar years, reflecting the newness of the Orthodox experience and the confusion of the Orthodox rabbinate. Should pulpit flowers be used? What was standard policy on congregational singing? On the height of the *mechitzah*? Should the Orthodox rabbi cooperate with the non-Orthodox and, if so, in what venues? Was the consumption of a dairy meal in a nonkosher restaurant, a practice otherwise known as "eating out," permissible? Unwilling or unable to respond on an ad hoc basis, Orthodox rabbis in the field demanded clear and unequivocal direction from their own leadership on how to proceed and called repeatedly and persistently for the establishment of a canon of rabbinic practice, one that would supplement their more theoretical RIETS training. "Many members of the younger orthodox rabbinate," explained one of that group, "are themselves confused. They are not able to determine which synagogue procedure is orthodox and should be followed ... and which is unorthodox and should be either not introduced or eliminated. . . ."[126] A professional imperative, the need for an overarching code of behavior with which to respond to the challenges of modernity governed much of the RCA's early activity as it sought, in the words of one of its officials, to become a "Rabbinic Tribunal."[127] In that connection, the RCA circulated memoranda, letters, and newsletters and even published sermon manuals to acquaint its membership with its thinking on matters of ritual behavior.

The litmus test of the RCA's emerging professionalism, however, was that of kashruth supervision, a symbol of the differences between the "old school" and "new school" rabbinates. Historically, kashruth supervision had been the preserve of an individual rabbi on whose authority the reliability of a product—be it meat or poultry or, in later years, a processed food item—would rest. For many European rabbis in the New World, the ritual supervision and endorsement of a product provided most of their livelihood; to secure this source of revenue, its rabbinic practitioners would often pass the position from family member to family member.[128] The RCA, both to show its Americanness and to restore the reputation of the Orthodox rabbinate, which had frequently been impugned because of the unsavory practices of some lax and fraudulent rabbis, sought to abolish the system of individual, private supervision and its "kosher commissars" and to replace it with a communal, nonpartisan system.[129]

Known as the Kashruth Commission, a staff of qualified kashruth investigators and certifiers worked under the aegis of UOJCA to analyze and check the kashruth of hundreds of food items. Those products that successfully passed inspection received the UOJCA seal of approval, a small "OU." In this decisive break with the past, with the traditional way of doing things, the RCA acted with the overwhelming consensus and approval of its constituents. When, in 1953, a referendum to the membership was circulated on whether to retain the individual, private system of *hasgacha* (ritual supervision) or its more modern substitute, more than three-quarters of those tallied favored the newer communal alternative.[130] Not surprisingly, opposition from the Agudat and those who preferred the traditional system was fierce and vitriolic. "Leave the responsibility for kashruth supervision to the *genuine rabanim*," insisted Rabbi Eliezer Silver, thereby casting aspersions on the expertise of the RCA rabbi. With the belief that the newfangled system of noncommercial, communal supervision would create more ritual problems than it could possibly solve, Silver even advanced the notion that the new system would cause more Jews to eat "trefa," or unkosher, a charge the RCA spurned as unfounded and scurrilous.[131]

Despite the ongoing divisiveness between the two camps, the more modern, RCA-sponsored method of ritual supervision took hold and the Kashruth Commission, with its OU imprint, became a highly regarded and widely used source of kashruth supervision. Although the noncommercial method of ritual supervision did not completely replace the older system, which persisted alongside of it, and which continues to dominate the kosher slaughterhouses, the modernized system eventually became the accepted norm among the observant Jewish community.[132]

As a forum in which the contemporary problems, both practical and theoretical, of the westernized Orthodox rabbinate could be comfortably addressed, the RCA gradually carved out for itself a professional ethos and identity. Under its aegis, tricky halakhic issues were considered and responsa drafted at the same time that guidance in administrative matters, like pensions and insurance policies, was dispensed. Despite the slow and frustrating nature of much of its activity and the considerable amount of hairsplitting and foot dragging that often characterized RCA proceedings, the American Orthodox rabbinate became increasingly more institutionalized and professionalized. The very fact of the RCA's establishment coupled with its attempt to set standards and to formalize what has been historically an elusive, not so easily codified, phenomenon tangibly marked the coming of age of the Orthodox community.

By the 1940s the English-speaking Orthodox rabbinate had suffered somewhat of a reversal and was forced to take stock of its future. Now muted, its characteristic buoyancy and optimism was succeeded by a barely disguised sense of thwarted expectations, especially pronounced among the second and third generation of RIETS students, as the interwar years gave way to wartime and the fifties. To the modernized Orthodox Jews, once confident that their form of Judaism would become the dominant religious expression of second-generation, Americanized Jews, it now seemed as if a true modernized Orthodoxy could be found only in isolated instances, in "pockets," and that the anticipated orthodoxization of middle-class American Jewry would not materialize.[133] "A lost cause," reflected a RIETS graduate of 1942, "Orthodoxy was not going anywhere."[134]

Barely out of its infancy, the new Orthodox rabbinate had not had much time to mature before it was confronted head-on with major threats not only to its much-anticipated domination of American Judaism but to the legitimacy of its self-perception and sense of worth as well, threats that it was unable to withstand completely. Challenges from both the left—an increasingly popular Conservative Judaism—and the right—a sizable postwar influx of Eastern European Hasidim and traditional Orthodox Jews—undermined its confidence and severely weakened its institutional base. The first to feel the pressures of tempered expectations, the English-speaking rabbinate had to watch in frustration as Conservative Judaism attracted its potential constituency and the emerging right-wing Orthodox questioned its authenticity.

With the suburbanization of much of New York Jewry in the aftermath of the Second World War, Conservative Judaism emerged, seemingly overnight, as American Judaism's fastest-growing denomination. The ideology and ritual of Conservative Judaism blended in neatly with the new suburban, class-based identities of second-generation American Jews and captured their institutional loyalty.[135] "Suburbanization brought with it the problem of the maintenance of Jewish identity," Marshall Sklare observed in his pioneering 1955 study, *Conservative Judaism*, "and it was to the synagogue that the new Jewish suburbanite tended to look . . . Conservatism exemplified the type of synagogue that was most appealing. . . ."[136] Having wholeheartedly and enthusiastically embraced the synagogue-center concept, the postwar Conservative synagogue provided a suitable context in which local Jewish residents could spend their leisure time. Geared to the needs of the entire family, the suburban Conservative synagogue developed into a successful vehicle for the neighborhood expression of Jewishness. The "agreeableness of its service," with its shorter length, mixed seating, and dominant English usage, correlated ritually with the middle-class orientation of its congregants, for whom, as Sklare has noted, Conservatism was "a response to the process of embourgeoisement."[137] At one point the Americanized Orthodox rabbi had entertained the notion that this group would be his constituency, that the middle-class second-generation Jew of European background would be drawn to his unique blend of the truly authentic and the modern. But the Conservative establishment, with foresight and imagination, took advantage of the incipient demographic shift from urban to suburban locale and moved quickly to establish synagogues and Jewish community centers in those emerging settlements. The 1950 decision of the Committee on Jewish Law and Standards to permit driving to services on the Sabbath, almost a necessity given the demographic realities of suburban living, further hastened the movement's appeal, legitimating ritually a practice that many congregants already engaged in, perhaps uncomfortably and guiltily.[138]

Made decidedly uncomfortable by the evident success of Conservative Judaism as more and more postwar synagogues clustered under its banner, Orthodox Jews denounced the movement in unequivocal terms as "the gravest menace to traditional Judaism."[139] Extremely outspoken in their criticism of the fast-growing denomination, they lambasted it for "tampering" with the text of the *siddur* (prayer book), "misleading" traditionally minded worshipers, "preying upon the Orthodox to win over converts," and "capturing" formerly Orthodox synagogues "via the deceptive path of mixed pews."[140] During the late forties and early fifties, hardly an issue of *Jewish Life*, the monthly magazine of the

American Orthodox community and a publication sponsored by the UOJCA, appeared without some kind of denunciation of Conservative Judaism. The frequency with which such criticisms appeared so troubled one reader that he discontinued his subscription, explaining that he had expected "more than innu-endos and back-handed slaps" from its articles and editorials. Interestingly enough, the magazine's editors felt compelled to respond to this disgruntled (former) reader and explained their persistent attacks as a moral obligation. "Since, however, the tenets and the very life of orthodox Jewry are constantly under attack from dissident Jewish sects," the editors related, "occasions must arise when it becomes *our duty* to inform our people as to the nature of this opposition."[141]

Even as Conservative Judaism took hold, the fortunes of RIETS took a downward turn, accelerating even more the sense that the destiny of an Ameri-can Orthodoxy was not propitious. With the sudden death, in 1940, of Dr. Revel, hopes for the future of the school and, with it, the success of the Orthodox rabbinate, plummeted.[142] The intramural squabbling between moder-ates and conservatives that had characterized Revel's tenure now burst forth unchecked as the Agudat determined to put its stamp on the institution by having its candidate appointed as Revel's successor. The unseemly jockeying for power that ensued extended even to the school's more liberal supporters as they split into rival factions, some promoting Joseph Lookstein as a candidate for the school's president and others touting the qualifications of Leo Jung. A demoral-ized faculty and an anxious student body watched as the power plays, coupled with the Depression's legacy of financial disarray, enervated the school. With all these factors pressing down simultaneously, the Seminary seemed for some to be an increasingly more viable alternative; of the class of 1938, a symbolic 20 percent enrolled at the Morningside Heights facility. "I think back to the period when my fellow students and I at the yeshivah, decided to make the break and become Conservative rabbis. . . .It was a great wrench . . . but we had to make it," recalled one of those who enrolled at the Seminary at this time. "We saw the future of Judaism in the Conservative movement."[143]

Though the moderates at the school held the day and appointed Samuel Belkin, a Yeshiva professor of both Talmud and Greek and a Revel-style intel-lectual, as the new president, that appointment represented a Pyrrhic victory, a stopgap measure. For it was not so much the threat of a powerful left wing that ultimately unsettled the American Orthodox rabbinate as it was the formidable challenge of an increasingly strengthened right wing. In the aftermath of the Second World War, adherents of an aggressive or "sectarian" Orthodoxy came into their own, sparking a fierce internal dispute within the ranks of the Ameri-can Orthodox as to their own authenticity and legitimacy. An accident of history, thousands of observant European Jews, among them some of European

Jewry's supreme arbiters of Jewish law and learning, settled in New York during the 1940s. "The orthodox community of America," commented RCA president Uri Miller in 1948, "has been greatly strengthened by the influx of [*European*] scholars and religious functionaries. . . ."[144] While that may well have been true both numerically and psychologically, it did not augur well, in the long run, for the more Americanized and happily modernized clergymen.

This influx to which Miller referred contained a number of highly influential rabbinic personalities. As a group, they wielded a formidable degree of authority, centered largely in charismatic rebbes like those of the Lubavitch or Satmar Hasidim or, alternatively, in the heads of recently transplanted yeshivas.[145] Giants in the field of *halakha* and widely revered because of their illustrious descent, or *yichus*, rabbinic personalities like Reb Aaron Kotler or Rabbi Moshe Feinstein could not be as easily dismissed as the prewar Agudat ha-Rabbanim or the Conservative rabbinate. Nor, for that matter, was the American Orthodox rabbinate inclined to ignore them. The ultimate standard-bearers of Jewish tradition and learning, these men, by their very lights, represented the essence of the Torah-true community and the very source of its continuity. Known collectively as the *gedolim*, the Torah giants, an appellation that succinctly attested to their impeccable and unimpeachable pedigree, they outranked the RIETS graduate, no matter how polished his oratory or broad his education. "Their overwhelming personality and stature as some of the greatest figures in world Jewry gave them a standing that could not be ignored. . . . Their scholarship, plus their worldwide following, combined to give them extraordinary standing in the community. . . ."[146]

Openly disdainful of the American Orthodox rabbi and his overwhelmingly pastoral orientation, the newer guard exceeded even the Agudat in its antipathy toward the members of that tribe. It did not take long before questions of credentials, standards, and moral authority, issues the American Orthodox thought had been laid to rest years before, were reopened. Standing on its head the modern interpretation of the Orthodox rabbinate, the postwar European rabbinate repeatedly challenged its American counterpart and some of its characteristic endeavors, such as interdenominational cooperation, as it sought, through not-so-subtle means, to undermine its authority. In a kind of throwback to the traditional, premodern European rabbinate, expertise in *halakha* and not one's pastoral or oratorical abilities became the overriding criterion of the Orthodox rabbi's success and public standing.

As the canons of evaluation changed, so too did the stature of the American Orthodox rabbi, even among his own kind. Ironically enough, the right wing's negative estimation of the representative RIETS rabbi came full circle and influenced the RIETS student body of the postwar era. Internalizing the right-wing critique of American Orthodoxy, the rabbinical students of the fifties and sixties adhered to a different standard of behavior and ideology than that cherished by the first generation of RIETS rabbis and their teachers.[147] They now viewed the elder statesmen of the Orthodox rabbinate with a somewhat jaundiced eye; to their way of thinking, the older generation was deficient in its knowledge of Jewish law, more concerned with the trappings of Orthodoxy than with its substance. Having readjusted their sights, the new rabbinical students regarded the older faculty as "minor figures," "lightweights," and their once highly touted popular courses on sermon construction or American Jewish sociology as "crap courses," an "easy A."[148] Like so much else connected with the pre–World War II Orthodox experience, the development of a modernized rabbinate was itself an exercise in style. But later generations simply did not see it in quite those terms and mistook the well-spoken minister so beloved by their parents as an insubstantial guide to the perplexities of their own era. In some respects, this kind of reevaluation was inevitable: the dismissal of an earlier generation of rabbis probably would have happened even without the intercession of the more aggressive sectarian Orthodox as one generation typically gave way to another with its own agenda and methodology. But in this instance, the overriding and incontestable strength of the right-wing rabbinate and its followers hastened the process, leaving a denomination that, as Norman Lamm, one of its postwar exponents, put it, suffered from a "collective inferiority feeling."[149]

The American Orthodox rabbinate did not simply throw up its hands in despair and abandon itself and its congregants to the right wing. RIETS alumni maintained, and at times fiercely so, their commitment to the notion of an indigenous, modernized Orthodoxy and their concomitant rejection of what one Orthodox spokesman termed "right-wing authoritarianism." Through the writings of such representative American Orthodox clergy as Lamm, Emanuel Rackman, and others, attempts were made to articulate formally an ethos of American Orthodox behavior. Still, in these attempts to reclaim the middle ground, or what was now being labeled as "centrist Orthodoxy," one cannot help but detect an edge of defensiveness, perhaps even of temporizing. What's more, some of American Orthodoxy's guardians like Joseph Lookstein found themselves thoroughly bewildered and disheartened by this seeming about-face in American Orthodox behavior. "You'll see," he remarked, cautioning a younger colleague about the excesses of the right wing, "this is a passing fad."[150] Correct about so many things, Lookstein, in this one crucial area, erred critically. His hopes, and undoubtedly those of many of his fellow clergy and laity, for the impermanence and evanescence of this newer, more aggressive Orthodoxy failed to materialize as the latter, now entrenched, grew from strength to strength.

Orthodox Jews at a wedding celebration, Hotel Astor, 1914. Resplendent in evening attire, male guests also donned black papier-mâché *yarmulkes*, "one of the latest inventions of modern Orthodoxy." (The Collection of Richard W. Joselit.)

Orthodox women in New York, ca. 1930s, observing the rite of *tashlikh* during the Jewish Penitential Period. (Samuel Zagat, photographer. Courtesy of the YIVO Institute for Jewish Research.)

Orthodox men in New York, ca. 1930s, observing the rite of *tashlikh* during the Jewish Penitential Period. (Samuel Zagat, photographer. Courtesy of the YIVO Institute for Jewish Research.)

The exterior of Congregation Kehilath Jeshurun, "undoubtedly one of the finest edifices ever erected by an orthodox congregation in America," after being remodeled in the late 1940s. An exterior double-sided staircase was removed in an attempt to modernize the synagogue. (Courtesy Congregation Kehilath Jeshurun.)

A few of the dignitaries at the cornerstone-laying ceremony of Congregation Kehilath Jeshurun, May 1902. The cornerstone was laid, the press reported, "amid great éclat." (Courtesy Congregation Kehilath Jeshurun.)

The sanctuary of the Jewish Center, "refined surroundings for Divine Worship," ca. 1930s. (Courtesy the Jewish Center.)

Attorney Street, 1908. Often located on the second or third story of a tenement, the typical immigrant synagogue, or *chevra*, presented "a most dour appearance." (Courtesy of The New York City Municipal Archives.)

Credo of the Kehilath Jeshurun Sisterhood, 1939. Auxiliary organizations like the sisterhood or the men's club provided the opportunity to pursue "sacred hobbies." (Courtesy Congregation Kehilath Jeshurun.)

The Jewish Center's board of trustees in the Center boardroom, 1942. (Courtesy the Jewish Center.)

Rabbi Moses Z. Margolies, ca. 1902. "The Ramaz," one family member recalled respectfully, "looked like Moses." (Courtesy Congregation Kehilath Jeshurun.)

Rabbi Joseph H. Lookstein shortly after assuming the pulpit at Congregation Kehilath Jeshurun. He symbolized the "new type, American type" of Orthodox rabbi. (Courtesy Congregation Kehilath Jeshurun.)

Rabbi Leo Jung, "the very epitome
of orthodoxy," in his study.
(Courtesy the Jewish Center.)

For careful wives with busy lives

KEEP IN SHAPE
WITH SHEFFIELD

Women like to be busy. But women don't like to be tired. A wife does a thousand things to make her house a home. But she doesn't mind — if she's fit. Milk is her helper. Milk builds energy as fast as she spends it. A quart a day keeps a sparkle in her eye . . . beauty in her cheek. And careful women say Sheffield before they say milk. EXTRA freshness means better flavor. Laboratory control insures Sheffield purity. 92 years of experience backs Sheffield practice. In short—you're sure of Sheffield! On the doorstep on-the-dot. Try it.

SHEFFIELD FARMS *Sealect* GRADE - A MILK

NRA

This advertisement for ritually supervised Sheffield Farms dairy products subtly links together fitness, shapeliness, and kashruth. (*The Orthodox Union*, October 1933.)

An Historic Event To The Jews of America

Inc.

Operating

One of the world's largest Candy Plants
and
227 Retail Candy Stores

Announces

The Authorization and Use of the Official Insignia
of the Orthodox Union

FOR *Loft* PURE CANDIES AND ICE CREAM

For 40 years, Loft has been nationally known for the absolute purity of its Candies
and Ice Cream, and is proud to announce the official endorsement by The Union of
Orthodox Jewish Congregations of America.

Loft is happy and ready to serve Jews
throughout America with its delicious and
fine Candies and Ice Cream. Now, *you* can
enjoy the large variety of confections, the
inspection of which, by the Rabbinical

Council of the Union of Orthodox Jewish
Congregations of America certifies that Loft
makes these products strictly according to
the dietary laws, and without any forbidden
ingredients or animal fats.

Inc.

FORTIETH AVENUE and NINTH STREET
LONG ISLAND CITY, NEW YORK

Loft's candies receive an Orthodox
stamp of approval. *The Orthodox
Union*, December 1934.)

A typical Lower East Side mikvah,
or "kosher bathing place," 1908.
(Collections of the Municipal
Archives of the City of New York.)

A detail from the previous photograph.

"Attention Mothers of Brides and All Jewish Daughters": An advertisement for the "model mikvah" touting its ultraviolet lamps, beauty parlor, and "other feminine needs." (*Morgen Zhurnal*, May 1941.)

The Ramaz Academy school bus. (Courtesy the Ramaz School.)

Enacting a Passover seder at school, ca. 1940s. (Courtesy the Ramaz School.)

Coeducation at the elementary-school level, ca. 1940s. (Courtesy the Ramaz School.)

Home economics, ca. 1940s. This course expressed best the modern day school's objective of creating an "integrated personality." While learning the principles of domestic science, students were also taught the "principles of kasherization." (Courtesy the Ramaz School.)

THE JEWISH PRIESTESS AND RITUAL

The Sacred Life of
American Orthodox Women

"Priestess of the Jewish ideal, Prophetess of Purity and Refinement," the American Jewish woman of the interwar years, it was widely believed, was a quintessential religious being.[1] Seen by the vast majority of American Jews of all denominations as the guardian of Jewish life, the safeguard of its future, it was she who upheld its standards and promoted Jewish ritual while seeing to the religious education of the children. And yet, it was not as a rarefied priestess or prophetess that the Jewish woman was most commonly esteemed and idealized; rather, it was in her capacity as mother and homemaker, as "queen of the home."[2] "The Jewish ideal of womanhood," one of its admiring students wrote, "is not the entrancing beauty of the queen of a knightly tournament nor the ascetic life of a virgin saint but wifehood and motherhood."[3] It followed, then, that the American Jewish woman most fully realized herself within her home, the staging ground for her "essential work."[4] Using language derived from the sanctuary, both male and female observers compared the housework of Jewish women to "service at the altar" and enjoined the American Jewish woman to "make of her home a miniature Temple" by consecrating it to religion.[5] The home, explained one popular Jewish text, "is the grandest of all institutions ... and woman its presiding genius."[6]

Despite this widely shared belief in the religious distinctiveness of the Jewish woman and in the centrality of the Jewish home, notions that would remain intact well into the 1960s, challenges to its hegemony began to appear during the interwar years, first among Reform and Conservative women and then, belatedly, among Orthodox women as well. With their newly acquired middle-class incomes and heightened secular awareness, affluent Jewish women of the interwar years began increasingly and more vociferously to articulate a need for broader "separate spheres" of communal involvement. "Conditions among Jewish women of culture have grown to be alarming," observed Mathilde Schechter, the founder of the Women's League and wife of the Jewish Theological Seminary's chancellor. She found her counterparts in 1918 turning aside

97

from Jewish tradition to "the opera, movies, the theater and society" for cultural fulfillment.[7] "The former queen of the home," complained an Orthodox observer, "has voluntarily reduced her rank and the Jewish home, the erstwhile temple in miniature is breaking down. . . ."[8] The etiology of this disaffection, or what several commentators labeled the "current spiritual unrest," was clear: it was not that modern Jewish women rejected the community's characterization of themselves as keenly spiritual personalities, for they did not; nor did they reject the community's characterization of the home as their primary "religious domain." Rather, they sought, in their designated capacity as spiritual and religious entities, to exercise their talents and capabilities in new and expanded directions: to involve themselves with a wider number of institutions and causes and to extend their influence beyond the home into the community at large. "The solution for much of the present domestic unrest," counselled Irene Wolff, an Orthodox Jewish writer, "is not to take women out of the home but to enlarge the concept of the home so as to bring into the home a widened interest."[9] Or, as one Reform advocate put it, the way to retain the interest and commitment of Jewish women was to put "Jewish womanhood on the road of highest usefulness to the cause of American Israel."[10]

Making use of the talents of modern Jewish womanhood by "enlarging the concept of the home" was yet another way of talking about the integration of the American Jewish woman into the larger Jewish community. A complicated process and one bound up with the modernization of the American synagogue, it entailed a gradual tempering and rethinking of the community's attitude toward women. "While the Jewish woman was honored as the priestess of the family hearth and the mistress of her home, her range of initiative ended there," remarked one observer.[11] But the modern American Jewish woman, the "new type of American Jewess," required a broader venue for her talents and one that was "beyond the shadow of her hearth."[12] Where some spoke of integration and others of the emergence of a new American Jewish woman, still others likened the would-be expanded communal involvement of the Jewish woman to a kind of coming of age of American Jewry and dubbed the process, somewhat fancifully perhaps, "deorientalization." The emancipation of the traditional Jewish woman from some of Judaism's allegedly "oriental inhibitions and constraints," deorientalization assumed a number of concrete manifestations: the abolition of the separate women's gallery and its replacement with mixed pews or family seating was one example, while the granting to women of full rights of congregational membership, and sometimes even inclusion within the synagogue's board, was another.[13] "Woman has at last found her niche in religious life as well as in civic and political work," observed one "new type of American Jewess" in 1924. "We do not find her today relegated to the gallery of the synagogue docilely watching the men of the congregation. Her voice is heard on the Temple Board, her advice is asked in the direction of affairs of the Sabbath School, she is in fact a force in the religious community. . . ."[14]

By far the most common example of "deorientalization" was the establishment of a synagogue sisterhood. Greatly expanding the "range of initiatives" available to the interested Jewish woman, the women's auxiliary harnessed her religious inclinations and organizational talents to the synagogue, providing a permanent and enduring outlet for communal affairs. Essentially a religious organization, the sisterhood of the interwar years pressed for greater ritual observance among its members even as it helped to render the American synagogue a warm, friendly, and accessible institution. Holding luncheons, equipping the synagogue kitchen, conducting Bible classes, decorating the sanctuary and the *succah*, raising funds, and publishing manuals on how best to administer a sisterhood and to have a "Jewish Home Beautiful," the American synagogue sisterhood sought to promote Jewish ritual observance both within and without the home.[15] An ally of the rabbi, perhaps even his "best friend," the synagogue sisterhood became an integral aspect of American synagogue life and, as such, marked "the ascendancy of women in the synagogue."[16] By World War II, hundreds of American synagogues of all persuasions maintained women's auxiliaries; in fact no self-consciously modern and proudly American congregation was without one. Referring to the synagogue sisterhood, one writer on contemporary American Jewish affairs remarked as early as 1925 that as an institution the sisterhood "was not singular nor unique. It is a transcript of the zeitgeist. . . ."[17] Putting it somewhat differently and less poetically, Orthodox rabbi Joseph Lookstein observed a decade later that "we cannot but be impressed by the invasion of all institutions and movements in Jewish life by the ever increasing numbers of women."[18]

Admittedly, this "invasion" was far more pronounced and widespread in Reform and even Conservative circles than it was in Orthodox ones. And yet, all throughout the 1920s and 1930s, the Orthodox community, abetted by several Orthodox clergymen and sustained by the grass-roots encouragement of well-educated and cultured Orthodox Jewish women, also began to take more and more notice of its women and their spiritual needs. In editorials with titles like "A New Deal for the Forgotten Jewish Woman," Jewish women were encouraged to attend synagogue, to establish sisterhoods, to acquire a firm Jewish education, and to practice Jewish rituals like kashruth and family-purity laws with interest and commitment.[19] Sensing growing disaffection among Orthodox Jewish women and determined to arrest it, the Orthodox community sought to integrate its women more fully within its boundaries. While the home remained the unquestioned lodestar of the Orthodox Jewish woman's spiritual and existential condition, Orthodox Jews become increasingly aware of the need to supplement the home with complementary alternatives and thus, in their own way, to "deorientalize" the Orthodox Jewish woman.

No doubt influenced, in part, by developments within the larger Jewish community and determined, as always, to keep abreast of them, Orthodox Jewry was beginning to realize that the traditional Jewish home was no longer immune to the blandishments of secular society. Insisting, as they had for centuries, on the primacy of the home, Orthodox Jews had not only failed to provide the observant Jewish woman with other communal and educational opportunities—preferring instead, as one rabbi put it, "to invest in manhood"—but they had also overestimated the home's durability.[20] "Formerly, the Jewish woman received her spiritual inspiration from the piety and religious fervor of her home. But in this age of scientific inquiry, children will not follow blindly in the footsteps and practices of their parents. Frequently do they question and even challenge the necessity for observing certain ceremonies."[21] Though such laments are a constant refrain in the Jewish historical experience, as each generation bemoans anew the failings of its successor, the frequency, passion, and gender specificity of these interwar complaints appears to reflect an altered set of circumstances: the emergence of a new generation of American-born women from observant families who were not only basically unlettered but also without the kind of nostalgic and atavistic attachment to ritual that had characterized their mothers. In the eyes of many communal leaders, the much-vaunted ideal of the ritually scrupulous and knowledgeable Jewish housewife and mother was fast becoming more of an ideal than a reality, a prescription of Orthodox behavior rather than a widespread social norm. "Do we wonder, then," asked Mrs. Rebecca Goldstein, the wife of one of Orthodoxy's leading young rabbis and herself a Barnard graduate, "that so many homes of today are un-Jewish? Why should a Jewish girl maintain a kosher home after she marries when she has never been taught the meaning of the dietary laws? Why kindle the Sabbath lights . . . ? Why observe the issue of Family Purity?"[22]

As the limits of the home became increasingly apparent, Orthodox leaders began to reevaluate that institution and, like Jewish leaders elsewhere, to redress its imbalances by providing suitable alternatives. Seeking to make more room within Orthodoxy for its women and, in effect, to develop (and ensure) a constituency of observant women, the community launched what in retrospect appears to have been a concerted effort to win their institutional loyalty. Its leaders addressed themselves to both the public and private spheres of the American Jewish woman's sacred or ritual life and in the areas of synagogue participation and ritual performance made determined overtures to her.

"Cultivating the synagogue attendance habit," as one Orthodox rabbi put it, was the most frequent, and easily attended to, feature of the community's efforts to render Orthodox life more appealing to the modern woman.[23] From the pulpit and the printed page, women were urged to make attendance at Sabbath services a regular and accustomed part of their religious ritual. Such encouragement was sorely needed, for the notion of an Orthodox female worshiper was somewhat of a novelty. Widespread in American Christian communities, female attendance at services was generally rare in traditional Jewish circles. For centuries, the American churchgoing public was largely female; as such, the church became the "property of the ladies" and church membership a "woman's activity."[24] But among America's Jews, especially those Orthodox in denomination, the attendance of women was occasional, limited to the High Holidays and those ritual moments on which *Yizkor*, the memorial prayer, was said. Despite the widely received notion that Jewish women were inherently spiritual, women simply did not attend services.

The absence of Jewish women from the traditional synagogue service was itself a kind of tradition. In the Old World, as in the New, women simply did not make synagogue attendance a part of their sacred lives. This is not to suggest that Jewish women did not pray—only that the context for their devotions was more private than public. The existence of *thines* (supplications), a rich Yiddish penitential literature designed almost exclusively for a female audience, suggests the multiplicity of occasions for female prayer. Women would routinely offer up a *thine*, often phrasing it in the first-person singular and inserting the personal names of loved ones, when they lit the Sabbath candles, buried the dead, gave birth, immersed in a mikvah (ritual bath), prepared holiday foods, and even when they cleaned house! In fact, the recitation of a *thine* tended to transform a routine and mundane event into more of a sacred moment. Suggestively enough, few *thines* were designed for recitation in the synagogue; most were recited in the intimate setting of the home.[25]

A striking departure, then, from established social convention, the presence of women in the Orthodox sanctuary had become, by the war years, a familiar and perhaps even normative practice, so much so that Orthodox girls who had come of age during the fifties could scarcely remember a time when they and their mothers were absent from the Sabbath service.[26] "The synagogue finds in woman not only a most generous supporter," commented Rabbi Lookstein, "but also a far more frequent worshiper than it finds in man. . . ."[27] At the urging and encouragement of their husbands, clergy, and peers, women went to synagogue more and more frequently, and, for many observant woman of the interwar years, attending services became an indispensable part of their ritual life, one they cultivated meticulously. "Going to services," recalled an Orthodox woman who grew up during the interwar years, "was a big deal."[28] Some, undoubtedly, simply "went along," attending services out of deference to their husbands' wishes.[29] Others, however, found synagogue attendance to their liking, not simply a marital obligation. Like their middle-class non-Jewish counterparts, for whom churchgoing was an approved and highly valued social convention, middle-class observant Jewish women construed synagogue attendance as a reflection and affirmation of their middle-class status as well as the "thing to do."[30]

Arriving between 10:30 and 11:00, toward the latter part of the service, women worshipers sat among friends or family members, exchanged news of the week, chatted about who was in attendance and who was not, and eyed one another's clothing. Dressing up, "getting *faputzt*," was an essential aspect of the ritual and one that attested concretely to the social significance of shul-going.[31] Almost as important a ritual as worship itself, dressing up afforded women the opportunity to display their finery and with it their financial status within a sacred context; it thus legitimated dress in a way that more secular venues like the theater or the opera could not. On an "ordinary Sabbath," women would don suits, gloves, hats, and "important jewelry," or, as one frequent Sabbath service attendee put it, look "*balebatish*"; young girls, generally those over the age of three, would be clad in hat, gloves, and a "good dress." Not surprisingly, synagogue attire developed into a complex ritual of its own with different requirements for different occasions: a regular Sabbath mandated one kind of uniform, while a *yontef* (holiday) called for slightly more fancy attire. The coup de grace, sartorially speaking, was Erev Yom Kippur, when women donned their very best. Fancy evening wear was customary: "cocktail dress was de rigueur," reported one contemporary, as was lavish jewelry and, if the weather permitted, even furs.[32] Reflecting the importance attached to dressing for these public ritual occasions, the purchase of new clothes often coincided with the Jewish calendar: it was customary to buy one's "fall" wardrobe in time for the Jewish New Year and one's "spring" wardrobe in time for Passover.

The sanctuary was not merely the setting for displaying one's finery; it was, after all, a venue for prayer. Despite the hum of gossip and the distraction of the beautifully clad, women worshipers did attend to their prayers. The architectural ambience of the modernized Orthodox synagogue sanctuary helped to focus their attention on the service. Historically, Orthodox synagogues (both in the Old World and in the New) were not known to give much thought, let alone much space, to their admittedly small female audience. Almost an afterthought, the women's section of the traditional New York synagogue was a "little shut-in stuffy gallery," barely more than an alcove.[33] Poorly ventilated, the "woman's precinct" was designed for a handful of visitors but expanded to "forty when necessary."[34] By the World War I years, however, the American Orthodox synagogue, now a dignified and often monumental structure, had begun to provide ample and capacious seating for its women. "Women have much to be thankful for in this new type of synagogue," one female eyewitness related. "To be sure, they still are not counted toward a quorum but they are not hidden behind a curtain. They have plenty of elbow-room."[35] The characteristically modernized Orthodox sanctuary accommodated its women worshipers, granting them ample "elbowroom" in one of two ways: either by providing a spacious upstairs gallery with clear sight lines or by situating the women on the main floor of the sanctuary and separating them from the men by a *mechitzah*, or partition. These architectural alterations or improvements made women worshipers feel more welcome than they had been when relegated to a little nook of the sanctuary. Including them within the architecture of the sanctuary gave them a sense, though perhaps one that remained unarticulated, that they were no mere appendages or occasional intruders but an integral or entirely welcome part of the ritual drama. No longer hidden behind a homemade curtain or grille, the female worshiper was able to observe the service firsthand, directly, and thus have a keener and clearer sense of the proceedings.

While it is sorely tempting to see in these altered spatial configurations of the interwar years, particularly in the *mechitzah* per se, evidence of a heightened sensitivity to the needs of the Orthodox American Jewish woman, corroborative evidence is hard to come by. Among Reform and Conservative Jews, seating patterns were often intertwined with questions of sexual equality. "Jews came to view the debate over the synagogue seating of women," observes historian Jonathan Sarna, "as a debate over the synagogue status of women. . . ."[36] But this was not the case among the Orthodox of the interwar years; nowhere do they associate a *mechitzah* or, for that matter, ample seating room with modernity or its corollary of deorientalization. The connection between the two apparently escaped them—or, if they did think in such terms, the link remained unarticulated. Unlike their Reform and Conservative counterparts, the Orthodox Jewish rabbinate simply did not view seating patterns as an avowedly women's issue and, in turn, as an index to their own modernity. Despite ample opportunity to make a case for the modernity of the Orthodox sanctuary, Orthodox synagogues during this period repeatedly failed to do so. Take, for example, the dedication, in 1918, of the Jewish Center, a showpiece of New York's Americanized Orthodox community, whose sanctuary employed a *mechitzah* on its main floor, in lieu of the more customary gallery, to segregate the sexes. Dedication exercises provided a tailor-made opportunity for trumpeting that congregation's modernity and parallel concern for its female members. And yet, neither the press, which generally seized on instances of nonconformity, nor Mordecai M. Kaplan, at whose behest and direction the sanctuary was designed, had anything to say on its novelty; the Center's somewhat unusual seating configuration—what Kaplan called a "kind of false gallery"—was a source of neither praise nor criticism. That it figures not at all in contemporary Orthodox records or even in the collective memory of Jewish Center congregants—folkloristic accounts of the intramural tensions that frequently accompany the construction of a synagogue have not been handed down—suggests, by indirection, that during the interwar years, Orthodox Jews themselves did not link synagogue seating patterns with their denomination's attitude toward women.[37] The most one can say with certainty is that a women's section with "more elbowroom" was more an incidental feature of the newly grandiose and monumental American Orthodox sanctuary of the interwar years than it was a direct consequence of modernity or conscious deorientalization. While the net result of these architectural alterations fed directly into and sustained Orthodoxy's experiment with deorientalization, the *mechitzah* per se was not a conscious part of that process.

It was only during the years following World War II, when the *mechitzah* became the yardstick by which American Jews distinguished an Orthodox from a Conservative synagogue—and the subject of increasingly vituperative debates between the two denominations—that Orthodox clergy picked up on the connection between seating patterns and attitudes toward women. Seeking to counter the claims of their more liberal coreligionists that Orthodoxy was inconsistent with modernity or, as one observer put it, to illustrate that segregated seating was "erroneously interpreted as a slur upon emancipated womanhood," Orthodox leaders raised the women's issue but only to refute it passionately.[38] The "foolish accusation hurled at the Orthodox synagogue, that its separate seating implies an acceptance of women's inequality," was dismantled, layer by layer, by Orthodox apologists.[39] Some drew on biblical and talmudic literature while others invoked anthropology to demonstrate the high regard in which Jewish tradition held its women. "It is simply untrue that separate seating in a synagogue, or elsewhere, *has anything at all to do with quality or inequality*," insisted Rabbi Norman Lamm, one of the postwar era's most eloquent rabbis.[40] The modern-oriented Orthodox clergy remained adamant on that point and energetically campaigned in the postwar period to maintain the practice of segregated seating, thus keeping their ideological boundaries intact and inviolate.

Whether consciously intended or not, the welcoming environment of the interwar American Orthodox synagogue provided the physical context in which women's attendance at the synagogue grew and developed. Within that context, the nature of the aestheticized Orthodox prayer service hastened the process still further. The introduction of decorum into the Orthodox sanctuary, a phenomenon described in an earlier chapter, had the effect of rendering the service even more accessible to the female worshiper than it had once been. Many of the new features of the Kehilath Jeshurun service, noted that synagogue's bulletin, had been instituted "in response to numerous requests coming especially from women who want to participate in the services in an intelligent manner."[41] As a by-product of the decorous service, the female audience was now better able to follow the Orthodox ritual and to participate more directly in it. Once English replaced Yiddish as the prevailing and public language of the service, the language in which announcements were made, sermons preached, and occasional prayers enunciated, the service was no longer foreign or mysterious; those without Yiddish or the requisite prayer skills—skills that native-born American Jewish women generally lacked—had no reason to feel ill at ease. Devotees of English responsive readings and of the rabbi's sermon, women had become, willy-nilly, more adept at following the rhythms of the service. Were they temporarily lost, the frequent announcement of pages in English helped them to reorient themselves; failing that, there were always one or two women congregants, *mishers* or page turners, who, approximating informally the Eastern European *zugerin* or *zugerke*, knew the ins and outs of that text. Congregational use of a common prayer book with English translations and transliterations also facilitated the woman worshiper's dexterity and familiarity with the prayer service, enabling her to feel at home within its pages.[42]

The transformation of the service from a wholly performance-oriented one, in which the cantor held complete sway as the congregation listened in silence, to a service in which congregants sang along at selected key moments also occasioned a greater sense of participation. "Teaching the congregation to join in, nay, even to maintain the service," was one way to enliven the proceedings and to banish apathy.[43] "The traditional melodies," Rabbi David De Sola Pool observed, "are all simple and of small range so that the least musical congregant may sing to them."[44] The Young Israel movement, one of the first organized religious expressions of modern Orthodoxy, took great pains to introduce congregational singing, then a novelty, into its pre–World War I service; its concerted effort to get women to join in the singing was even perceived, at the time, as somewhat "revolutionary" and radical. More established congregations like the 85th Street Shul and the Jewish Center also actively promoted congregational singing, even going so far as to sponsor coeducational classes in Jewish music or to institute a choral group to familiarize worshipers with the new tunes. "We must ask the support of women in the choral circles," Rabbi De Sola Pool explained, "so that they also may swell the melodious cadence of prayer in the synagogue. . . ."[45]

As they lifted their voices in song, listened attentively to the sermon, keenly participated in the responsive readings, and managed the prayer ritual, female worshipers became an integral and expected fixture of the Orthodox synagogue. Ultimately, what brought women into the synagogue and then kept them there was its transformation from an exclusively prayer-oriented and male-centered institution into an active social center geared toward the entire family, a phenomenon described at length in an earlier chapter. Once the Orthodox synagogue sought determinedly to become a hub of community life, a center for extradevotional activities like classes, sports activities, teas, and luncheons, women felt increasingly more comfortable within its sacred precincts. By more broadly defining its role within the community, the Orthodox synagogue enabled the American Orthodox woman to feel that the synagogue was as much her institution as it was her husband's or her son's.

In large measure, the sisterhood was the agent of this transformation. Assigned the "inner life, the housewivery" of the synagogue, sisterhood women applied their domestic sensibilities to the task, making of the synagogue a miniature home.[46] Much as she cultivated a spirit of warmth and hospitality within her private life, the sisterhood woman was expected to cultivate a spirit of good feeling and hospitality within the synagogue. As the "backbone" of the congregation's social spirit, the sisterhood institutionalized the natural impulse toward confraternity and, in that way, helped to build a community or, as Rabbi Lookstein liked to say, "weld[ed] [the] congregation into a happy family unit."[47] In the characteristic premodern Orthodox synagogue, there was little sense of a community whose interests extended beyond that of prayer; whatever fraternizing existed was informal and largely outside (both literally and figuratively) of the shul. The proudly modern Orthodox congregation, however, transformed socializing into one of its integral functions, an essential ingredient in its modern makeup. Through a continual round of social events—teas, dances, luncheons—the sisterhood kept alive and nourished the healthy social spirit that developed into the hallmark of the American Orthodox synagogue. "Serv[ing] in large measure as *the* cultural and social arm of the congregation," sisterhood women were made to feel not only welcome in but important to the success and vitality of their local synagogue.[48]

As more and more Orthodox women took to the synagogue during the interwar years, making the sisterhood their "fortunate cause"[49] and emerging as active participants in American Orthodox synagogue life, the Union of Orthodox Jewish Congregations of America (UOJCA), American Orthodox Jewry's umbrella organization, began to take note of them and their efforts. Alerted to the potential of this increasingly numerous and articulate element in the community and eager to tap its resources, the UOJCA in 1923 developed a women's division, known succinctly as the Women's Branch, much as Reform and Conservative Jews had established comparable organizations years before. Coordinating and overseeing the activities of the local synagogue sisterhoods, the Women's Branch unified these discrete entities into one centralized unit, and in that way provided Jewish women with an organizational framework in which they could pursue their interests as observant Jews. With the backing of dozens of local New York Orthodox sisterhoods and hundreds nationally, Women's Branch grew to represent an Orthodox female constituency and one, moreover, that sought to define the Orthodox Jewish experience from a woman's perspective.[50]

On the simplest level, Women's Branch assisted the local synagogue sisterhood with its administrative and cultural programming. After all, most Orthodox women of that time were newcomers to organizational ventures like the sisterhood and keenly in need of advice on how best to administer their organization and keep it afloat. As a clearinghouse of information on the workings of an Orthodox sisterhood, Women's Branch provided direction to the sisterhood movement and systematized its efforts from the top on down. Dispensing detailed, generous advice, the Women's Branch helped fledgling sisterhoods to get off the ground, even going so far as to provide them with a model constitution, complete with preamble and articles of incorporation. It also published a series of "how to" pamphlets and manuals, like the popular *Manual for Sisterhoods*, in its attempt to develop "an efficient sisterhood."[51] Women's Branch was the place to turn with questions on cultural and social activities; here the organization lent its expertise and collective wisdom in cultural and social programming and provided step-by-step or, more precisely, month-by-month advice. December, explained the *Manual*, might be an appropriate time to celebrate the rededication of the family to the synagogue with a "dutch supper," while a February tea on the theme of American patriotism might be worthwhile; May, the *Manual* noted, was a promising time for an extended discussion on women's place in Judaism.[52]

Not everything associated with the local sisterhood was frivolous or lighthearted. The members of the Women's Branch took themselves seriously and were most sensitive to the importance of developing not only a committed but also a knowledgeable female Orthodox population. "To make orthodox women convincingly articulate in discussing Jewish tradition," Women's Branch encouraged them to attend classes in Hebrew, Bible, religious ceremonies, literature ("The Jewish Classics"), sociology, family problems, and housewivery"— the latter an in-depth course in kashruth and cooking.[53] Where no classes existed, the Women's Branch created them and provided instructors, syllabi, and recommended reading lists as well as speakers for special lectures. But the fashioning of an articulate and well-read Women's Branch member was only part of that organization's overall agenda. Even more to the point was the creation of a highly motivated *observant* American Jewish woman, a "faithful Jewess." "An awakened observance of Jewish tradition," an editorial on the Women's Page related, "would result from a revival of Jewish learning."[54]

Women's Branch did everything it could to awaken Jewish ritual observance among its members. As a vehicle for the promotion of greater and better-informed religious practice, Women's Branch worked in concert with local sisterhoods to encourage the Jewish woman's performance of her ritual obligations. Like Reform and Conservative national sisterhood organizations, it too defined itself in religious terms, as an institution making for enhanced religious observance or, as one spokeswoman would have it, as "a force for Jewishness."[55] In its efforts "to nurture spiritually the adolescent and grown-up tradition-true daughter of the American Jewish home," Women's Branch campaigned energetically for synagogue attendance and holiday observance; published a series of slender volumes with such titles as "Marriage and the Home: A Jewish Guide for Marital Happiness," and "Yes, I Keep Kosher," an "attractive one page leaflet on the Woman's View of Kashruth" that touted the benefits of Orthodox ritual; and increasingly, toward the end of the thirties and in the early forties, crusaded for Jewish education for girls and women.[56] "There are over a million Jewish women in this country," observed the founder and president of Women's Branch, Mrs. Herbert S. Goldstein, in 1925. "Do all of them attend divine services on the Sabbath? Does each woman see to it that her children are raised strong in the faith of our fathers? Does each woman observe all the ceremonials of her religion? . . . Till this can be answered in the affirmative," Mrs. Goldstein firmly concluded, "we must concentrate all our efforts. . . ."[57]

In an attempt to reach the unobservant Jewish woman, Women's Branch published and widely disseminated guidebooks or, more accurately, primers in Jewish ritual observance. Keenly aware, perhaps from personal experience, that most American Jewish women of that period were somewhat deficient in their ritual knowledge, Women's Branch sought to reacquaint them with their tradition through the publication of what one contemporary labeled "an abridged shulkan aruch for women."[58] Lucidly written, texts like *Symbols and Ceremonies of the Jewish Home* took the reader by the hand and guided her, point by point, step by step, through the basics of Jewish ritual observance: *Shabbos, yomtovim,* kashruth, mikvah.[59] Grounding the reader in the particuliarities of Jewish ritual observance, these guidebooks made explicit and clear what, in all probability, had been implicit, widely shared assumptions of the Jewish homemaker of an earlier generation.

At its heart, this emphasis on the ritual education of Women's Branch members reflected the sorry state of Jewish educational opportunities then available for women. Though a few afternoon Talmud Torahs for girls could be found throughout the city—Williamsburg, for example, was home to the Brooklyn National Hebrew School, while the Herzliah Hebrew High School was located in Manhattan—most Jewish girls received a minimal and spotty Jewish education, schooled at home by a parent or a tutor. "Reading Hebrew," related Mrs. Elizabeth Gilbert, herself the daughter of a rabbi, "was considered enough."[60] "What have most American-born observant Jewish women been taught?" asked one writer on the topic of the religious training of the adolescent girl. "The reading of a few prayers? A few Biblical stories? Some superstitions of an East

European ghetto?"[61] Once an unquestioned norm, this informal and superficial kind of Jewish education became the subject of increasing criticism during the interwar years, which culminated, some years later, in the formation of coeducational Jewish day or parochial schools, a topic treated elsewhere in this volume. "In the past," observed Rabbi Lookstein, "the primary concern of Jewish education has been the Jewish boy. . . .His Jewish sister had to be content with a few private lessons at home and with rudimentary instruction in the religious duties of Jewish wifehood and motherhood. The inevitable result was generation upon generation of righteous women, but not of learned women."[62]

The creation of a new modern generation of "learned women" became the mandate of the Women's Branch as it sought "to get off the educational double standard and offer to women the educational advantages that hitherto seemed to be only man's prerogative."[63] Beginning in the 1930s and gaining momentum in the years following World War II, as the Jewish parochial or day school came into its own, girls were increasingly offered these educational advantages. In the interim, "hundreds" of American Jewish girls "of fine families" attended the Hebrew Teachers Training School, a Women's Branch enterprise that prepared college-age women for careers as Hebrew teachers.[64] For their mothers, however, it was too late to do anything more than apply stopgap, remedial measures to make up for their educational deficiencies. For the older generation, guidebooks and supplementary adult education were the sole avenues by which to acquire the "necessary tools" for being observant Jews.[65]

The need to define both the practice and the rationale of selected religious rituals was most clearly demonstrated when it came to the observance of kashruth. Responsibility for adhering to the dietary laws evolved organically from the Jewish woman's role as homemaker and consumer; Jewish tradition also viewed it as one of her specific ritual obligations, "the mandate of the Jewish woman . . . a duty that falls naturally and almost exclusively within the women's sphere."[66] Given the primacy of kashruth in the sacred life of the traditional Jewish woman, it was not surprising that Women's Branch focused on its promotion. Keeping kosher became a test case of the inherent adaptability and relevance of ancient Jewish ritual to modern urban America. Repeatedly, Women's Branch leaders urged their constituent sisterhoods to press for the observance of kashruth, likening its promotion to a "sacred rite."[67] Under its aegis, classes were held on the divine origins of the dietary laws, instruction in kosher cooking sponsored, and the publication of sisterhood kosher cookbooks widely encouraged. "The dietary laws," explained *Jewish Home Beautiful*, a widely published ritual guide and a household staple, "must find their first expression in the home and the Jewish woman must be their exponent."[68]

In the attempt to convince the modern Jewish woman to be the "exponent" of the dietary laws, the rationale for kashruth observance was thoroughly recast and, in a very real sense, reinvented. Neither halakhic nor biblical precedents for the observance of kashruth were invoked, for these explanations, kashruth advocates knew, were likely to be of limited appeal. Instead, arguments in favor of kashruth were couched in terms believed to be of interest to the modern, middle-class American woman. Keeping and cooking kosher, according to the new interpretations proferred by their interwar exponents, were symbols of refinement and civility, of high moral tone and character. "On the whole," one authority noted, "nothing has refined the Jewish character as much as the dietary laws."[69] "Abstinence from foods permitted to others," it explained, "develop[s] and strengthen[s] self mastery and control."[70] Helping to build moral Jews, keeping kashruth also helped to build healthy Jewish bodies, for kashruth, its adherents boasted, induced greater immunity from disease and promoted longevity. But of all the explanations for keeping kosher, the one most favored held that kashruth was nothing less than an artistic opportunity, an occasion to demonstrate the aesthetic sensibility of the modern ritually observant Jewish woman. "A fine art," cooking kosher challenged the artistry inherent in the Jewish woman.[71] "Living as Jewess, is more than a matter of faith, knowledge or observance," stated one popular ritual text. "To live as a Jewess, a woman must have something of the artist in her."[72] Kashruth, then, was the instrument by which that talent and artistry could be revealed.

In their new idiom, these arguments for keeping kosher sought unmistakably to make the point that observance of the dietary laws was as consonant with middle-class life as handsomely appointed apartments or visits to the opera. The terms and conditions, as well as the language, of bourgeois life, were now freely extended even to traditional Jewish rituals. "Increased substance and status has found expression, among the Orthodox, as often in elegance of cuisine and dining ritual as in the greater modishness of matters pertaining to the synagogue," observed the author of a *Commentary* article on the success of Barton's, the kosher candy manufacturer. "It is perhaps not inconceivable," he noted somewhat glibly, "that a 'Jewish' taste, which had to satisfy itself until recently with such things as kosher delicatessen, has now found an additional source of satiety in Continental candies."[73] And, this author might have added, in Continental cuisine. From the kinds of questions kosher consumers put to experts on such matters in the pages of the *Orthodox Union*, one sees evidence not only of a sophisticated palate but also of interest in "eating American." Is caviar kosher? Housewives from Brooklyn, the Bronx, Long Island, and Manhattan wanted to know. What about capers? Sturgeon? Is smoked fish permissible? Anchovies? Nestlés chocolates? Ovaltine? Or Aunt Jemima pancakes? (In most of the instances cited, the Union affirmed the kashruth of the product in question. But when it came to the reliability of Nestlés and Hershey's chocolates, they responded: "We are investigating and will let you know as soon as possible.")[74]

Advertising campaigns for kosher food products reinforced the message that kashruth married well with urbane America. Bold and contemporary in their graphics, there was nothing hesitant or diffident about the promotion of matzoh, shortening, or baked goods. Displaying young, cheerful, and trim cooks as they made use of kosher canned goods or desserts, the ads affirmed the notion that in modern America, the dietary laws were no obstacle to full gastronomic enjoyment. Thus a 1936 advertisement for Spry, whose copy read "Orthodox Women Hail New White Kosher Shortening," noted that the kosher consumer's affinity for the product made perfect culinary sense: "No wonder! For now you can use a beautiful White shortening and *still* keep the Dietary Laws."[75] The promotion of ritually supervised Sheffield Farms dairy products had this to say: "Keep in Shape with Sheffield: Women like to be busy. But women don't like to be tired. A wife does a thousand things to make her house a home. But she doesn't mind—if she's fit. Milk is her helper." Thus fitness, shapeliness, and kashruth were subtly linked all together in one product.[76] Purveyors of kosher services like restaurateurs and caterers similarly capitalized on the newly heralded modernity of kashruth by explicitly connecting matters of taste with the kind of ritual services they made available. The logo of Max Braun, a Harlem caterer, affirmed "Catering with a taste to families of taste and refinement," while those of other kosher caterers, with such elegant-sounding and decidedly subtle names as Patrician and Carlton, boasted of their access to New York's best hotels, once again tying kosher food to sophistication and elegance.[77] Describing the "social life" of New York's Orthodox community, the *Jewish Forum* in 1927 noted the existence of kosher restaurants (and hotels) that not only served kosher food "but . . . effect[ed] a refined home-like atmosphere." Such establishments, the paper explained, "encourage not only the aesthetic but also the vitally religious needs in Jewish life."[78]

The kosher cookbook, often a sisterhood project, delivered this message even more graphically and concretely.[79] Though concerned explicitly with food and its preparation, these cookbooks can be read as social statements that reflected and sometimes even created a set of attitudes toward the observance of the dietary laws. Through the medium of a recipe, the inherent suitability and adaptability of kashruth to modern times was directly conveyed. After dispensing with a few general comments about the laws of kashruth, the kosher cookbook provided dozens, sometimes even hundreds, of recipes divided by type: appetizers, main dishes, desserts, condiments. In the vast majority of instances, the recipes cited were examples not of Ashkenazic, representative Jewish food but rather of basic American middle-class culinary fare: corn fritters, oatmeal cookies, stews, steamed puddings, marshmallow salads, creamed soups. Only the subtle, barely perceptible, substitution of almond milk for the real thing or vegetable oil for lard indicates that these dishes were inherently unkosher.[80]

Explicitly familiar, Jewish foods were set aside, relegated to a different section of the cookbook where they were associated with ceremonial and distinctive occasions: Jewish food, it seemed, was special fare to be consumed on the Sabbath and holidays but not on Tuesdays. In fact, foods associated with the Sabbath and the holidays were frequently hailed, in lavish, often emotional prose, as distinctive. Items like *charoset* and *russel*, one text observed, urging their consumption on wary readers, "acquire a dignity, bordering upon sanctity which elevate them to the status of religious traditions. . . ."[81] Among other religious culinary traditions were borscht, "an ambrosial dish," and blintzes, customarily prepared for Shavuot. In the latter instance, serious cooks were urged to arrange the blintzes "like the two Tablets of the Law"; by sprinkling cinnamon on their surface in two parallel lines, the text advised, one could even "suggest the Ten Commandments themselves."[82]

Though many of the specifically Jewish recipes and the circumstances under which their preparation was detailed may strike a slightly silly note, the sisterhood cookbook or its extension, the kosher cookbook, was a high-minded endeavor. An attempt to create, if only culinarily, a traditional Jewish community with shared norms and values, the kosher cookbook promoted the exchange—and consumption—of recipes and in that respect bound together its readers and practitioners into a community with a shared culinary preference and, even more to the point, a shared ritual.

Whether in the form of an advertisement or of a recipe, the implicit and subtle message in this marriage of the contemporary and the hoary was their inherent compatibility. Keeping kosher, it seemed, was not inconsistent with modernity; the two could be comfortably accommodated to each other. Kashruth posed no barrier to participation in the wider world. Through actual physical substitutes, on the one hand, and intellectual reinterpretations, on the other, it was made part of that world. "In a Jewish home, a perfectly prepared meal, daintily served is not enough," Jewish housewives were told. "It may satisfy the physical desires and the esthetic sense but *to be perfect*, it must be kosher."[83]

Concern for rendering kashruth compatible with modernity took observant women out of the kitchen and into the marketplace. Bringing to bear their sensibility as astute consumers and assiduous homemakers even as they fulfilled one of the most fundamental of their ritual obligations, Orthodox women of the Women's Branch not only encouraged the observance of kashruth but also sought to make it more viable by expanding the range of available kosher food products. "We have within our power to give these kosher products nationwide sanction and publicity," explained Women's Branch members as they exerted concerted pressure on food manufacturers to produce kosher food products.[84]

No doubt tired of a limited number of kosher canned and processed goods and perhaps even more weary of having constantly to tell their children what they could not eat, Women's Branch explored the possibility of having a wider array of kosher foodstuffs at their disposal and on their table. Women's Branch groups visited factories and manufacturing plants, defrayed the costs of expensive laboratory analyses, and ultimately secured a broad number of kosher food products by convincing manufacturers of the financial benefits likely to accrue from the kosher market. Thanks to their labors, the UOJCA became increasingly known for its sophisticated approach to ritual supervision; its discrete seal, OU, inconspicuously situated on the base of a food item, emerged during these years as a synonym for careful and reliable *hasgacha* (ritual supervision). "The women," related a former Women's Branch president, "made the OU," referring to the barely noticeable seal, while "the OU," explained one kosher Upper West Side hostess, "made Passover and kashruth."[85]

Kashruth observers eagerly awaited the addition of a new American foodstuff to the list of ritually sanctioned items and avidly followed the often complex negotiations that attended the process. Widely publicized in the Orthodox press, the news that one or another American food manufacturer had agreed to ritual supervision of his products was an occasion for excitement and hyperbole. When, in 1935, the manufacturer of Loft's ice creams and candy agreed to cooperate with the OU, one periodical hailed the news as "an historic event for the Jews of America."[86] A symbolic as well as a gastronomic success believed to represent the coming of age of the kosher market, the kasherization of one of America's most popular ice cream and candy manufacturers was formally marked by a celebration dinner at the Hotel Biltmore. Loft's gentile president was the guest of honor at this occasion, singled out by the OU for his role in seeking ritual supervision. Congratulating the food executive for his "broad and humane vision," the OU officials extolled "his foresight in anticipating the tremendous goodwill which will redound to the benefit of his already well-known company as a result of his cordial cooperation with the OU in this enterprise."[87] By the late thirties, the number of American food manufacturers that "cooperated cordially" with the OU by submitting to the ritual supervision of their products was substantial. As a result, the kosher consumer had a wide array of products from which to choose: breads, dairy products, cereals, candies, desserts, mayonnaise, mustards, oils, shortening, noodles, and soups. The OU's "Kashruth Directory," a list of ritually sanctioned items, took up a full single-spaced page in the *Orthodox Union* and included a who's who of American food manufacturers, among them Pepsi-Cola, Wrigley's, Dugan's, and Heinz Good Foods, of whose 57 varieties, the *Union* noted solemnly, "26 were kosher."[88]

Orthodox women of the interwar years by no means exhausted their organizational energies and talents in pursuit of the efficient sisterhood or exemplary kosher recipe. Throughout the 1920s and 1930s, the cause of Zionism or, to be more precise, that of religious Zionism, increasingly engaged them as well. The Mizrachi Zionist Movement, also known to some as "clerical Zionism," fused the political pragmatism of secular Zionists with the religious ideology of observant Jews and as such formally represented the interests of religious Zionists within the world Zionist movement.[89] Established in Europe in 1902, Mizrachi was launched in America in 1913 by its president, Rabbi Meyer Berlin, who had traveled to the New World in search of funds. When stranded by the outbreak of the Great War, Berlin turned his attentions to the creation of an American branch of the world Mizrachi movement.

The involvement of Orthodox women in the affairs of the American Mizrachi did not get under way for another decade. Organized in 1925, the Mizrachi Women's Organization of America grew quickly and, despite its late start, encompassed close to fifty chapters nationally by the mid-thirties; by 1950, it boasted of fifty thousand members in thirty-eight states throughout the country. On the local level, virtually every Orthodox community in Brooklyn, Manhattan, and the Bronx contained a Mizrachi chapter whose whirl of luncheons, inventively named "Tikvah Teas," bazaars, and cultural "Palestinian Evenings" contributed much-needed moral and financial support to the Yishuv, the Jewish settlement of Palestine.

Like the sisterhood, members of American Mizrachi Women applied their special feminine qualities as mothers and homemakers to the upbuilding of Palestine. "We realized that the home has always been the logical starting place for the carrying out of ideas," explained Mrs. Jesse Ginsberg, the organization's president, echoing a common refrain as she reflected on its history. "We realized that it is the mother who makes the home what it is. It is not surprising therefore," she concluded, "that we decided to concentrate our efforts on the adolescent girl who is the Jewish mother of the future."[90] Accordingly, American Mizrachi Women built a series of academic, agricultural, and vocational institutions throughout Palestine to house and instruct young girls in such fields as child care, education, farming, gardening, dressmaking, and dietetics, all typically female enterprises.[91] Later, the organization broadened its base to include recently arrived émigrés from Hitler's Europe, smoothing their course of adjustment to life in the Middle East. Male Zionist circles did not always understand the exclusively domestic focus of American Mizrachi Women, finding its Judaic version of "Kinder und Kuchen" difficult to take seriously. Those of an antireligious bent were even more pronounced in their criticism. "I have heard very often from other organizations," reported a Mizrachi representative stationed in Jerusalem, "of how they have tried to paraphrase the work of the Mizrachi Women as kosher kitchens. Kosher Kitchens!" she exclaimed, taking umbrage at the description.[92] "Mizrachi," retorted another of its devotees, "is not just an interest in kosher meat."[93]

To some, participation in a Mizrachi chapter was an expression of support for the Zionist experiment; for others, it afforded yet another opportunity, one beyond that of the sisterhood or Women's Branch, to assert their affiliation with American Orthodox causes. The Mizrachi Women's Organization, insisted one of its charter members, "is the very organization in which [Jewish women] may reveal and confirm their orthodoxy."[94] Whatever the rationale for membership, the association of Orthodox women with Zionist affairs helped to render Zionism a socially acceptable enterprise in middle-class circles and, as an institutional outlet, a close second to the sisterhood. Admittedly, the Mizrachi Women's Organization never quite achieved the kind of social cachet and prominence that the Hadassah Women's Organization, established in 1912, had already attained. Rivals for the affections and dollars (or, in this case, the "shekels") of the middle-class American Jewish woman, the two organizations maintained cordial, if cool, relations with each other. Publicly, they stressed the extent to which they worked in tandem, "through common channels and . . . along a common path."[95] Privately, though, the Mizrachi Women's Organization bridled at the notion that it was a poor cousin to the older and more established Hadassah. "Whereas it is fashionable and respectable to be a Zionist or to belong to a Hadassah," one contemporary observed, "it is queer and quaint to belong to Mizrachi. It is associated with old people and old interests and old methods."[96] American Mizrachi Women sought, however, to overturn that widely prevalent view of their organization and, like so much else associated with the interwar Orthodox experience, to recast even religious Zionism in acceptable, bourgeois terms. American Mizrachi Women, explained a member in 1937, "is our answer to the question of how orthodox Jewesses take care of their own."[97]

While the ritual observance of kashruth was attended with constant publicity and the promotion of religious Zionism actively encouraged, the observance of the Jewish family-purity laws, as central a ritual in the Orthodox woman's sacred life as kashruth, was treated with considerable diffidence. Rarely the subject of a public lecture, extended editorials, or sisterhood get-togethers, *taharas hamisphaca*—a practice that entails a period of sexual abstinence culminating in immersion in a pool of rainwater—was not a popular topic of discussion. A disturbing "hush of silence" enveloped the performance of this *mitzvah*.[98] "Nobody talks about it," one practitioner related, "probably because it is a private kind of ritual, unlike keeping a kosher home. Rabbis tend not to talk openly about it. Parents don't speak of it. People feel it's an archaic custom."[99] In part, the community's tacit and widely shared silence on the subject derived from a certain amount of discomfort inherent in any public discussion regarding sexual mores; it was one thing to speak out about kitchen rituals and quite another to discuss those relating to the bedroom. Then, too, the community's uneasiness reflected its discomfort in rationally making sense of a phenomenon that was, as one woman put it bluntly, "an unnecessary relic of ancient times."[100] The Jewish family laws simply did not lend themselves to the kind of reinterpretation that was so successfully applied to kashruth observance and, as such, proved to be a vexing issue for those Orthodox Jews determined to prove the ongoing consonance of Orthodox tradition with modernity. Here was one ritual that appeared to resist the highly valued equation between modernity and religious traditionalism.

Despite their unquestioned centrality within Jewish tradition, the family-purity laws appear to have been among the first rituals to be unceremoniously abandoned by the American Jewish woman, so much so that when European rabbinical authorities wished to point to the "trefa-ness" of America, they pointed to the absence of mikvahs as dramatic proof.[101] "If it is true that Orthodoxy in America is the great unknown," an Orthodox sympathizer wrote as late as the 1940s, "then *taharas hamispocha* is the greatest unknown."[102] Another lamented that in the New World, the practice was "on the verge of extinction."[103] Given the intimate nature of the practice, it is hard to know with certainty whether statements like these actually mirrored reality or were instances of exaggerated Orthodox fears. To put it differently, discovering what constituted normative levels of observance is all but impossible: few, if any, mikvahs maintained attendance records; what's more, oral history interviews yield few clues, for people are extremely uncomfortable in discussing their personal observance of this ritual and tend to shy away from or discourage questions on this score. But if contemporary published accounts are to be believed, and there is no reason why they should not be, it would seem that the perception of widespread neglect of the family-purity laws was an accurate one, at least when it came to its more public aspects: immersion in a ritual pool. "While sex hygiene is taught in school and public discussion of sex quite open," observed Rebbetzin Mrs. Moses Hyamson in 1927, "the use of the mikvah at the prescribed periods is more honored in the breach than in the observance."[104] In a striking number of instances, the prescribed prenuptial visit to the mikvah remained, for most women, their sole encounter with the ritual bath. While sexual abstinence may have been maintained, the monthly "dip" was not. The family-purity laws were not one of those rituals that Orthodox women eagerly embraced.

Disturbed that *taharas hamisphaca* was rapidly becoming, or in fact had already become, more of a matter of limited individual observance than of normative practice, a number of Orthodox rabbis and a few of their wives attempted to reverse the situation. Some, like Rabbi Jung of the Center, actively and inventively campaigned for the promotion of family-purity laws; Jung was one of the few rabbis who made a point of personally meeting with the bridal couple expressly to discuss the ritual.[105] Sometimes visiting with the couple together and at other moments meeting with them individually, Jung lyrically extolled the value of sexual restraint, which he believed promoted marital happiness and physical well-being. Hoping to appeal to his generally affluent constituency on its own terms, he urged the husband to purchase a special pearl necklace or pin for the wife which she would don as a sign of her ritual impurity. Despite his passion for this ritual and his resourceful way of defining the practice, Jung did not always make headway. His smart, college-educated or college-bound audience found the gentle rabbi's admonitions "sweet," "caring," but hopelessly old-fashioned and irrelevant.[106]

Unlike Rabbi Jung, most Orthodox clergy liked to deal with the topic from a distance, when they dealt with it at all, and preferred the printed page to the personal encounter. Creating a new genre of American rabbinic and prescriptive literature—modern marriage manuals that were dispensed shortly before the marriage ceremony—they sought to make a case for the inherent viability of the traditional Jewish marriage laws. Written in Yiddish or, more commonly throughout the interwar years, in English, these manuals carried such titles as *A Handbook for the Jewish Woman, The Duty of the Jewish Woman*, or *The Ways of Her Household: A Practical Handbook for Jewish Women on Traditional Customs and Observances*, and were composed almost exclusively by men for an exclusively female audience.[107] Interestingly enough, though both men and women were enjoined to observe the laws of family purity, women (then as now) "managed" that ritual, seeing that its intricacies of time and performance were fully observed. It was to them alone that these texts were addressed.

Compact and often prettily illustrated booklets (biblical or pastoral scenes were the most common illustrations), the mikvah manuals sought to make accessible the laws of family purity to an audience increasingly unaware of them. Surrogate parents and educators, mikvah manuals replaced the more traditional avenues of ritual instruction and, ironically enough, became in their own way an index of modernization. Jewish parents and educators, the authors of these texts complain, had abdicated their responsibility for teaching their daughters and students respectively even the most basic facts about the ritual. As a result, even in those households where scrupulous attention to other aspects of Jewish tradition was maintained—where "the womenfolk believe in the power of the Almighty and the sanctity of the Torah . . . where milk and meat are separated and chametz removed during the Passover holiday. . . .even in such households, mikvah is not observed. How," asks the author of this passage, "how could this be?"[108]

Assuming absolutely no knowledge of the laws of family purity on the part of the intended female reader, these guidebooks, as their name implies, provided a detailed description of each phase in the ritual cycle, leading the reader, step by step, through the process (the first thing you do is this, the second is that, and so on). Such detail was also designed to dissuade the reader from the obvious temptation of relying on the bathtub as a ritual substitute, thus suggesting that many, perhaps even most, observant women did just that. Invoking rather strong, even indelicate, language, many guidebooks carried the admonition that a bathtub was unequivocally verboten. "There is as much difference between the bathtub and the mikvah pool," women were told, "as there is between trefa . . . and kosher meat."[109] Following, at times, in the Ashkenazic literary tradition of the *seder mitvas nashim*, whose premodern Yiddish tracts explained, in plain and direct language, the ritual responsibilities of the Jewish woman, these American mikvah manuals contained chapters on the remaining womanly commandments of Shabbos and kashruth, put forward helpful and encouraging words to the bride-to-be, and provided a list of appropriate *thines*, or supplications, to be said before, during, and after immersion; the more modern and forward-looking texts even provided a "Personal Ritual Calendar" to be used for jotting down relevant "personal ritual" dates.[110]

Where the language explaining the laws and legal niceties of family purity was controlled and neutral, the narrative accompanying them was unabashedly propagandistic. Designed to convince their readers of the relevance of mikvah to the modern world, the mikvah manuals of the interwar years marshalled arguments to meet the modern, middle-class American Jewish woman on—and in—her own terms. Employing language more commonly found in popular women's magazines of the 1920s and thirties, mikvah manuals stressed those issues likely to be of most concern to the middle-class woman: issues of marital happiness, physical well-being, mental health, and beauty. "The laws of abstinence," explained one text, bring about mutual marital happiness and "serve as a safeguard against the disadvantages, dangers and pitfalls of married life."[111] The discipline exacted of the married couple, in turn, was said to render them strong and fit to withstand the rigors of modern urban living. Addressing itself to the "Psychological Value" of the family-purity laws, *Jewish Family Life*, one of the most popular and enduring of mikvah manuals, suggested that the observance of this ritual "provides a sense of renewal, fulfillment and purification."[112]

In what must have seemed to the authors of mikvah manuals to be the most convincing argument, or what they liked to call "rationale," of them all, science was harnessed to ritual, and medicine pressed into the service of the sacred. The medical benefits of family purity, it seemed, were unquestioned: not only did mikvah-going enhance the possibility of conception, timed as it was to coincide with the ovulation cycle, but it also allegedly prevented cervical and uterine cancer. "Many physicians," the modern mikvah manuals note, "are of the opinion that it is the observance of the Mosaic ritual laws . . . which accounts for the low incidence of [these diseases]."[113] Influenced by the eugenics movement of the interwar years, some guidebooks even went so far as to suggest that "the sturdiness of the Jewish stock is directly due to the [Jewish family laws]. Jewish law feels that healthy Jewish offspring, physically fit to cope with life's many problems, can only come from healthy, physically fit mothers . . . and the law of monthly separation . . . takes every precaution to safeguard the mother's health."[114] More to the point, observance of mikvah was thought not only to produce physically fit mothers and children but also, it was said, to enhance woman's physical attributes: Mikvah observance, *Jewish Family Life* proclaimed in what must have been one of the stronger selling points, "prolongs [the woman's] youth, beauty and attractiveness."[115]

For all their insight into the needs of the modern American Jewish women, these texts apparently did little to reestablish the primacy of the mikvah; women in record numbers bypassed the experience entirely or, at best, substituted the bathtub for the mikvah plunge. However convincing mikvah manuals may have been, they were no match for the unpleasant and uninviting reality of the public mikvah. "It is true," admitted Benjamin Koenigsberg, one of the interwar years' most active Orthodox crusaders, in 1940, "that a great many of the mikvahs . . . were not too inviting. It may be that women may have been alienated from this fundamental mitzvah because of repelling features in some of the older establishments."[116] Rabbi Jung concurred, noting that he was "profoundly shocked" by the condition of the American mikvah, which was commonly in "an abominable state of filth."[117]

So unappealing, in fact downright unsanitary, were these ritual institutions that the New York City Board of Health in the years prior to World War I publicly branded them a "menace" to the health of Jewish New Yorkers and strongly recommended that its devotees find another venue for their "ablutions."[118] Of New York's approximately forty mikvahs, or what city officials dubbed "kosher bathing places," most were little more than rusty iron tanks located in the basements of immigrant Jewish neighborhoods.[119] Because the water in these pools was rarely changed—an average of three hundred people, health investigators estimated, used the mikvah before its water was replaced—the latter contained an inordinately and dangerously high bacteria count. Towels were conspicuously absent, forcing mikvah users either to bring their own, to share with others, or, more commonly still, to purchase them from local pushcart vendors who loitered outside of the mikvah in the hope of making a sale. Disturbed by the mikvah's potential spread of contagious disease, New York's health officials worked in concert with concerned Jewish laity to eliminate the worst offenses and offenders. A Mikveh Owners Association was established, before World War I, to define a high sanitary and moral code. To qualify as a member, one had to answer affirmatively to the following questions, questions that give a very concrete sense of the quality of the New York mikvah:

> Will you empty your plunge after every 15 baths? Will you disinfect the baths by adding chloride of lime every 3 hours? Will you insist on bathers taking preliminary soap baths? Will you sterilize towels after use?[120]

For middle-class ritually concerned Jewish New Yorkers, the unsanitary conditions of the ritual bath simply would not do. Keenly attentive to their own personal hygiene, the proud owners of spacious, clean, and well-appointed bathrooms, they knew all too well that mikvah observance would fast fall into disuse were not strong remedial measures taken. Beginning in the late 1930s, a series of more sanitary mikvahs or what were then proudly termed "model mikvahs" were built throughout the greater metropolitan area in an effort to encourage the observance of family-purity laws.[121] "Realizing the importance of inviting externals," the sponsor of one such model mikvah recounted, "rabbis and concerned laity have succeeded in constructing modern, sanitary, hygienic mikvaoth which meet the requirements of even the most fastidious."[122] Or, as one rabbi would have it, the creation of handsomely appointed and hygienic mikvahs proved that "*there is room* for aesthetic Orthodoxy in [this] country."[123]

Built to conform with New York City building and health codes (that itself being a new development in American Jewish history) and to satisfy the "aesthetic needs of the modern woman," the model mikvah was a far cry from its tenement predecessor. The Courland father-and-son team of architects, following upon lengthy and complex negotiations with both building and health officials, developed a paradigm for New York's model mikvahs, one that was later adopted throughout the country. From the certificate of occupancy and other legal forms that New York's first model mikvah, located at 313 East Broadway, was compelled to file (!), one clearly sees the emergence of a conscious attempt to develop a middle-class, modern American ritual institution.[124] The following features were soon standard: individual fonts or pools "to ensure privacy"; bathrooms with colored tubs, tile floors, and walls lined with beveled mirrors; ultraviolet lamps, "beneficial to health and used for sterilizing freshly laundered linen"; ever-changing water to "insure a fresh supply for each visitor"; and modern beauty parlors with "hairdriers and other feminine needs."[125] These model mikvahs, one observer related, "represent near-perfection in privacy and sanitation."[126]

Concomitant with the new internal structural refinements, the model mikvah acquired a new name: either the highfalutin and august "ritualarium," a term that endowed the institution with a kind of grandeur and importance, or the "Jewish

Women's Club," a term suggesting a feminine and warm environment, a home away from home where women could relax, socialize, and tend to their feminine needs even as they fulfilled their ritual obligations.[127] Suggestively enough, however, the mikvah's formal name was known only to its initiates. No signage defined the building, giving a clue to its character or use. However handsome and distinguished the interior, the exterior deliberately called no attention to itself; one could walk by the building without ever knowing it housed a mikvah. The discreet, unobtrusive quality of the model mikvah contrasted dramatically with the unrelieved publicness of its predecessor, whose existence was boldly heralded through large, hand-lettered signs announcing, in Yiddish or Hebrew, "Koshere Mikve far Bnos Yisroel" (A Kosher Mikvah for All Daughters of Israel). "The unsightly descriptive signs," noted one advocate of the model mikvah, "repelled many from entering the building."[128] In its clublike, almost secret, promotion of itself, the new mikvah had evolved into a thoroughly bourgeois social institution, the very model of discretion and politesse.

Hailed by its creators and sponsors as "the very last word in modernity . . . in beauty of design and hygienic construction," the model mikvah, it was hoped, would quickly overcome the modern Jewish woman's reluctance to make use of it.[129] Or, as one writer put it at the time, "No longer will there be any excuse or reason for any daughter to decline to observe this fundamental mitzvah on any *logical basis*."[130] Ultimately, it was precisely the absence of logic or reason or, to put it differently, the absence of westernness in the observance of family purity that prevented its observance from becoming as accepted and widespread a Jewish woman's ritual as, say, kashruth. Where modern Jewish women took to the promotion of kashruth, making it their special preserve, many stood aloof from mikvah observance; with the exception of a few comments sprinkled here and there throughout the Women's Page of the *Orthodox Union* quietly urging women to avail themselves of the "handsome and sanitary mikvah," women's voices were still. They simply didn't take to it: neither the beautifully appointed mikvah nor the well-reasoned arguments of the mikvah manual could overcome objections to what was seen as the fundamentally oriental nature of the practice. Meanwhile, those who observed the ritual did so grudgingly and unhappily and perceived ritual immersion as one of the things one simply had to do. "Grin and bear it," was how one sophisticated Orthodox woman described her attitude toward the mikvah; another explained with a shrug that "this, too, was Judaism."[131]

In the long run, whether it was the practice of abstinence per se, immersion in a pool of rainwater, or both (and contemporaries remain too embarrassed to say) the entire ritual called into question and conflicted with the middle-class American Jewish woman's much-vaunted sense of herself as modern, urban, and westernized. In certain instances—as in kashruth or synagogue participation—

some of Judaism's "oriental" rituals were comfortably and successfully reconciled with a modern outlook. Efforts to render mikvah compatible with secular society fell wide of the mark. That the ritual of kashruth could be reinterpreted and reworked to fit the canons of the modern woman's sensibility, where mikvah could not, highlights the essential differences between the two and illustrates the complexities of being a modern observant Jewish woman. Where kashruth had a kind of transforming power, allowing the middle-class Jewish woman to feel a part of western culture, mikvah simply held her back. Where kosher recipes could be accommodated to a Western palate, there was no analogue in the modern world for the mikvah pool. Mikvah, observed one Orthodox rabbi, "is associated with something obsolete and consequently appears to have *no place* in modern life."[132] Unable to situate the family-purity laws within a modern urban context, many modern American observant woman chose to forego their observance. "The spirit of the age," lamented one rebbetzin, "is not quite as ready to accept the hardships our mothers and grandmothers endured. The youth of today longs for greater ease and comfort, for more beauty in its surroundings." Because the mikvah experience failed to satisfy such needs, its practice fell into disuse and disregard. "The observance of mikvah," she concluded with a telling phrase, "has become the *Cinderella of Jewish Rituals.*"[133]

For the American Jewish woman of the interwar years, modernity brought with it considerable opportunities for an expanded religious life: Orthodox Jewish women were now actively encouraged to attend synagogue regularly, to form sisterhoods, to exert pressure on the marketplace, and to have a voice and a presence in Orthodox communal affairs. And yet, if a boon in some instances, in others modernity carried with it considerable challenges. As the interwar history of mikvah observance makes clear, modernity posed a serious threat to the hegemony of tradition and often entailed a reinterpretation, and at times the abandonment, of selected ritual behaviors, even among those who considered themselves Orthodox.

Through it all, "a new personage" had emerged eager to avail herself of modernity's challenges and complexities. "As there is a new woman," noted the author of a 1925 text on American Judaism, "there is also a new Jewess . . . They are finding themselves . . . glorifying in their birthright."[134] Experimenting with a new and often perplexing ritual identity and with emerging forms of communal involvement, the interwar generation of Orthodox women was as involved with defining the limits and possibilities of their own sacred lives as their daughters and granddaughters have been, most recently, with theirs.

"THE SCHOOL OF TODAY AND TOMORROW" THE MODERN YESHIVA

"My child goes to Jewish parochial school," explained author Harold Ribalow in 1954, as he attempted to enlighten the readers of *Commentary* regarding the yeshiva experience, a "rather bewildering phenomenon." Describing his seven-year-old daughter as a well-adjusted and bright child, extremely secure in her Jewishness, Ribalow, himself the product of a more traditional and apparently unhappy yeshiva upbringing, sought to make a case for the viability of day-school education in postwar America. At the same time, he could not help but contrast his daughter's experience with his own. "How different it used to be! When I went to yeshiva, a yeshiva student was a 'freak' even in New York City. . . .and pleasure was unknown."[1]

The fastest-growing Jewish educational system of the postwar era, the Jewish day or parochial school had changed markedly since the time Ribalow had attended one, some fifteen years earlier. Not only had the numbers of such institutions increased dramatically since the interwar years—by 1949, the Empire City was home to fifty-eight such institutions, where two decades earlier there had been only fifteen—but they had become "progressive," physically attractive institutions where the arts, dancing, painting, drawing, and singing were "taught freely and joyously" alongside the more traditional Hebraic curriculum.[2]

To many postwar observers, the Jewish day school appeared to be not only the fastest-growing American Jewish institution but "the most exciting and hopeful phenomenon in Jewish life in America."[3] In a startling about-face, New York Jewry of the postwar era began to reverse its once firmly antagonistic stance toward the day school and to embrace Jewish parochial education as a legitimate, viable, and consonantly American enterprise. Taking the Orthodox community by storm during the 1950s, the day-school movement began to make considerable inroads among Conservative Jews during the sixties and seventies and even among Reform Jewry a decade later. To the Orthodox especially, the day school represented a most attractive educational opportunity, a guarantor of Orthodoxy's future and key to its continued viability as an American religious movement. As early as 1917, the (few) advocates of a parochial school education roundly touted its benefits, claiming that it and it alone would be the basis for an ongoing, flourishing traditional Jewish culture in the New World. "The only salvation for orthodox Judaism in America," insisted Samuel Hurwitz, a leading prewar Jewish educator and principal of the Talmudical Academy, New York's first modern yeshiva high school, "is in the creation of a national system of Jewish parochial schools." Bemoaning the prevailing educational system for its inability to do little more than teach "Judaism in fragments," Hurwitz maintained that only an all-day program would "make complete" the life of the Jewish child. Hurwitz even went so far as to argue, in a stunning play on the dominant critique of the day school, that the Jewish parochial school was itself "a great Americanizing agent . . . in that it helps to bridge the gap that exists in the life of an immigrant child between an ultra-Oriental Judaism and an ultra-Occidental Americanism."[4]

Admittedly, most interwar Jews, even those who included themselves proudly within the Orthodox camp, did not see matters quite that way and preferred to educate their children in the city's public schools or, in some instances, in its most advanced and sophisticated private academies like Horace Mann or the Dalton School. Putting it differently, few even contemplated the possibility of a yeshiva education for their children. Committed passionately to the public school as the sine qua non of their acculturation or, as one put it, the "rock bottom" of their commitment to America,[5] interwar Jews were committed equally as strongly to the notion that Jewish education could legitimately be only supplementary in nature: either in the form of the afternoon talmud torah or Hebrew school or alternatively, for those with means, a private tutor. Few were inclined to challenge what had emerged both tacitly and overtly as a matter of communal consensus.

Those concerned with Jewish education went along with this consensus and effected an elegant synthesis between the religious school and the public school. Yielding unhesitatingly to the primacy of the latter, they claimed a secondary role, that of junior partner, for the talmud torah, which would "work hand in hand with the public school. . . ."[6] "The accepted formula," Alexander Dushkin, perhaps the interwar's leading Jewish educational authority, would write as late as 1940, "is for Jewish education to be supplementary to the public schools. We have accepted wholeheartedly the primacy of the public school. . . ."[7]

The Jewish community's idealization of the public school had serious and deleterious consequences for Jewish education: as the *Judisches Tageblatt* noticed sarcastically, "Jews Neglect Jewish Education and Blame America."[8] For one thing, the number of Jewish school-age children receiving a formal Jewish education was startlingly low. A 1918 study, conducted by Dushkin for his Columbia University dissertation, revealed that more than three-quarters of Jewish elementary school children received *no* Jewish training whatsoever or, as another disgruntled Jewish educator put it, were "never shown the face of an Aleph"; the proportion increased even more strikingly among Jewish adolescents. Among the latter, Dushkin found that approximately 1 percent kept up with their Jewish studies. What's more, the proportion of culturally illiterate Jewish schoolchildren remained more or less constant well into the 1930s despite the efforts of Jewish educators and concerned laity to improve matters.[9]

That the Jewish schools were in a sorry state of disarray surely did not help. Whether the symptom or the cause of the community's benign neglect of the issue, the Jewish educational scene, for much of the pre–World War II era, was characterized by an absence of professional standards and widespread "disorganization and anarchy." A seemingly jumbled array of institutions competed for the meager student body: *kaddish* schools, bar mitzvah and *brocha* schools, Sunday schools and charity schools, "schools housed in shacks, in apartment houses, in the rebbe's bedrooms, in temples that rival the neighborhood's newest banks in their Grecian splendor."[10] This slightly exaggerated depiction of the range of extant educational options hinted at but did not fully elaborate on the overwhelmingly poor physical qualities of most interwar Jewish educational facilities. Like the immigrant synagogue with which it was often compared, the typical talmud torah was not exactly a salubrious affair; as one educational expert noted in 1918, the statistics "tell a tale of wretched accommodation."[11] Housed in basements, dreary rented quarters, or the vestry rooms of a synagogue, few afternoon schools maintained their own building. "Even the best of [vestry rooms]," an obviously inspired Dushkin observed, "have a dark, dank, subterranean atmosphere which chills enthusiasm and is detrimental to the welfare of both teachers and pupils."[12] Concerned educators and parents drew the same conclusion from the inhospitable accommodations of the typical talmud torah as they had from those of the immigrant synagogue: the physical defects of the plant would invariably lead the younger generation astray. "What can our children think of Judaism," Samson Benderly, head of the newly established Bureau of Jewish Education, wondered in 1918, "if after their stay in the modern public school buildings, we offer them Jewish classrooms which are badly ventilated and poorly lighted, and which are very often not kept clean?" Jewish children, the educator concluded, "are bound to interpret the entire heritage of our people in the terms of the physical side of the classroom."[13]

Irrespective of its venue, the Jewish educational experience was at best a minimal affair. Limited to Sunday mornings and weekday afternoons, following the students' dismissal from public school, the talmud torah sought, against great odds, to instill a degree of working knowledge of and affection for things Jewish. Instead, as both educators and students conceded, the best one could hope for was "a smattering of Hebrew and a few vague memories of a few books of the Bible."[14] In the few hours allotted to Jewish studies, little that was comprehensive or systematic could be attained, despite the claim that everything from "aleph-bes to bar mitzvah" was taught.[15] In many, perhaps most, instances, Yiddish was the lingua franca of instruction while Hebrew, or "Ivra," in its most common and corrupted usage, was reserved for the acquisition of ritual skills, notably bar mitzvah preparation. "We never learned anything," an alumnus of one Lower East Side talmud torah recalled. "We never got out of Bereshis [the Book of Genesis]. . . .The schooling," he added, "was from Hebrew to Yiddish which further added to the misery. . . ."[16]

Most measured the success of the talmud torah in utilitarian and not educational terms: how well it primed one's son for his bar mitzvah. Though often disdained, the greatest and most constant incentive for attendance at Hebrew school was ritual preparation for the bar mitzvah. Bar mitzvah classes drew the largest number of students and sustained their attendance for the longest period of time—some two years—at the conclusion of which the drop-out rate reached inordinately high proportions. "Our generation," one disheartened rabbi observed in 1947, "has inherited a laity whose Jewish education stopped at age thirteen."[17] The average talmud torah, a layman related, is a *baruch shepatarani* institution," a clever reference to the traditional prayer invoked by the parents of a bar mitzvah in which they are newly released from personal and ritual responsibility for their son's deeds. "Simultaneously with the father's saying of the blessing, the child leaves the Jewish school and Jewish interests."[18]

The deficiencies of the interwar talmud torah were by no means lost on the Jewish educational community. At times, it seemed as if no one had a kind word to say about the talmud torah, neither its advocates and teachers nor, least of all, its reluctant student body, who viewed the after-hours program as "a theft of time that might better be used in playing stickball."[19] No less an advocate of the supplementary school than Dushkin himself criticized the prevailing system as "a liability rather than an asset."[20] During its heyday and even retrospectively, the talmud torah figured in the Jewish collective imagination more as an object of derision than as a source of pride. Far from enhancing the middle-class American Jews' appreciation of their ancestral tradition, the afternoon Hebrew school, in the harsh words of one critic, was responsible "for the larger part of dislike for things Jewish."[21]

For all that, though, few were prepared to abandon the supplementary system in favor of a more intensive kind of Jewish education such as the yeshiva, the Jewish parochial school. The latter, in fact, came close to being anathema to New York Jewry's middle class and its representative educators. Its champions dismissed either as religious extremists or as hopelessly old-fashioned "kleinshtetlach" Jews, the day school was perceived as a singularly inappropriate educational response to modern-day America. At best, the Jewish parochial school was grudgingly accepted as a highly specialized kind of institution, a "pre-vocational" school for the extremely religious children of extremely religious parentage destined to embark on careers as rabbis or educators. But under far more general circumstances, cautioned one educator, the day school was not "to be considered as a *normal* type of American Jewish school."[22]

Although by the twenties only a handful of day schools had been established in New York and elsewhere throughout the country, their existence upset the status quo, the "accepted formula," and as such engendered fierce, often acrimonious, debate. Attacks on the parochial school came from different quarters and assumed different forms. The strongest challenge to its legitimacy came from those who feared that the school retarded assimilation or, worse still, endangered the status of the American Jewish community. Raising the "cry of separatism," opponents of the day school branded it as an agent of segregation, willfully creating a distinct and separate class composed of "alien Jews."[23] The parochial system, Dushkin added dramatically, "is fraught with danger for America and for American Jews. . . ."[24] Then there were those who, worried about the ramifications of a ten-hour school day, believed that the day school hampered the physical development of its young charges. A 1924 study of some 750 yeshiva students found that they suffered far more from physical handicaps than public-school children of comparable age. As a group, yeshiva students were "undersized and undernourished," experienced "undue eye strain," and had greater tonsil and adenoidal trouble. The potential health risks of yeshiva attendance, concluded the study's author, were enormous, for in his estimation the yeshiva population constituted the "human material out of which will develop some of the tuberculars, the cardiacs, the neurotics and other physically and nervously decrepit."[25] Yet others, perhaps more representative of the grassroots attitude toward the parochial school than were public health officials or Jewish civic leaders, grounded their objections in class concerns. It was not so much fear of contracting disease or of endangering one's status as an American that kept their children from attending day school as it was concern lest the day school hamper and limit access to the middle class. Addressing the issue in a roundabout way, upwardly mobile, first-generation American parents voiced concern that their children might fail to "get into" a good college; more palpably still, they worried that the English acquired in day school would be heavily accented, without "the clear English ring." "People were not so anxious to send their children to a yeshiva," recalled one rather courageous mother whose sons attended such a school. "I had friends who had sons my age, everyone was kosher, everyone was religious . . . and some of them would never think of going to a school like Ramaz," a reference to one of the more successful of the latter-day parochial schools.[26]

In the absence of suitable alternatives, the supplementary school system remained the option of choice. Despite the manifold and readily apparent flaws of the talmud torah, no one was prepared to jettison that institution. The problem, as Jewish educators understood it, lay not so much with supplementary education per se as with its archaic methods and uninformed administration. Whatever was wrong with the afternoon Hebrew school could be fixed: what was needed, one educator explained succinctly in 1918, was "systemized instruction by well trained teachers under sanitary physical conditions. . . ."[27] On the eve of America's entry into the First World War, New York Jewry could boast two modern talmud torahs whose innovative approach to the teaching of Jewish culture would come to dominate and revolutionize modern Jewish pedagogy: the Uptown Talmud Torah and the Central Jewish Institute (CJI).

Likening themselves to a "laboratory," and an "experimental station for Jewish education," these two schools held out great promise for the future of a modern Jewish educational system. Suggestively enough, words like "modern," "efficient," "up-to-date," and "standardized" adorned their literature, pointing up a collective fascination with the modern era. With the proud determination to harness the best of modernity to traditional subject matter, they made much of their licensed, professional staff as well as such "decided innovations" as the stereopticon machine, a particular favorite. Before they fell victim to dwindling student bodies, the consequence of rapid demographic shifts in both Harlem and Yorkville, the CJI and Uptown Talmud Torah, between them, presided over the education of several thousand school-age children and raised Jewish education to a level of unprecedented sophistication.[28]

Established in Harlem at the turn of the century as a talmud torah in the traditional sense, the Uptown Talmud Torah on East 111th Street transformed itself into one of the more advanced Hebrew schools of the pre–World War I era. Under the direction of Samson Benderly, a man lavishly praised by the characteristically ungenerous Kaplan as "the most constructive force in American Jewish life," second only to Zionism, the Uptown Talmud Torah was the first afternoon school to be linked formally with Benderly's newly established Bureau of Jewish Education.[29] A "model" school, it sought to render Jewish education attractive to a broad-based, economically diverse Jewish population by establishing "preparatory" classes for girls, the first institution to do so, and forming a West Side Branch, on West 115th Street, to attract the children of the affluent. "An up-to-date talmud torah run along the most modern and efficient system," the school endowed the talmud torah system in New York City with newfound dignity and self-assurance.[30]

Heir to the Uptown Talmud Torah, the Central Jewish Institute opened its doors in the spring of 1916. None other than Louis Marshall hailed the institute as an "oasis in the desert of education," while New York papers like the *Hebrew Standard* dramatically observed that, with its opening, "Orthodox Jewry is practically on trial."[31] That a great deal of hyperbole attended the school's opening is not surprising: the culmination of more than five years of trial and error at both the Uptown Talmud Torah and the Bureau of Jewish Education, the institute represented the most polished embodiment of the modern talmud torah ideal. Fortunately, a wealth of extant files allows us to reconstruct the early history of the school.

Everything about the institution, which was literally next door to Kehilath Jeshurun on East 85th Street,[32] from its determinedly handsome edifice to its up-to-date curriculum, reinforced the notion that Jewish education could be appealing and relevant to the needs of contemporary Jews. "A protest against the old, ineffective form of Jewish education," the CJI hoped, in its own words, "to blaze a new path."[33] With the logo "Judaism and Americanism" emblazoned on its portals, the CJI modified the traditional form and content of the Hebrew school to make it better suited to American life. "Children run away from Judaism," one CJI official observed, "because most of the Talmud Torahs do not teach Judaism in a very modern way. While the children are playing you can teach them Judaism."[34] Eschewing the traditional pre–bar mitzvah curriculum, CJI staff taught Bible and Jewish history through the use of songs and the stereopticon machine; Jewish tradition through arts and crafts and dramatic productions. One former instructor recalled how he became adept at using visual aids, almost "expert in 'splicing' bits of biblical history films, obtained from whatever sources were then available, and in rearranging pictures, cut out from sundry books on the Bible and Jewish history, for use in overhead projection."[35]

By far the most striking innovation of the CJI curriculum was the use of the "Ivrith b'Ivrith" method of instruction, a technique associated so intimately with Samson Benderly that it was often called simply "Dr. Benderly's style." The use of Hebrew as the language of instruction marked a radical departure from what was then current practice. In the vast majority of talmud torahs, Hebrew was regarded more as a dead language, "an ancient relic," than as a linguistic signpost of a vibrant culture. One maskilic educator, Uriah Engelman, put it even more bluntly: writing in the *Menorah Journal* in 1929, he characterized the Hebrew school as a classic misnomer: "Hebrew is the least and last thing wanted here."[36] Benderly sought to put an end to that notion. For him, the "natural method" of instruction not only enlivened the proceedings, attracting and retaining the interest of the child, but was also the quickest and most efficient way to instill Jewish knowledge or, as he put it, "the shortest and most attractive road to the Bible and the prayerbook."[37] Through extremely imaginative means—the use of flash cards and moving-picture images, a student dictionary and Hebrew games—he further encouraged the acquisition of Hebrew as a spoken language; reading, Benderly believed, would follow as a matter of course.[38]

In its cultivation of the Ivrith b'Ivrith method of instruction, the CJI drew heavily on the talents of Benderly's students, a "small army of young collegemen."[39] One hundred and ten strong, these largely American-born, college-trained recruits, known popularly as the "Benderly boys," served in the vanguard of a new highly educated class of Jewish teachers. Earlier, few Hebrew teachers had much knowledge of the rudiments of teaching; all that a teacher needed, a contemporary observed, "was a siddur in his pocket."[40] Benderly's talmidim, however, followed a rigorous program of instruction: after graduation from college, they went on to pursue advanced degrees both in pedagogy, from Teachers College or comparable "American schools of Pedagogy," and in matters Jewish, from the Seminary's Teachers Institute. In the process Jewish education was transformed into a profession. For the first time, recalled Dushkin, one of Benderly's star pupils, Jewish education possessed the characteristics of a profession: "group mind, adequate training and critical, scientific study."[41] Imbued with the secular philosophy of John Dewey and the cultural Zionism of Ahad Haam, Benderly's students, in one generation, recast the prevailing image of the Jewish educator. Typical Hebrew schools, observed a contemporary, "were not schools in the American sense. They were not conducted by teachers who were qualified from a pedagogical standpoint . . . but rather were staffed by kindly, well meaning but completely unqualified old men."[42] But Benderly's students, wresting control from these kindly, if unqualified old men, effected a quiet revolution, molding the traditional talmud torahs into "American Hebrew schools."

Throughout this period of "enthusiastic anticipation," Benderly's success in professionalizing Jewish education, in making the field a desirable and legitimate one for American-born, college-trained young men, spawned a number of teacher-training institutes.[43] With the peripatetic Kaplan at its head by 1909, the Seminary's Teachers Institute worked hand in hand with Benderly's Bureau in providing trained personnel. Yeshiva followed suit a few years later by integrating the Teachers Institute, a fountainhead of Mizrachi Zionism, into its orbit. With Pinchos Churgin as Kaplan's opposite number, the more avowedly Orthodox T.I. sought to provide certified, professional, and observant "Men of Hebrew letters" for its afternoon Hebrew-school system.

A rather startling consequence of Benderly's innovations was an influx of young women into the field of Jewish education. In a 1912 report on the activities of the Bureau, Benderly lamented the limited educational opportunities then available to Jewish women and called for the expansion of those opportuni-

ties, including the training of female Hebrew teachers. "If the Public Schools
suffer from over-feminization," he wrote, "our schools, particularly the Talmud
Torahs, suffer from over-masculinization."[44] With the introduction of elementary-level "preparatory" classes for girls followed by a program of high-school
study, Benderly made room for them within his educational community. The
Bureau's director even went a step further and encouraged female high-school
graduates to take up teaching as a career. "Every season several hundred young
Jewish women graduate from the High Schools of New York. Many of them
take up stenography or some other office work. . . . It would be a great gain to
Jewish schools and homes if we could encourage, every season, a number of
such young women to take up this work," meaning Jewish teaching.[45]

Thanks to Benderly's encouragement, a number of women—Libbie S. Berkson, Rebecca A. Brickner, Dvorah Lapson—could be counted among the first
and second generation of the "Benderly boys." What's more, by 1930, women
made up a sizable one-third of the teaching staff in New York afternoon
schools.[46] In the aftermath of the war, the proportion grew higher still, leading
Jewish social critic Midge Decter to state categorically, "The New Hebrew
Teacher is a woman."[47] Young, generally unmarried women from observant
backgrounds, "armed to the teeth with technique," replaced the poorly trained
male immigrant teacher of the premodern talmud torah and, in a considerable
number of instances, his scientifically trained successor as well.[48] What Decter
called the "feminization" of Jewish communal life unfolded against the background of Benderly's innovations. Before World War I, the notion of Jewish
women as educators, recalled one of their number, was "something new."[49] In
the aftermath of the war, however, it became quite normative as New York's
Orthodox community formed their own teacher-training institutes. The Hebrew Teachers Training School for Girls, established in 1926, led the way. A
creation of the Women's Branch of the UOJCA, it claimed to have trained some
one hundred women annually to be "capable women pedagogues for Talmud
Torahs and synagogue schools."[50] Meeting, symbolically enough, at the CJI, the
Training School, later to be incorporated into Stern College for Women, provided systematic instruction in Hebrew and Jewish culture and qualified its
graduates as licensed Hebrew teachers.[51] The Herzliah Teachers Training
School, formed at approximately the same time as the Hebrew Teachers Institute, was yet another facility designed to provide teachers for the primary
grades. An outgrowth of the National Hebrew School, one of the few talmud
torahs to have educated Jewish girls before World War I, Herzliah was created
by maskil Moshe Feinstein to provide National Hebrew School graduates with a
more advanced education; by the mid-twenties, it had expanded its roster of
courses to include a teacher-training program. Located first on the Lower East
Side and then moving to West 91st Street in 1943, Herzliah viewed itself as a

kind of "folk-school" in which "maximum Jewish education" was promoted.[52] "Jewish history, we believe," the editors of the *Orthodox Union* wrote in 1937, "will surely credit our generation with this one contribution to Hebrew education: recognition of the place of women in our school system."[53]

Not unexpectedly, opposition to the "up-to-date, modern, and efficient talmud torah" and to its licensed, professionally trained staff arose within ultra-traditional circles. Some were confused by the rhetoric fancied by its devotees and cognoscenti. "We receive many complaints from neighborhood parents," record the CJI minutes, that "the teachers we have here are too modern. They want a certain type of teacher. They do not understand Jewish consciousness and atmosphere."[54] Others were distrustful of its methodology. Deriding the "Ivrith b'Ivrith" method as a "lot of nonsense," Yorkville rabbi Moses Hyamson explained his opposition before a meeting of the CJI Talmud Torah Committee. "I believe in the old school, in making the foundation religious. I do not believe in this system at all."[55] Then there were those who, vexed by the modern technology of the model talmud torah, engaged in a classic act of machine bashing. Dramatizing their dislike of the stereopticon machine, which neatly combined in form and function the much-touted modernity of the curriculum, a few Uptown Talmud Torah board members, latter-day Luddites, proceeded to cut its wires, thus preventing the airing of a slide-show lecture on the Bible. The Benderly "boys," charged the *Morgen Zhurnal*, "made a 'show' of the Torah and our holy prophets. They changed these spiritual giants into moving picture heroes. . . ."[56] Harshest criticism by far emanated from the rabbinic quarter, which accused the bureau not only of trivializing tradition but of promoting *apikorsos*, hereticism, and, more damning still, possibly even apostasy, a charge that made headlines in the traditional Yiddish press. "Rabbinical Meeting," observed the *Tageblatt*, "Declares War on the Kehillah's Bureau of Education."[57]

Though rabbinic opposition to the bureau's methods made quite a stir, its impact was limited. "Influential enough to evoke controversy and to sap energy away from constructive efforts, the rabbis," writes Arthur Goren, "were too weak and bewildered to offer a viable alternative."[58] Ultimately, Benderly's success in professionalizing the field of Jewish education and in generating a corresponding sense of esprit de corps and optimism contained the opposition. Writing to Harry Fischel, a former president of the Uptown Talmud Torah who had resigned his post because of opposition to his progressive methods, Jacob Schiff dramatically insisted that those who stand "in the way of Modern Jewish Education, [will find] that the Community will sweep over them like the ocean over a little islet in its midst."[59] Small comfort at the time to the aggrieved Fischel, Schiff's hopes for the eventual triumph of progressive Jewish education did, in fact, materialize. Benderly's efforts, then "revolutionary," had become so integral and "routine" a part of the Jewish educational scene by the 1940s that they generated absolutely no comment.[60]

Staunch advocates of the supplementary school, American Jewish educators like Dushkin, Berkson, and other "Benderly epigones," remained unswervingly loyal to the afternoon talmud torah well into the postwar era.[61] By that point, the heyday of the CJI, of the school center they had vigorously championed, had long since passed, eclipsed by the growing popularity of the congregational Hebrew school. In its courtship of the nuclear middle-class family, the synagogue had assumed responsibility for the education of its younger members, a development heralded by some and feared by others.[62] Yet another development, or "happy augury," that radically transformed the Jewish educational community during the twenties and thirties was the flowering of the Jewish day-school movement.[63] As alternative voices within Jewish educational circles began to make themselves heard, the formerly unquestioned consensus regarding the nature of American Jewish education began, little by little, to break down. Drawn, for the most part, from the ranks of the Americanized Orthodox community and the Zionistically inclined, advocates of the interwar day-school system had become increasingly frustrated by the "half-hearted" education prevalent in the supplementary system; finding it wanting, they looked more sympathetically upon a modernized day school and saw in it the antidote to widespread Jewish ignorance. "Will we be content with just a smattering of Jewish knowledge, with just a glimpse of Jewish culture, and just a bird's-eye view of Jewish history? Is it possible to develop sturdy Jews in that way?" they asked.[64]

For some, the decision to establish an all-day Jewish school grew out of personal motives. Joseph Lookstein, the founder of the Ramaz School, relates in his unpublished autobiography that many of his colleagues believed that the need to find proper schooling for his young son lay behind his creation of that institution. "Why did Ramaz come into being?" he asks. "A few good friends with a sense of humor maintain to this day that the school was founded for 'Rabbi Lookstein's son.' Subconsciously that may have been the motivation."[65] Others were far more explicit in their acknowledgment of a personal or autobiographical imperative: the founders of the Brooklyn Jewish Center School, for example, were eager to avoid the "inner conflicts, the maladjustments, the emotional strains, to which we ourselves were subjected in our childhood."[66] Rejecting the bifurcation of their lives into separate Jewish and American components, interwar parents were "in search of a synthesis," hoping to find it within the day school.[67]

That New York City witnessed the formation of twenty-three day schools between 1917 and 1939, a veritable efflorescence of the Jewish parochial system, suggests that the phenomenon of the day school was as much generational as it was personal or idiosyncratic. Throughout the Empire City, in Flatbush and Crown Heights, the Upper East Side and Washington Heights, in Borough Park and the Upper West Side, personal concerns joined with larger social ones in breaking with established precedent. "I felt that the times called for a different kind of educational institution. There was need for a type of school that would resemble the private progressive school more than the classical yeshiva," Ramaz's founder observed.[68] The formation of the Jewish Center School, the Hebrew Institute of Borough Park, the Shulamith School, the Yeshiva of Flatbush, the Brooklyn Jewish Center School, and the Ramaz Academy suggests he was right.[69]

Though it often bore the title "yeshiva" on its letterhead, the modernized day school bore little resemblance to its predecessor. The modern day school, one educator explained, "in no way resembles the traditional Jewish parochial school, neither in form, substance, character, nor curriculum."[70] Where, say, the Rabbi Jacob Joseph School or Yeshiva d'Harlem functioned as a traditional European yeshiva in which secular studies, when provided, were "thrust into the tail-end of a long day devoted largely to Hebrew, Bible and Talmud," the modernized day school gave equal play to secular and Judaic subjects.[71] Pioneering the notion of a "staggered curriculum," in which Hebrew studies alternated with secular ones throughout the school day, the modern yeshiva sought to create an integrated and total personality, a complete, happily adjusted American Jew. "From my own Yeshiva experience," recalled an alumnus of the Rabbi Jacob Joseph School, "I developed the feeling that from eight thirty in the morning when the Jewish studies began, till three thirty in the afternoon when they ended, I was a Jewish person. And from four in the afternoon till seven in the evening when the 'English' studies were offered, I was a different kind of person. That is not a healthy feeling, nor is it a desirable educational practice."[72]

In their creation of an "integrated personality," the educators and parent body of the modernized day school, partners in its evolution, fully recognized the duality inherent in being both American and Jewish and sought to reconcile the two. The American Jewish child, explained Fannie Neumann, a founder and parent of the Brooklyn Jewish Center School, in 1930, is heir to two traditions, one Judaic and the other American. Between them, she affirmed, there is "no conflict, no incompatibility."[73] The curriculum reinforced the absence of conflict, providing a "balanced intellectual diet."[74] A course in world geography embraced material on the geography of Palestine while one in domestic science included sections on kashruth, the "methods of kosherization," and how to manage a kosher home; the latter was an especial favorite of Ramaz's principal. Asked by an interviewer, in 1940, to show how his integration theory was put into practice, Lookstein selected "Home-Making" as an example. This course, he explained, "was the best one I can think of."[75]

The Hebraic curriculum was also the source of considerable innovation. With the Ivrith b'Ivrith method at its core, Judaic studies made a strong case for cultural Zionism, or what others liked to call "biculturalism." In fact, it was within the nascent day school that Zionism received the strongest expression throughout the interwar years. Synagogues would occasionally introduce a Zionist leader as guest lecturer or sponsor a course in Palestinian folk music or dance as part of their cultural programming; financial appeals for a Palestinian yeshiva or charity were also quite common, reflecting, in turn, the characteristically philanthropic nature of American Zionism.[76] But these Zionist-flavored activities were more a reflection of the rabbi's personal interests or inclinations than anything else and could hardly be called a sustained and consistent part of the synagogue's agenda. Surely it is no coincidence that interest in Zionism flagged outside of the synagogue as well: during the interwar years membership in the Zionist Organization of America declined markedly. When Brandeis headed up that agency, membership had reached an all-time high of 200,000; by 1940, the ZOA could claim only 50,000 dues-paying members.[77] If and when middle-class American Jews thought of the Jewish homeland, they tended to exoticize the phenomenon, a tendency reinforced by the heavily romantic treatment of Jewish Palestinian affairs by the Jewish press. Travelogues, "Impressions of Present Jewish Life in the Land of Israel," were the staple of popular magazine articles on life in that far-off corner of the world, supplemented occasionally by capsule biographies of Zionist leaders and English translations of Bialik short stories.[78] By the late 1930s, however, the sobering realities of Hitler's Europe led to a heightened concern with the politics of Zionism and, in turn, a downplaying of the Zionist mystique.

In contrast, the Zionist ideal was central to the emerging modern day-school movement: making cultural Zionism the very linchpin of its curriculum, the day schools transformed the notion of a Jewish state from a somewhat quaint and distant possibility into a tangible cultural reality. In part, this emphasis was a function of the day school's Hebrew teachers, many of whom were aligned, both formally and informally, with the then-emerging American Mizrachi movement. Guardians of traditional Judaism in Palestine, the members of Mizrachi reconciled the politics of Zionism with the demands of ritual, or as Jessie Sampter explained in a pamphlet on Zionism, the Mizrachi "square Zionism with Orthodox Judaism."[79] With a three-point program, American Mizrachi under the leadership of such rabbinic and educational personalities as Meyer Berlin, its first American president, and Professor Pinchos Churgin, its president in 1949, sought to ensure the continued presence of religiously minded Zionists in the Yishuv and in the Jewish Agency. At the same time, Mizrachi leaders believed in the importance of sparking a religious cultural revival, both within and outside of Palestine. In this respect, perhaps the most tangible contribution of the American Mizrachi movement was its creation of the Teachers Institute, which supplied many of the personnel to the ranks of emerging day-school educators.[80] Then, too, the formal association of many of the day-school founders with Mizrachi—both Lookstein and Churgin served jointly as national vice-presidents as well as members of the editorial board of the *Jewish Outlook*, Mizrachi's English-language periodical—indirectly ensured the introduction of a strongly Zionist-centered Hebraic curriculum. Committed personally and politically to the ideal of a vibrant Orthodoxy in the Jewish homeland, they took great pains to encourage a Zionist cultural revival within the corridors of the elementary school. The widespread use of Hebrew as the predominant language of instruction was a case in point; so too was the attention given, through assemblies, dramatic productions, and special projects, to the promotion of a potent cultural awareness of Eretz Yisrael.[81]

Although the centrality of Zionism within the modern day-school curriculum betokened a break with the past, it was with its student body, the projected audience for these programs, that the modernized day school departed most radically from common practice. Once an educational haven for would-be Jewish communal servants, what Dushkin called a "priest class,"[82] the day school now sought to cultivate an average middle-class Jewish constituency and one, moreover, that consisted of both boys and girls. Broadening its base, the modernized day school sought to make day school acceptable and even fashionable, attracting those intent on sending their children to fine public schools or private academies. Writing of his decision to establish the Ramaz School, Lookstein noted, "I was not in competition with Tifereth Jerusalem or with Torah Voda'ath," referring to two traditional yeshivahs, "but with Horace Mann and Ethical Culture."[83] Eager to tap that population, yeshiva educators launched an intensive public relations campaign and in handsome, well-designed brochures that spoke of a "progressive and dynamic educational environment" and "spacious, well-equipped" facilities made their pitch to the affluent and acculturated. This promotional literature, one social observer commented, "reads like an invitation to send your child to an American Jewish Eton."[84]

Throughout, the modern day school maintained a welcoming and positive stance toward the outside world and secular culture. Despite the commonly repeated charge that the day school was little more than a hotbed of segregation, of un-American sentiment, its supporters believed otherwise and went to great lengths to express their patriotism. Making a case for the viability of the day school as an American institution, its proponents seamlessly bound together such concepts as democracy, cultural pluralism, and the American spirit. In their formulation, cultural pluralism was no longer a quirky or farfetched intellectual concept but rather "the very essence of the American way of life," while the modern day school, building on the foundations of cultural pluralism, was itself, as Lookstein liked to say, an "institution of democracy."[85] In statements invoking the time-honored link between Hebraic culture and the founding fathers of the United States, the advocates of the day school missed few opportunities to underscore the inherent consonance and mutuality of interest between their school and the national culture. Some even went so far as to avow that attendance at such a school was an act of patriotism. "It becomes the patriotic duty on the part of the American Jew," the *Jewish Forum* editorialized, "not only to resist absorption but to keep alive and to foster the Jewish spirit"; what better way to do so than to support Jewish day schools.[86]

Extremely conscious of and sensitive to public opinion, educators like Lookstein at Ramaz or Joel Braverman at the Yeshivah of Flatbush sought not only to anticipate objections to the day school but to neutralize them. They listened carefully to the arguments invoked against the day school, internalized these arguments, and then stood them on their head. Its modern-day founders made over the day school into a quintessentially bourgeois institution and tended to stress those facets of the school likely to appeal to a bourgeois clientele. Emblematic of this posture was the decision to hold no classes on Sundays or national legal holidays and to provide for winter and spring vacations that coincided with those taken by the public schools; in the obvious, bold way of sharing in American holidays, the modern day school demonstrated its commitment to being an intrinsic part of America. "I did not want the children to feel excluded or disadvantaged," Lookstein wrote of his then-controversial decision to hold no classes on Sunday and to provide for a winter break that coincided with Christmas. "I was striving for integration not isolation."[87]

In still other respects, the modernizing of the day school paralleled that of the synagogue. Its advocates put much stock in the physical accoutrements of the school buildings, boasting of "light and airy classrooms" and of furniture that was the "last word" in style and durability.[88] Such things counted for a great deal: one parent recalled that she had sent her sons to Ramaz because of the sensitivity of its principal to the needs of his middle-class constituents. "He wanted the gold knockers on the door, he wanted the children from the upper middle class."[89] Not only were the handsome and well-appointed classrooms a source of considerable pride, but, like the features of the modern synagogue building, they served effectively to rebut those who argued that the day school, like its forebear the *cheder*, was unsanitary, unappealing, and ultimately un-American. Much as the reconstructed monumental synagogue did much to sanitize, and recast, the image of the Orthodox, so too did the handsome school; the two efforts were of a piece.

Even the names by which many interwar day schools were known sought to reassure supporters and constituents alike that the day school was a normative American institution and one, moreover, that had high-class pretensions. "I wanted once and for all to remove the stigma of a 'ghetto school,'" Lookstein explained as he named his modern American yeshiva the "Ramaz Academy"; by 1942, it had changed its name to the even more neutral-sounding Ramaz School.[90] Ramaz Academy, the Jewish Center Day School, the Manhattan Day School—each of the names chosen to adorn the modernized day school was at one and the same time ambiguous and high-toned. One parent active in the formation of a number of day schools recalled that the general appellation "day school" was widely chosen because it was "classy, reminiscent of the exclusive Christian private school."[91]

The founders of the day school in New York relied heavily on external indices of success to promote their institutions and, undoubtedly, on a certain level to reassure themselves and others as well that day-school students were not suffering from Jewish parochial education. For one thing, they were apt to encourage site visits from leading non-Jewish educational authorities—usually professors of education from universities of high repute—whose professional evaluation, it was hoped, would lend unquestioned validity to their enterprise. Delighting in the words of experts who extolled the "uniformly fine spirit" of such a facility and its steadfast maintenance of "higher and higher standards than those of schools operating on a conventional basis," day-school administrators would widely circulate these reports.[92] Internally, a close watch was kept on the academic achievements of day-school students: repeatedly, institutional minutes proudly recorded that the student body was of the "highest caliber," that students scored well on standardized tests, or that the average IQ "far exceeded" the average of students in either public or private schools. That many of these comparisons could be grounded in cold statistical evidence was even better still; as a result, the habit soon developed of busily comparing the performance of yeshiva students—on IQ tests, Regents exams, and later still, college acceptances—with those of other schools and proudly publishing the resulting statistics. "Jewish Education At its Best," exclaimed the *Jewish Forum*, as it recorded, on its editorial page no less, the following statistics: 82 percent of the Talmudical Academy student body in 1926 passed the Latin Regents, as compared with 56 percent elsewhere; 86 percent passed Math, as compared with 54 percent elsewhere; and so on.[93] Figures on college acceptance were, however, the ultimate validation: the extent to which graduates of yeshiva high schools entered the Ivy League graphically demonstrated, as little else could, that attendance in a modern yeshiva high school was no barrier to educational excellence and, in turn, complete acculturation. Much as the members of the Young Israel movement a generation earlier had proudly affirmed that "one could be *shomer shabbos* and go to college," the current generation took this notion a step further and argued that one could be a product of a Jewish day school and yet attend Harvard. No wonder then that a standard feature of the Ramaz annual report, the "Principal's Report," and the newsletter was a chart depicting the range of college acceptances. "Harvard, Yale, Princeton Accept Ramazites," boldly proclaimed the front page of the *Ramaz Mirror*, a publication of the Ramaz Parents Council. "This year's high school graduating class can really give itself an academic pat on the back."[94] That its students could be accepted to stellar institutions of higher education not only underscored that particular school's success but validated the modern yeshiva experience as a whole in secular, worldly terms.

The first modernized day school to "break the geographical barrier," the Ramaz Academy, established in 1937, was located on East 85th Street, in the heart of the Upper East Side. Unique not only by dint of its geography but in the circumstances of its establishment as well, the Ramaz Academy enjoyed a symbiotic relationship with Kehilath Jeshurun.[95] The latter, as proof of its "undiminishing vigor" during its seventieth year as a modern American congregation, launched the school.[96] Though synagogues had previously sponsored afternoon Hebrew schools, they had never before sponsored a Jewish parochial school, and KJ, not surprisingly, approached the task with considerable trepidation, much of it financial: after all, the projected school was to become a reality only a few years after the synagogue had fallen victim to the Depression. Recalling the heated discussions regarding the establishment of the school, one of its most ardent supporters quoted the synagogue's president, initially opposed to the notion, as saying that he would not put "a healthy head into a sick bed."[97] The power and persuasiveness of Rabbi Lookstein's arguments, however, overcame the doubts of the opposition, and, in a gesture reminiscent of noblesse oblige, the shul agreed to support the school. "If you divorce the educational function from the congregation," Lookstein explained in an effort to win the board's ongoing support for his school, "you are removing the foundation from under its feet and the roof from over its head. What will remain will be desolate walls enclosing empty and gaping benches."[98] With the board's imprimatur and the gift of $500, the Ramaz Academy came into being; tuition, private donations, and gifts from the KJ sisterhood provided additional revenue. Administered by a committee of the board known initially as the "Ramaz Academy Committee," the school was also housed, during the first few years of its existence, in the synagogue's vestry rooms.[99]

Joseph Lookstein, the school's founder and principal, was no stranger to the world of Jewish education, having served as the principal of the Hebrew Teachers Training School for a number of years and, concomitantly, as professor of homiletics at Yeshiva. Following a gestation period, which by Lookstein's own admission lasted ten years, the Ramaz Academy was established in the fall of 1937 as a lasting memorial to the young rabbi's grandfather-in-law and senior colleague, Rabbi Moses Z. Margolies, after whom the school was named (RAMAZ is an acronym of that name). The notion of a coeducational, high-level day school grew out of Lookstein's experiences in the field. For one thing, his tenure at the Hebrew Teachers Training School alerted him to the urgency of providing systematic and quality Jewish education for girls. A "modest" effort, that school, he would write, "served to call attention to the problem of the higher Jewish education of women."[100] For another, the rabbi's personal involvement with the KJ community dramatized the importance of cultivating a middle-class constituency. "I think that it is time that we declare that a child from a rich Jewish home also has an inalienable right for a full and comprehensive Jewish education," he explained somewhat passionately.[101] Then, too, one cannot discount more personal factors: the Ramaz Academy provided the energetic and ambitious young rabbi with a canvas for his own talents: as his son recalls, the senior Lookstein would often say that "he did not enter the rabbinate just to preach sermons or teach a class."[102]

The "pilot class" consisted of twelve students, three of whom were youthful members of the synagogue family: the president's daughter, the *shamas*'s daughter, and the rabbi's son. As it grew, the Ramaz Academy rented a few classrooms from the CJI next door. By 1945, having expanded to well over one hundred students, the academy purchased the CJI building and, in that same year, added on a high school. With fifteen classrooms and "specialty rooms," a large auditorium with a fully operational stage, a well-equipped gymnasium, and two science laboratories, the Ramaz Academy could hold its own with other, more established New York City schools. "You will be interested to know," a trustee informed his fellow officers in 1939, "that the District Superintendent of the Board of Education visited the school early last term and found it so satisfactory that she openly admitted it to be on a par with such advanced private schools as Lincoln, Horace Mann and Ethical Culture."[103]

Determined to have his school rank with the best, Lookstein assembled a team of highly regarded educators to chart its course, among them Paul Klapper, dean of City College's School of Education and later president of Queens College; Professor Joseph Cohen, dean of Brooklyn College's School of Education; and Pinchos Churgin, dean of TI and, subsequently, the founder of Bar-Ilan University. Together, they drew up a curriculum for both the secular and Judaic subjects that reflected the latest in educational theory. In fact, much was made of the successful adoption of the principles of the then-popular "New Education," in which the curriculum was organized in the form of "units of work." Study was further enriched, Lookstein reported to the Board of Regents, by the use of visual aids such as lantern slides, sound films (shades of

Benderly!), museum trips, dramatic presentations, school assemblies, and a course in citizenship training.

The teaching staff reflected Lookstein's commitment to high standards. Beginning with two teachers in 1937, one for the kindergarten and the other for the first grade, Ramaz's faculty grew to seventeen persons a decade later: six full-time general studies teachers, six full-time religious studies teachers, and five part-time specialty subject teachers. Both the English and the Hebraic studies teachers were college graduates with "professional training that included both special and general pedagogy."[104] Often, as Lookstein liked to boast, they were drawn from the same pool of candidates that supplied the prestigious New York private schools. "We obtain them from the same sources and through the same channels used by the leading private schools of the city," he proudly told a group of supporters.[105] Many of the teachers, "typical American young men and young women," were trained in Mizrachi-oriented institutions, where they honed their pedagogical skills in a staunchly Zionist ambience.[106] To ensure their fealty to the school, Lookstein paid his teachers salaries comparable to those of elementary-level public-school teachers and introduced high cost-of-living bonuses. "You see then," he wrote to the head of the Hebrew Teachers Union in 1945, "we are not only doing the right thing at the present time, but are planning to do even better in the future."[107]

Ramaz expected its faculty not only to be well trained but to be able to serve as models of integration, the leitmotif of its curriculum. Both within and without the classroom, in matters of dress, conduct, and orientation, they were expected to demonstrate the viability of synthesis between Jewish and American culture. "Above all," Lookstein related, "I sought teachers who were themselves committed to bi-cultural education and who could serve as examples of the integration of Judaism and Americanism."[108] With such teachers as models, Ramaz students would be "exposed to a wholesome and integrated American Jewish personality."[109]

The school's commitment to what it somberly called the "principle of integration" was demonstrated in yet other ways, most notably by infusing the study of the Bible and religious customs with music, arts, and crafts. "In the arts and crafts room, in the music room, at the assembly, in the dramatic performance, no opportunity is missed for a subtle and almost imperceptible integration of the secular and the sacred," Lookstein pridefully explained before a somewhat skeptical audience.[110] "Incidentally," Lookstein told a panel of Regents reviewers at about the same time, resorting to technical lingo, "each of these expressional arts is taught by the same specialist throughout the day, thus providing continuity in the development of techniques, appreciation and creative abilities."[111] The school's avowed dedication to integration culminated in regularly scheduled assemblies in which "numerous opportunities present[ed] themselves to emphasize the relation of American and Jewish ideals."[112] Thanksgiving Day served as an occasion for linking the words of the Prophets with those of the Pilgrims, while the Passover assembly stressed not only the liberation of the Israelites from bondage but also the striving of mankind for liberation from opposition. In each instance, the objective was to create "a school atmosphere in which a child live[d] throughout the school day as a Jew and as an American at one and the same time."[113]

Classes ran from 9:00 A.M. until 3:00 in the afternoon and were thoroughly integrated, one with the other. Determined to teach Judaic and secular subjects, "not alone side by side or under one roof but as a synthesized and composite unit," the school departed from the customary practice of devoting the morning to Hebraic matters and the afternoon to English ones.[114] Instead, the two fields alternated one with another: beginning with a *chumash* (Bible) lesson, a child would move on to a class in arithmetic followed by a lesson in Hebrew literature. Though the staggered system of instruction occasioned considerable criticism, especially from those who objected to teaching "goyishe" subjects in the time traditionally reserved for more sacred matters, Lookstein held his ground. For him, the integration of the two curricula lay at the heart of his educational experiment.

To allay the fears of those who worried lest a day-school education shortchange their children, Ramaz's English curriculum paralleled that of the public school and guaranteed that "when their course of study is completed, they will *of course* in their English studies be prepared to enter any of the high schools of their choice. . . ."[115] "General studies" included arithmetic, arts and crafts, health education, music, language arts, literature, science, and social studies. The Hebrew curriculum, conducted almost entirely in the Ivrith b'Ivrith method, entailed Jewish history, literature, "important sections of the Talmud and Mishnah," as well as the Pentateuch and the Prophets. With a strong Zionist orientation, the school even devoted an entire unit to Palestine, in which students prepared an "imaginary trip through the land," interviewing British and Jewish officials, building a miniature model of a typical settlement, and utilizing their Hebrew.[116] "It is of course needless to add," a school trustee added, "that they will be able to use the Hebrew language as a speaking medium with the same ease that they use English."[117] A lively extracurricular program—with a G.O. (student government), Social Service Fund, school publications—and a profound commitment to athletics rounded out the program. Contrary to the traditional yeshiva, Lookstein boasted to a colleague, "we go in a great deal for physical education."[118] Years later, basketball games and proms were grafted on to the high school's roster of extracurricular activities. "We learned how to dance in school," one alumnus recalled. "The Girls' gym teacher taught us how to dance in homeroom. I remember learning the fox trot and the rumba."[119]

The school, under Lookstein's watchful eye, was diligently monitored; nothing escaped his notice. The style of dress fancied by the teaching staff, the health of his young charges, even the heating conditions of the building were subject to intense scrutiny. One cold winter morning, Lookstein went on an "inspection trip" of the school building and, much to his dismay, found many of the rooms underheated. Drafting a lengthy memo to the school's administrator, Lookstein took him to task, citing chapter and verse: "Room 303: The room thermometer read fifty degrees. Half of the radiators in the room were cold. Room 402: The room thermometer read sixty-five degrees. Twenty-five percent of the radiators were cold. This time," the principal concluded, "I regret to say that I am not interested in *explanations*. I am concerned about *performance*." He then proceeded to issue a series of firmly worded directives.[120] Ramaz's principal scrutinized financial reports and intelligence tests as eagerly as he monitored the building's maintenance. As each year brought a fresh batch of statistics, Lookstein and his staff anxiously tabulated them, watching closely for signs of success or, conversely, a slight falling off in performance, numbers of students, or financial stability. Lookstein's penchant for statistical rigor, exhibited earlier in his administration of the KJ synagogue, was given full rein in his school; not surprisingly, the physical and mental mettle of the student body was frequently put to the test and the results compiled in the form of booklets for each individual child. In these "biographies," which neatly summarized the child's "elementary school career," every measurable fact, from scholastic ability to work habits, general appearance, and emotional stability, was fully documented.[121] Proud of the results, the school would widely disseminate this information in school publications, annual reports, and fund-raising dinner journals. Thanks to these efforts, considerable publicity attended Ramaz's success, and soon the institution was widely hailed as "the school of today and tomorrow."[122]

"The school is an American school in every sense of the word," one of its supporters noted in 1951. "You would see a classroom that looks physically like the classroom of an American or private school. You would see teachers, educated in American universities. . . .You would see children studying, learning, behaving just as children do in the American public or private schools. . . .In short, you would see children absorbing the American spirit in every sense of the word."[123] Undoubtedly music to Lookstein's ears, this laudatory description of the Ramaz School, then entering its second decade, masked what must have been a source of considerable consternation to its principal: the absence, in both relative and absolute terms, of Upper East Side Jewish students. Despite the apparent Americanism of the school and its evident academic success, Lookstein was not nearly as successful as he had hoped to be in drawing to his academy the "neglected children" of the upper middle class and the Upper East Side.[124] Institutional minutes make a point of emphasizing the solid middle-class complexion of the student body: children, we are told, come from the "loveliest homes"; "prominent people," one report noted proudly, "were sending their kids to the Ramaz Academy."[125] But these "lovely homes" were located across the park, on the Upper West Side, then a vibrantly middle-class Jewish enclave. A 1950 study of the "geographic distribution of our students" revealed that while youngsters from Manhattan accounted for more than 60 percent of the entire student body, those who lived "in the city" were drawn overwhelmingly from the Upper West Side.[126] They were not, however, drawn from the ranks of Lookstein's own constituents, the supporters and benefactors of the shul and the school. Prepared to support the school generously, Lookstein's "own people" stopped short of making the ultimate contribution: their children.

The absence of Upper East Side children at Ramaz can be attributed, in part, to demographics: there were simply not that many Jewish school-age children on the Upper East Side during the interwar years, a fact that, a decade earlier, had prompted CJI's president to bemoan his school's "mal-location."[127] But then, it was also a matter of class. When it came to the schooling of their children, KJ congregants "were not willing to take a chance."[128] One stalwart of the congregation recalled how the decision not to send her son to Ramaz wounded its principal. Having officiated at this young man's *bris*, Lookstein was heard to exclaim with delight that he was now "going to get another Ramaz student." When, for a variety of personal and financial reasons, this would-be Ramaz student was sent to public school, Lookstein "never forgave" the family.[129] Not until the sixties were students drawn from the immediate vicinity. By 1969, 196 students from a total student body of 682 were "locals," an increase of about 60 percent in five years. "It might well be," commented a Ramaz publication, "that Ramaz is becoming a factor in bringing Jewish residents to this area."[130]

Ironically enough, given the school's projected image as a staunchly American institution, many Ramaz students during the first two decades of its existence were the children of refugees. With a strong tradition of parochial-school education—those from Belgium, for example, were themselves graduates of the *tachkemoni*, or Mizrachi educational system, "a gymnasium in the European sense of the word"—and sufficiently affluent to afford the costs of private education, the Ramaz parents of this era were neither unfamiliar with nor threatened by what Lookstein and his colleagues sought to accomplish.[131] "The people who really made it possible for the school to grow," one contemporary related, "were the refugees. . . .they came along with the tradition and with their funds."[132] (It is also worth noting that the absence of a comparable institution in their own neighborhood—the Manhattan Day School was not established until 1943—spurred the trek across the park.) A stabilizing force, the Europeans sustained the school during its earliest years and as such, recalled

Mrs. Lookstein, "were really the backbone of the school."[133] Their support for the modern American yeshiva was in fact so pronounced that it gave rise, quite unexpectedly, to a real, if short-lived, anxiety on the part of many native-born parents that the American day school was becoming "too European."[134] Yet in this instance, as in so many others, "grave misgivings" about the appropriateness of Jewish day-school education ultimately subsided.[135] "The ultra-American reader," historian Abraham Duker observed in a 1949 article on Ramaz students, "need not worry about their pronunciation of English, their interest in baseball or love of hot dogs, kosher ones, of course."[136] The modern day-school student, he seemed to say, was as inherently American, and normal, as the fellow next door.

Once seen as an "exotic phenomenon,"[137] and not a highly esteemed one at that, the day school had succeeded in overcoming its benighted reputation to emerge as the most dynamic and celebrated Jewish institution of postwar America. Building on the momentum generated during the interwar era, the day-school movement nationally created more than one hundred new schools between 1942 and 1952, over half of them in New York City alone. The extremely rapid, and at times unsystematic, development of the American day school led, in fact, to the formation of a number of umbrella educational agencies—Torah Umesorah among them—to coordinate their growth and, in a real sense, tame what had emerged as a grass-roots phenomenon.[138]

A number of factors account for this "ever-increasing galaxy" of day schools.[139] The influx of European Jewry with a strong tradition of parochial education provided a pliant student body at a time when native-born Jews were hesitant to send their children to a Jewish parochial school. The creation of the State of Israel, following on the Holocaust, gave Jewish education an incontestable moral imperative. Then, too, the reputation of the modern day school was no longer in doubt; thanks to the efforts of the pioneer generation, it had acquired a considerable social, cultural, and educational imprimatur, perhaps even cachet. An institution like the Manhattan Day School, reflected Mordecai Kaplan, who lived in its neighborhood, "will do to Orthodox Judaism [in America] what S. R. Hirsch succeeded to do with the Jewish school which he established in Frankfurt am Main."[140]

As it developed into the postwar generation's primary object of attention, the day school supplanted the modernized synagogue in the Orthodox community's hierarchy of institutions. Orthodoxy today, observed Emanuel Rackman in 1956, is "transferring its prime emphasis from the synagogue to the school."[141] A generation earlier, the synagogue sought to standardize and order the religious behavior of its congregants, rendering Orthodox worship attractive, modern, and suitably American. The day school sought to do much the same thing, but on a larger scale. Operating in a different sphere from the synagogue sanctuary, the day school articulated both a behaviorial and an intellectual standard for middle-class New York Jewish children. The modern yeshiva not only strengthened the educational foundations and emotional ties that bound New York Orthodox Jews to their ritual but led, in turn, to greater homogeneity in religious conduct and religious orientation. In its own way, then, the modern New York day school reflected the coming of age of American Orthodoxy. As an extension of the American Orthodox ethos beyond the four walls of the sanctuary, the modern day school served as an index of that denomination's continued vitality.

POSTSCRIPT

"We face three dangers to the development of a pure and enduring orthodoxy," insisted a leading postwar European rabbinical authority in 1956: "Reform Judaism, Conservative Judaism and the modern orthodox."[1] That "modern Orthodoxy" could be lumped together in the same spirit (and in the same sentence) with its own rivals and, worse still, that it could be construed as a danger to Judaism gravely undermined the status of the indigenous American Orthodox community, playing havoc with its carefully worked out accommodation with modernity.

In what has been termed the hasidification of American Orthodoxy, a more aggressive or sectarian Orthodoxy came into its own in the aftermath of World War II, sparking a fierce internal debate within the American Orthodox world as to the legitimacy of the prewar phenomenon.[2] Challenging the indigenous, happily modernized Orthodox community at its very core, the newer element disdained the education of the New York–trained rabbi, mocked the community's preoccupation with manners as *narishkeyt* (silliness), and spurned its religious culture as ill conceived, inconsistent, and, most damning of all, inauthentic. Virtually everything championed by the interwar Orthodox, from English-speaking rabbis to "modern yeshivas," was anathema to the emerging right wing. In due time, not surprisingly, a social chasm developed between the two groups by mutual consent. As they warily eyed each other across this chasm, it became increasingly clear that if the two factions were not radically different phenomena, then they shared an Orthodoxy with neither a sense of kinship nor a common past.

The disjunction between the prewar and the postwar Orthodox reflected, in part, a shift of demographics: in many instances, the postwar Orthodox were not the descendants of those who, a generation and a war earlier, had proudly built monumental Orthodox synagogues on the Upper East Side, in Harlem and Borough Park. Though the children of that culture maintained, in large measure, their parents' commitment to a modernized Orthodoxy, they found themselves overshadowed, outnumbered demographically, by the children of refugees or those of the "survivors" who took up residence in New York during the thirties and in the wake of World War II. At that time, the presence of thousands of premodern and, in many cases, passionately antimodern Eastern European Jews, with a remarkable sense of institutional cohesiveness, significantly altered the demographic and geographical face of New York Orthodoxy. Their re-creation in New York of tightly knit, highly structured Jewish communities with intensely lived Jewish ambiences and stellar rabbinic personalities—the German Breuer community of Washington Heights, the Lubavitch Hasidim of Crown Heights, the Satmar of Williamsburg, along with a handful of powerful yeshiva communities are a few of the best-known and most successful of the postwar circles—redefined the communal structure of the New York Orthodox. With their dense, heavily populated constituencies and strong, pervasive sense of community, the "new" Orthodox could not help but make their presence felt within the Empire City.[3]

But then, the social chasm between the two groups is more than a matter of a different set of genes or different geographical origins; at its most basic, it reflects and is rooted in an altogether different approach to and understanding of religious behavior. In no uncertain terms, the postwar element rejected New York Orthodoxy's rapprochement with modernity, substituting its own, far more negative, point of view. With Yiddish as their public and private language and clad in distinctive dress, the postwar Orthodox proved to be far more stringent in their ritual observance and unswerving in their opposition to social integration than their American predecessors had been. Initially, the postwar element kept to itself, but by the mid-1950s, it had become more vocal in its castigation of American Orthodox practice and sought to impose its standards of behavior on the community as a whole. "I just don't like the feeling one gets in their company," observed an American Orthodox Jew of his Hungarian neighbors in Williamsburg, "that they are the ones who represent Orthodoxy and everyone who looks or acts differently just isn't as good a Jew."[4] Though many indigenous New York Orthodox doubtless agreed with this assessment, they too ultimately modified their behavior, bowing unhappily to a new consensus, and adopted more stringent patterns of observance. Prohibitions against such formerly commonplace behavior as mixed social dancing and mixed swimming or going about publicly without a head covering or wearing sleeveless attire gradually became normative, even among the typically American Orthodox of the interwar years. Reflecting on some of these changes, Elizabeth Gilbert, the daughter of a leading and widely revered prewar Orthodox rabbi, Dr. Philip H. Klein, and herself a lifelong Orthodox Jew, noted that until recently she had "never even heard of many of the behaviors" associated with the Orthodox community in New York.[5]

Arguably a short-lived success, the "older" Orthodoxy turns out to have been a phenomenon of limited duration, the product of a very defined span of time and a particular community of Jews with which it was inextricably bound up. Through little fault of their own, New York's Orthodox were brought up short by the rapidly changing complexion of American Orthodoxy following World War II, caught off guard by the emergence of an especially potent challenge from the right. Having devoted themselves conscientiously to building the institutions of American Orthodoxy—a rabbinical seminary, a congregation, an appropriate architecture, a day school, and even, one of its promoters noted, a language—that generation had given little thought to making its assumptions explicit, to developing an overarching philosophy of American Orthodoxy. For them, the construction of community was sufficient in and of itself. "What is the next stage of traditional Judaism?" asked Rabbi Lookstein during the 1950s, as he delivered a talk on the evolution of American Orthodoxy. "I think the next stage will be characterized by . . . an expansion and a growth and second, an ideological interpretation of the position of traditional Judaism in connection with which we have still been negligent. We didn't have time to write books, dear friends," the clergyman explained to his audience, members of the New York Board of Rabbis, "because we were too busy building institutions . . . We didn't have time to write books," he reiterated, "because we were too busy making lives."[6] Perhaps with time, a considered philosophy of American Orthodoxy might well have emerged as the second generation of RIETS-trained rabbis and a more educated laity, the beneficiaries of a day-school education, built on the foundations of the original pioneers. No such opportunity, however, was forthcoming. Triumphant and self-assured during the 1920s and 1930s, Americanized Orthodoxy emerged shaken and troubled by its encounter with the postwar Orthodox, unable to hold its own in the face of withering criticism. In the absence of an intellectual tradition, the American Orthodox rabbinate, the focus of much of the animus of the postwar Orthodox, "failed to interpret itself to itself," even as the culture as a whole suffered a distinct and "collective inferiority feeling."[7]

Suggestively, one of the most powerful indices of change in the complexion of the contemporary New York community resides in the language of Orthodoxy. Now a part of current parlance (even among the non-Orthodox), words like "halakha," "halakhic," or "frum" (exactingly observant) were hardly, if ever, used by the interwar American Orthodox. Similarly, the liberal usage of Yiddish, a practice the interwar generation studiously avoided, has also become a linguistic commonplace. "Among the Orthodox of the 1920s and 1930s," recalled a Jewish Center congregant of that era, "one did not toss around the word 'frum.'"[8] As for the use of the term "halakha," another congregant related that "nobody even knew what it was."[9] Revealingly, it was also during the postwar era that the term "modern Orthodox" came into widespread use.

Though used sparingly during the interwar years as a descriptive phrase, the label became increasingly more popular during the postwar years—but this time, as a term of derogation. The right-wing element, or the "extremists," as one staunchly American Orthodox rabbi would have it, used the expression as a form of derision to poke fun at or castigate the actions of their more liberal counterparts.[10] "Ah, he's a *moderne*," was said, often condescendingly, of clean-shaven rabbis given to lengthy English sermons or presiding over coeducational day schools. The implications of this new turn of phrase were far-reaching and, to those so designated, extremely disturbing.

For close to half a century, the indigenous American Orthodox, the congregants of Kehilath Jeshurun and the West Side Institutional Synagogue, those of the Mt. Eden Jewish Center or the Young Israel of Williamsburg, had viewed themselves unabashedly as "Orthodox," as the authentic and sole practitioners of traditional Judaism in the New World. Now, in the aftermath of World War II, the members of this community were being told point-blank that their collective claim to being Orthodox and wholly traditional was not merited and that their behavior was simply not up to snuff. At best, they were America's "modern" Orthodox, a subdivision or possibly even a dissident sect of traditional Jews but certainly not the denomination's authentic standard-bearers. Pressured into redefining themselves, the prewar Orthodox had become merely the modern Orthodox. The authentic Orthodox, the true believers, it seemed, were to be found elsewhere.

A Note on Sources

The sources used in this study ranged from archival material to oral-history interviews with both clerical and lay members of New York's Orthodox community. In reconstructing the day-to-day affairs of such institutions as the synagogue and the day school, the primary materials consulted consisted of minute books, internal correspondence, and organizational records. Sadly, the archival record is not nearly as complete as one might hope. Despite an oftentimes acute historical sensibility, Orthodox synagogues tended to be notoriously poor record keepers and failed, for the most part, to maintain a watchful eye over the documents of their past. Diminished by the vagaries of time, poor storage conditions, and migration, extant synagogue records, as well as those chronicling the early years of the modern day school, are few and incomplete. The best single source remains institutional minutes. When successfully preserved, this material serves as a treasure trove of information on administrative and financial matters as well as on issues of social conduct such as synagogue etiquette.

Admittedly, minutes are not without their own built-in limitations. Deliberately terse and clipped in tone, these documents represent an artful, perhaps even an artificial, construction of events and personalities in which heated issues are rendered calmly, in neutral language, and long-simmering controversies or personality clashes neatly compressed and smoothed over. And yet, if mined carefully and thoroughly, they yield up an astonishing array of detail and information. The minutes of Congregation Kehilath Jeshurun, which date back to the turn of the century, have been preserved in a set of bound and accessible volumes and thoroughly document the evolution of that institution from a humble Eastern European *chevra* to a stately American Orthodox congregation. Those of the Eldridge Street Synagogue, recently translated from the Yiddish by Fruma Mohrer, provide a detailed, if at times unintentionally humorous, look into the Americanization of one of the Lower East Side's most prestigious congregations between 1890 and 1916. Synagogue bulletins, souvenir anniversary journals, and an occasional pamphlet, flier, or invitation help to round out the picture of grass-roots congregational life.

The bound minute books of the Ramaz School, along with an arbitrarily preserved set of "early" files and a recently assembled photograph collection, document the school's evolution. As part of its semicentennial celebration, a number of Ramaz School students conducted interviews with several of the key players in the school's creation. The transcripts of these interviews served as an extremely useful, and colorful, aid in detailing that institution's past. Also of considerable use in getting a sense of New York Jewish educational matters were the files of the Central Jewish Institute, now the property of Cejwin Camp. Though a good portion of this archive, including the private papers of Albert Schoolman, was destroyed in a fire, what remained was rich, vivid, and hitherto untapped.

The private papers of those who labored on behalf of Orthodox institutions in New York were yet another heavily drawn-upon source. The Harry Fischel Collection of the Agudath Israel Archives, which consists largely of the corre-spondence of this leading Orthodox philanthropist, along with a sampling of his speeches, provided insight into the workings of an Orthodox layman. The papers of Rabbi Joseph Lookstein, in turn, reflect his fifty years in the pulpit and as such contain valuable correspondence, sermons, drafts of articles and, from time to time, revealing in-house memoranda. The Lookstein collection, housed at Congregation Kehilath Jeshurun, also contains important information on the establishment and early years of the Ramaz School. Yet here too, the archival record is not nearly as systematic or as comprehensive as a researcher would hope. Taken as a whole, the data tend to be weighted toward the latter part of Rabbi Lookstein's tenure—during the 1960s and seventies—rather than provid-ing an ongoing chronicle of his interwar career. Sadly, the records of Look-stein's contemporary, Rabbi Leo Jung, and his synagogue, the Jewish Center, do not seem to have survived or, alternatively, remain inaccessible. A private col-lection of Jewish Center synagogue bulletins was made available, as were scat-tered organizational minutes and drafts of Rabbi Jung's sermons and public addresses, dating from the 1920s.

Ironically enough, some of the most helpful information in reconstructing the Orthodox experience has come from a most unlikely source: the pen of the Reconstructionist founder, Rabbi Mordecai M. Kaplan. His multivolume hand-written diaries, in the collection of the Jewish Theological Seminary, were compiled over more than half a century, from 1914 through 1971 (!), and record Kaplan's intimate knowledge of behavior among New York's Orthodox bour-geoisie. Having served that community, in one capacity or another, for much of the pre–World War I and immediately postwar eras, Kaplan had much to say about his erstwhile congregants. His sharp-tongued, acerbic impressions of personalities, events, and institutions not only make for wonderful reading but provide a vivid, fresh, and hitherto unquoted perspective on Orthodox life of the time. Joseph H. Lookstein's far milder unpublished autobiography, "God

Owes Me Nothing," offers a less vitriolic, but still personal, first-hand perspective on the emerging New York Orthodox experience.

The Anglo-Jewish and Yiddish press provided a continuous source of information, especially the sympathetic *Hebrew Standard*, a weekly English-language newspaper, and the *Jewish Forum*, a monthly magazine that saw itself as "the voice of cultured orthodoxy." Chronicling the cultural, religious, and recreational interests of New York's Orthodox Jewry, or editorializing on one or another aspect of institutional affairs, the two periodicals were invaluable to this study. Often overlooked by students of American Jewish history, the *Hebrew Standard* and the *Jewish Forum* reveal, in considerable detail, the complexities of the modern Jewish urban experience. The *Orthodox Union* and its successor, *Jewish Life*, the *Jewish Outlook*, *Mizrachi Women's News*, and the published proceedings of the Union of Orthodox Jewish Congregations of America and the Rabbinical Council of America reflect the slightly more parochial concerns of American Orthodoxy's leading lay, Zionist, and rabbinic interests, although at times they too contained much helpful material on prevailing religious practice. The pages of *Jewish Education*, a professional journal for American Jewish educators, were replete with information on the then-dominant supplementary school system of Jewish education and fairly bristle with hostility toward the Jewish day or parochial school. Published marriage guides suggested the unlimited possibilities of wedding traditional rites with modern hygiene.

Finally, this study made extensive use of oral-historical information culled over a five-year period from interviews with a great many of the participants in New York's Orthodox community prior to World War II. Lasting generally two or more hours, each interview ranged over such topics as ritual performance, synagogue seating patterns, lay-rabbinic relations, Jewish education, recreational pursuits, and, perhaps most important of all, community gossip. With few exceptions, virtually everyone who was interviewed freely shared his or her memories—and opinions—of past events and personalities. The insights and observations of those who, on both the grass-roots and institutional levels of New York's Orthodox life, fashioned its religious culture greatly enhanced this study.

Abbreviations

AH	*American Hebrew*
CJI	Central Jewish Institute
HS	*Hebrew Standard*
JF	*Jewish Forum*
JTS	Jewish Theological Seminary
KJ	Kehilath Jeshurun
OU	*Orthodox Union*
PAJHS	*Proceedings of the American Jewish Historical Society*
RCA	Rabbinical Council of America
RIETS	Rabbi Isaac Elchanan Theological Seminary
UOJCA	Union of Orthodox Jewish Congregations of America

154

Notes

INTRODUCTION

1. Natalie Gittelson, "American Jews Rediscover Orthodoxy," *New York Times Magazine*, September 30, 1984; see also Edward Shapiro, "Orthodoxy in Pleasantdale," *Judaism* 34 (Spring 1985): 163–170; C. Jakobson, "The New Orthodox," *New York*, November 17, 1986, pp. 52–60.

2. Joseph H. Lookstein, "The Place of the Rabbinical Council in the American Rabbinate," typescript, n.d., p. 3, KJ Archives; see also Joseph H. Lookstein, "Orthodox Judaism," in *Fireside Discussion Group of the Anti-Defamation League* (New York, 1940), p. 9.

3. Bernard Drachman, *The Unfailing Light* (New York, 1948), p. 279.

4. Quoted in Elias Solomon, "Downtown Synagogues," manuscript, n.d., p. 17, JTS Archives.

5. Leo Jung, "Modern Trends in Judaism," in *Jubilee Publication of the Mizrachi Organization of America*, ed. Pinchos Churgin and Leon Gellman (New York, 1936), p. 38.

6. Max Etra, "President's Report," 1943, KJ Minutes.

7. "A New Era in American Jewish Life," *JF* 11, no. 5 (May 1928): 238.

8. Mordecai M. Kaplan Diaries, September 13, 1914. All quotations from Kaplan's diaries appear courtesy of the Library of the Jewish Theological Seminary of America. Charles Liebman, "Religion, Class and Culture in American Jewish History," *Jewish Journal of Sociology* 9, no. 2 (December 1967): 230.

9. Mordecai M. Kaplan Diaries, January 3, 1929.

10. "The Advance of Orthodox Judaism," *HS*, June 14, 1907, p. 8.

11. Quoted in the *Jewish Gazette*, June 17, 1898, p. 2.

12. Many Jews of this period were what might be called "accidental" Orthodox Jews. Oftentimes living in neighborhoods where the absence of a Conservative synagogue forced them to choose between a familiar Orthodox synagogue or a more foreign and daunting Reform congregation, they became members of Orthodox synagogues. Orthodox Jews by dint of convenience or circumstance, they are not the focus of this study.

13. See, for example, Jeffrey Gurock, *The Men and Women of Yeshiva: Higher Education, Orthodoxy, and American Judaism* (New York, 1988), and Steven M. Lowenstein *Frankfurt on the Hudson: The German-Jewish Community of Washington Heights, 1933–38, Its Structure and Culture* (Detroit, 1989).

14. See, for example, Jenna Weissman Joselit, "Modern Orthodox Jews and the Ordeal of Civility," *American Jewish History* 74, no. 2 (December 1984): 133–42; Samuel Heilman, *Synagogue Life: A Study in Symbolic Interaction* (Chicago, 1975); and William Helmreich, *The World of the Yeshiva: An Intimate Portrait of Orthodox Jewry* (New York, 1982).

15. Meyer Waxman, "American Orthodoxy—The Fifth Unknowable," *JF* 8, no. 10 (October 1924): 650.

16. Joseph H. Lookstein, "Problems of the Orthodox Rabbinate," typescript, n.d., p. 12, KJ Archives.

17. *JF* 4, no. 2 (February 1921): 719.

18. Edward S. Shapiro, "The Missing Element: Nathan Glazer and Modern Orthodoxy," *American Jewish History* 77, no. 2 (December 1987): 268.

19. Marshall Sklare, *Conservative Judaism: An American Religious Movement* (New York, 1972), p. 73.

20. Benny Kraut, *"American Judaism*: An Appreciative Critical Appraisal," *American Jewish History* 77, no. 2 (December 1987): 220.

21. Sklare, *Conservative Judaism*, p. 266.

22. *Jewish Outlook* 4, no. 3 (November 1939).

1. THE "REASONABLE" ORTHODOX

1. Samuel Levy, "Orthodox Jewry Rises to the Occasion," *Yeshiva University, Historical Souvenir Journal*, 1925, p. 1.

2. Ibid., p. 2.

3. A. A. Roback, "The Rise of Orthodox Influence in America," *JF* 8, no. 8 (September 1925): 396; "The Yeshivah's Surprising Success," *JF* 7, no. 12 (December 1924): 759.

4. Ibid.

5. Jonathan Sarna, ed., *People Walk on Their Heads: Moses Weinberger's Jews and Judaism in New York* (New York, 1982), pp. 5–6.

6. "Seventieth Anniversary of the Beth Ha-Midrash Ha-Gadol," *JF* 4, no. 6 (October 1921): 975.

7. Ray Stannard Baker, *The Spiritual Unrest* (New York, 1909), p. 101.

8. Quoted in the *Jewish Gazette*, June 17, 1898, p. 2.

9. Baker, *Spiritual Unrest*, p. 117.

10. Moses Rischin, *The Promised City: New York Jews, 1870–1914* (New York, 1962), p. 146.

11. Quoted in the *Jewish Gazette*, June 17, 1898, p. 2.

12. One of the issues that bedevil historians of American Jewish religious behavior is when to date the emergence of Conservative Judaism. Moshe Davis's book, *The Emergence of Conservative Judaism* (Philadelphia, 1963), suggests a mid-nineteenth century origin for that denomination. In his review of that work, Charles Liebman argued that those Davis placed within the Conservative camp were to be seen more accurately as Orthodox Jews. See Charles Liebman, "Orthodoxy in Nineteenth-Century America," *Tradition* 6, no. 2 (Spring/Summer 1964): 132–40. Most recently, Jonathan Sarna's re-evaluation of the Reform Pittsburgh Platform of 1885 points to the existence of a community of traditionally oriented American Jews even at that time. See "New Light on the Pittsburgh Platform," *American Jewish History* 76, no. 3 (March 1987): 358–68.

13. Rev. Meldola De Sola, *Jewish Ministers?: An Arraignment of American Reform Judaism* (New York, 1905), p. 31.

14. Ibid., p. 28.

15. Rev. Meldola De Sola, "The Duty of Orthodox Congregations," 1887, p. 15; reprinted in *Jewish Ministers*.

16. Jacob Katz, "Orthodoxy in Historical Perspective," in *Studies in Contemporary Jewry*, vol. 2 (Bloomington, Ind., 1986), p. 4.

17. J. H. Hertz quoted in "Conference Thoughts," *Jewish Gazette*, June 24, 1898, p. 2.

18. Joseph H. Lookstein quoted in "What's in a Name," *Jewish Life* 19, no. 6 (July/ August 1952): 3.

19. Leo Jung, *What is Orthodox Judaism?* (New York, 1929), p. 5.

20. Joseph H. Lookstein, "Orthodox Judaism: The Name and its Implications," in *Fireside Discussion Group of the Anti-Defamation League* (New York, 1940), p. 1.

21. "What's in a Name," p. 4.

22. *American Israelite* 34, no. 12 (September 1887): 4. The synagogue's dedication exercises were something else: noisy, disorderly, and rambunctious. "I wish I could speak as favorably of the dedication exercises," the newspaper's reporter declared, as he pointed to the prevailing lack of decorum. "This, I regret to say, cannot be done." Not only did the noise emanating from the men's and women's sections "baffle all description," but the program's musical selections "were not from Beethoven, but from some operetta, suiting well enough the behavior of the audience, but not becoming the sacred place." The only saving grace, as far as the *American Israelite* was concerned, was the performance of the cantor, who "recited very well and did not rock himself too much during the Eighteen Benedictions."

23. Gerard R. Wolfe and Jo Renée Fine, *The Synagogues of New York's Lower East Side* (New York, 1978), p. 90.

24. On its history, see Abraham Karp, "New York Chooses a Chief Rabbi," *American Jewish Historical Society* 44 (March 1955): 129–98, especially p. 136. See also Jenna Weissman Joselit, "What Happened to New York's 'Jewish Jews'?: Moses Rischin's *The Promised City* Revisited," *American Jewish History* 73, no. 2 (December 1983): 163–72.

25. "The Orthodox Congregational Union," *Jewish Gazette*, June 17, 1898, p. 1. Detailed coverage of conference proceedings was furnished by this newspaper, the English supplement of *Judisches Tageblatt*.

26. Ibid., p. 2.

27. "Report of the Committee on Organization," *Jewish Gazette*, June 17, 1898, p. 2.

28. "Union of Orthodoxy," *AH*, January 4, 1901, p. 228.

29. De Sola, *Jewish Ministers*, p. 33.

30. Quoted in "Committee on Organization," p. 2.

31. "Our Position," *Jewish Gazette*, June 24, 1898, p. 1.

32. An eminently workable solution to a nettlesome and emotionally charged issue, the presence of a Yiddish translator at the OU's first general convention in 1901 engendered rather negative comment on the part of one less than sympathetic reporter. Somewhat snidely, he noted that not only were "English speaking orthodox Jews but few in number," but that "few of the delegates present understood enough of the English language to enable them to discuss the questions presented." "Union of Orthodox Congregations," *AH*, January 4, 1901, p. 235. A week after this report appeared, the *American Hebrew* carried a letter from a convention delegate who took great exception to that paper's "unfriendly" coverage of the event. See Albert Lucas, Letter to the Editor, *AH*, January 11, 1901, pp. 257–58.

33. "Report of the President—H. Pereira Mendeṣ," in *Sixth Annual Convention, UOJCA*, June 29, 1913, p. 19.

34. See, for example, Herbert S. Goldstein, "A Year of Orthodoxy," *JF* 8, no. 10 (December 1925): 557–65.

35. David De Sola Pool, "Forty Years of American Orthodoxy," *OU* 5, no. 6 (March 1938): 4.

36. "Where is the Union?" *JF* 13, no. 1 (January 1930): 3.

37. Rabbinical Council of America, *Rabbinic Registry* (New York, 1945). See also *Rabbinic Registry* (New York, 1949) for a listing of those Orthodox rabbis in service during the immediate postwar era.

38. *HS*, August 5, 1904, p. 11.

39. *HS*, April 23, 1909, p. 5; June 3, 1904, p. 14.

40. *HS*, January 13, 1911, p. 7. Prior to his stint as cantor of the Henry Street Synagogue, Rev. Herlands had served briefly as the cantor of the Eldridge Street Synagogue. Minutes of the Eldridge Street Synagogue, December 20, 1893, vol. 1, pp. 120, 122–24.

41. *Judisches Tageblatt*, March 9, 1906, p. 10; see also *HS*, March 17, 1905, p. 14.

42. Kate Claghorn, "The Foreign Immigrant in New York City," in *Report of the United States Industrial Commission on Immigration*, (Washington 1901), vol. 15, p. 477.

43. Quoted in the *Thirtieth Annual Report and Yearbook of the YMHA*, 1904, p. 68.

44. Claghorn, "The Foreign Immigrant," p. 477.

45. Minutes of the Eldridge Street Synagogue, April 23, 1903, vol. 2, p. 377; July 1, 1909, vol. 2, p. 498; July 22, 1909, vol. 2, pp. 499–501; December 21, 1909, vol. 2, pp. 509–10; April 23, 1911, vol. 2, p. 510; April 30, 1911, vol. 2, pp. 511–14.

46. Herbert S. Goldstein, ed., *Forty Years of Struggle for a Principle: The Biography of Harry Fischel* (New York, 1928), p. 57.

47. "Observations on the East Side," typescript report, June 1941, p. 2. Works Progress Administration. Historical Records Survey. Federal Writers Project. "Jews of New York." The New York City Municipal Archives.

48. Maurice Samuel, *The Gentleman and the Jew* (New York, 1950), p. 103.

49. Aaron Frankel, "Back to Eighty-Sixth Street," *Commentary*, August 1946, p. 171.

50. *Jewish Center Bulletin*, February 15, 1946, p. 4.

51. Isaac Berkson, *Theories of Americanization* (New York, 1920), p. 183.

52. Mordecai M. Kaplan Diaries, July 24, 1923. Kaplan was not always given to such negative opinions of the middle-class American Jew. Extremely fond of A. E. Rothstein, one of the founders of the West Side Jewish Center, whose son, Arnold, went on to become one of the interwar period's most renowned Jewish criminals, Kaplan wrote of him that "if the bourgeoisie can produce saints, he certainly is one." Mordecai M. Kaplan Diaries, April 10, 1915.

53. Baker, *Spiritual Unrest*, p. 112.

54. Mordecai M. Kaplan Diaries, April 21, 1918.

55. Delmore Schwartz, "Shenandoah," in *Poetic Drama*, ed. Alfred Kreymborg (New York, 1941), p. 843. See also James Atlas, *Delmore Schwartz: The Life of an American Poet* (New York, 1977), especially pp. 4–5, 188. Atlas quotes Schwartz as having believed that he possessed a "Washington Heights view of our time and country."

56. Interviews with Mr. Isaac Friedman and Mr. Hyman Bucher.

57. Roback, "Rise of Orthodox Influence," pp. 394, 396.

58. *Jewish Gazette*, June 17, 1898, p. 2.

59. "Jews Who Have Made Their Mark," *HS*, October 27, 1916, pp. 10–13; December 1, 1916, p. 10.

60. Goldstein, *Forty Years*, p. 57.

61. Mordecai M. Kaplan Diaries, September 13, 1914.

62. Harry Fischel, Foreword to Goldstein, *Forty Years*, p. xvii.

63. Favorable comments on the book, like those of Rabbi Hertz, were collated and reprinted in a section entitled "Comments" that preceded the book's table of contents.

64. Gaylord S. White, "The Upper East Side—Its Neglect and Its Needs," *Charities* 12, no. 29 (July 16, 1904): 748.

65. Ibid., p. 749. See also Walter Laidlaw, *Statistical Sources for Demographic Studies of Greater New York*, vol. 1 (New York, 1910); Caroline Moore, "How Can Yorkville Survive? The Effect of a Luxury Building Boom on an Old-World Community" (Master's thesis, Columbia University School of Architecture, 1969).

66. Will Irwin, "The Melting Pot of the Rich," in *Highlights of Manhattan* (New York, 1926–27), p. 221.

67. Transcript of the Stenographic Minutes of the Board of Directors, CJI, November 12, 1925, p. 3.

68. Albert Wald to Samuel Ungerleider and S. G. Rosenbaum, November 26, 1928, Harry Fischel Collection, Agudath Israel of America Archives.

69. Interview of Joseph H. Lookstein by Dr. Elmer Offenbacher, 1975.

70. "Observations on the East Side," p. 6; see also "Our Own Women: Mrs. Edward Epstein," *United Synagogue Recorder* 6, no. 2 (March 1926).

71. Transcript of Stenographic Minutes, CJI, p. 6; "Report of the Talmud Torah Committee," CJI, January 7, 1926. Caroline Fajans, untitled ten-page typescript, December 1940, p. 1. Works Progress Administration. "Jews of New York. Population."

72. "Membership Meeting," KJ Minutes, April 26, 1921.

73. KJ Roundtable Discussion, November 10, 1987; Joseph H. Lookstein's "Sabbath Service Impression Notecards," KJ Archives.

74. KJ Minutes, January 21, 1943.

75. KJ Minutes, May 22, 1947.

76. Mordecai M. Kaplan Diaries, December 14, 1952. See also Selma C. Berrol, "The Jewish West Side of New York City, 1920–1970," *Journal of Ethnic Studies* 13, no. 4 (1987): 21–45.

77. Quoted in James Trager, *West of Fifth: The Rise and Fall and Rise of Manhattan's West Side* (New York, 1987), p. 5.

78. Quoted in Jeffrey Gurock, *When Harlem Was Jewish, 1870–1930* (New York, 1979), p. 153.

79. Mordecai M. Kaplan Diaries, October 26, 1922.

80. Frankel, "Back to Eighty-Sixth Street," p. 170.

81. Ruth Sapin Hurwitz, "The Emigres," *Menorah Journal* 44 (Spring 1956): 96.

82. Four-page typescript report, May 19, 1941, p. 3. Works Progress Administration. "Jews of New York, Population."

83. Ibid., p. 4. Washington Heights, in upper Manhattan, was the site of another large-scale German Jewish colony during the thirties. In what became known, somewhat ironically, as the "Fourth Reich," the members of the Frankfurt am Main Orthodox community, under the leadership of Rabbi Dr. Joseph Breuer, reconstructed the highly elaborated communal structure characteristic of the Hirsch community. Keeping very much to themselves, the members of the Breuer community developed an independent network of Orthodox educational and religious institutions, including its own supply of kosher meat and food products. The history of the Breuer community, which was less an American social phenomenon than a transplanted European one, lies outside the scope of this book. It is, however, treated in Steven M. Lowenstein, *Frankfurt on the Hudson: The German-Jewish Community of Washington Heights, 1933–38, Its Structure and Culture* (Detroit, 1989).

84. Mordecai M. Kaplan Diaries, November 14, 1952.

85. Interview of Joseph H. Lookstein by Dr. Elmer Offenbacher, 1975; author's interview with Dr. Bender of Bar-Ilan University.

86. Interviews with Mrs. Sylvia Kramer; Irma and Clarence Horwitz.

87. Joseph Kaminetsky, "Boro Park," *Jewish Life* 21, no. 1 (September/October 1953): 19.

88. Oral history interview with Harold C. Wilkenfeld, November 29, 1973, conducted by Mrs. Evelyn Greenberg for the Oral History Program at the University of Maryland, p. 2. I would like to thank Mrs. Greenberg for making this transcript available to me.

89. Walter Goodman, "The Hasidim Come to Williamsburg," *Commentary*, March 1955, p. 269; "Table Showing the Distribution and Salient Characteristics of Synagogues in the Eighteen Kehillah Districts," *The Jewish Communal Register of New York City, 1917–*

1918 (New York, 1918), p. 123. See also Gershuni, "A Daitcher in Williamsburg," *Jewish Life* 21, no. 2 (November/December 1953): 17.

90. Wilkenfeld interview, p. 4.

91. George Kranzler, *Williamsburg: A Jewish Community in Transition* (New York, 1961), p. 40.

92. Ibid., p. 62.

93. Wilkenfeld interview, pp. 20–21.

94. Quoted in Kranzler, *Williamsburg*, p. 17.

95. Wilkenfeld interview, p. 19.

96. Gershuni, "Daitcher in Williamsburg," p. 17; Kranzler, *Williamsburg*, p. 37.

97. Isaac Marks, "The Phenomenal Growth of Borough Park," *JF* 7, no. 4 (April 1924): 240–41; G. S. Roth, "Philanthropy in Borough Park," *JF* 7, no. 4 (April 1924): 266–67.

98. Marks, "The Phenomenal Growth"; Joseph Barondess, "Achievements and Failings of Borough Park," *JF* 7, no. 4 (April 1924): 243.

99. Roth, "Philanthropy," p. 267.

100. Ibid.; Marks, "The Phenomenal Growth," p. 241.

101. Kaminetsky, "Boro Park," p. 23.

102. Interview with Professors Naomi Churgin Miller and Bathia Churgin.

103. Katz, "Orthodoxy in Historical Perspective," p. 4.

104. Ibid., p. 5.

105. Joseph H. Cohen quoted in Mordecai M. Kaplan Diaries, July 30, 1950.

106. Mordecai M. Kaplan Diaries, August 25, 1917.

107. Transcript of interview with Mr. Lawrence Kobrin, Ramaz School Oral History Project, 1986; author's interview with Rabbi Louis Engelberg.

108. Transcript of interview with Mrs. Hortense Kobrin, Ramaz School Oral History Project, 1986, pp. 2, 4. For parallels with British Jewry, see Steven Singer, "Jewish Religious Observance in Early Victorian London, 1840–1860," *Jewish Journal of Sociology* 28, no. 2 (December 1986): 117–37.

109. Transcript of interview with Rabbi Haskel Lookstein, Ramaz School Oral History Project, 1986, p. 2.

110. Ibid.

111. Ibid.; interviews with Mrs. Gertrude Lookstein, Professor Nathalie Lookstein Friedman. One New York Orthodox resident of the time recalls hearing that Ramaz students were instructed during fire drills to remove their head coverings before proceeding outside. Though perhaps apocryphal, the story points to the seriousness with which Rabbi Lookstein viewed the public display of one's religious identity. Interview with Mrs. Irma Horwitz.

112. Aesthetic considerations may have also played some part in the collective decision not to don a *yarmulke* publicly. Before the emergence of the knitted *yarmulke* or *kippah*, an Israeli invention, ritual head coverings were rather ungainly and unattractive items. Made out of a cheap rayon material, they were often several sizes too large and perched awkwardly on small heads. On the Israeli knitted *yarmulke*, see Suzanne Baizerman, "The Kippa Sruga as Cultural Artifact," (Student paper, The University of Minnesota, Department of Textiles and Clothing, 1982). I would like to thank Ms. Baizerman for sharing her work in progress.

113. Trude Weiss-Rosmarin, "Where Orthodox Jewry Has Failed," *Jewish Spectator*, June 1944, p. 7.

114. Mordecai M. Kaplan Diaries, June 26, 1923. Interview with Clarence and Irma Horwitz.

115. Mordecai M. Kaplan Diaries, April 10, 1915; September 13, 1914.

116. Interview with Mr. Clarence Horwitz.

117. Interview with Judith Gottesman Friedman. Inevitably, a comparison with the founders of Conservative Jewry suggests itself. Before such comparisons can be fully developed, one needs to know more about the first generation of Conservative Jews in New York. The available extant information, however, suggests a number of linkages between the two denominations, in some instances personal and familial links and in still others institutional ones. Surely it is no coincidence that the founder of the Jewish Center, Joseph H. Cohen, and Louis Cohen, founder of the Brooklyn Jewish Center, one of the interwar period's leading Conservative synagogues, were brothers; both modernized Orthodoxy and Conservative Judaism, it seems, drew on the same population. What's more, talk of merger between the Jewish Theological Seminary and Yeshiva's RIETS during the twenties suggests a kind of fluidity, on the institutional level, between the two denominations. Mordecai Kaplan, following a meeting with JTS president Cyrus Adler, related that a number of Orthodox Jews had raised the possibility of a merger with JTS or, in Kaplan's words, "intimated the possibility of a rapprochement between the Seminary and the Yeshiva." The former Orthodox rabbi was considerably shaken by the prospect of a potential alliance by the two institutions and confided in his diary: "O ye Gods! That's all I need." Mordecai M. Kaplan Diaries, June 27, 1925; March 10, 1926. For Yeshiva's perspective, see Aaron Rakeffet-Rothkoff, "The Attempt to Merge the Jewish Theological Seminary and Yeshiva College, 1926–27," *Michael: On the History of the Jews in the Diaspora* 5, no. 3 (1975): 254–79.

2. "BIGGER AND BETTER" ORTHODOX SYNAGOGUES

1. "Cornerstone Laying," *HS*, May 9, 1902, p. 4; "Laying of the Cornerstone of Kehilath Jeshurun," *AH*, May 9, 1902, p. 750; "Programme at the Laying of the Corner Stone, Congregation Kehilath Jeshurun," Sunday, May 4, 1902.

2. "Kehilath Jeshurun Cornerstone and Jacob H. Schiff," *HS*, May 9, 1902, p. 6.

3. Mordecai M. Kaplan Diaries, February 7, 1959; *AH*, September 12, 1902, p. 473; WPA, Historical Records Survey, Federal Writers Project, Inventory of Records and Churches: Congregation Kehilath Jeshurun, New York City Municipal Archives, Box 3751.

In 1910, KJ expanded by acquiring two adjoining brownstones, which it subsequently tore down to make room for a new "Community House." Over thirty years later, the congregation embarked on extensive architectural alterations to upgrade and modernize its overutilized and somewhat run-down facilities. When all the renovations are completed, wrote Lookstein to a congregant, "we will have a cathedral synagogue." The substitution of a direct, street-level entrance into KJ for the more traditional double-sided stairwell was perhaps the most dramatic of these alterations. See Joseph H. Lookstein to Renee Margareten, October 22, 1947, KJ Archives.

4. *HS*, May 9, 1902, p. 4.

5. Sarah Schack, "O'Leary's Shul—and Others," *Menorah Journal* 16, no. 5 (May 1929): 464.

6. Ibid.; Interview with Mrs. Iris Spiro, October 21, 1987; Mordecai M. Kaplan Diaries, January 25, 1914.

7. *OU* 3, no. 8 (May 1936): 1.

8. "Remarks of Rabbi David de Sola Pool," KJ Minutes, May 13, 1947.

9. "An Interview with Rabbi A. Landesman," May 1941, typescript, p. 3, Works Progress Administration, The Jews of New York, Population: Brooklyn, New York Municipal Archives; Schack, "O'Leary's Shul," pp. 462–63.

10. Schack, "O'Leary's Shul," p. 463.

11. Ibid.

12. Elias Solomon, "Downtown Synagogues," manuscript, n.d., p. 4, Elias Solomon Collection, JTS Archives. Sometime prior to World War I, Elias Solomon, then a young Seminary rabbinical student, wrote what is perhaps the fullest and most incisive extant critique of the "downtown" immigrant synagogue. See also Rabbi Leo Jung, "The Jews and Jewishness in America, Part Two," *JF* 9, no. 5 (July 1926): 275.

13. *AH*, September 12, 1902, p. 473.

14. De Sola Pool, "Remarks." See also Ray Stannard Baker, *The Spiritual Unrest* (New York, 1909), chap. 3, especially pp. 101–41; Charles Bernheimer, *The Russian Jew in the United States* (Philadelphia, 1905), pp. 149–55.

15. "Article Two: Membership," By-laws of the Congregation Kehilath Jeshurun, 1903, pp. 3–4, KJ Archives. See also "Privileges of Membership in Congregation Kehilath Jeshurun," KJ Minutes, May 18, 1944.

16. Aaron Frankel, "Back to Eighty-Sixth Street," *Commentary*, August 1946, p. 170.

17. Mordecai M. Kaplan Diaries, November 11, 1917.

18. Ibid., November 10, 1950; November 11, 1917.

19. Recalled by Mordecai M. Kaplan Diaries, January 4, 1914.

20. Herbert S. Goldstein, "The Younger Orthodox Rabbis in America," *HS*, June 18, 1915, p. 2.

21. Joseph Kaminetsky, "Boro Park," *Jewish Life* 21, no. 1 (September–October 1953): 20. Temple Beth-El, Kaminetsky wrote, "is a 'temple' only by virtue of its gala physical appearance; it is one hundred percent orthodox."

22. Mordecai M. Kaplan Diaries, February 7, 1959.

23. Quoted by Aaron Rothkoff, "The Sojourns of Ridbaz: Religious Problems within the Immigrant Community," *PAJHS* 57, no. 4 (June 1968): 561–62; Mordecai M. Kaplan Diaries, April 24, 1966.

24. *HS*, October 7, 1904, p. 7. For one congregant's understanding of the contretemps, see "Communications," *AH*, October 7, 1904, p. 549.

25. *AH*, September 30, 1904, p. 516.

26. Mordecai M. Kaplan Dairies, January 17, 1929. On Kaplan's tenure at KJ, see Mel Scult, "Controversial Beginnings: Kaplan's First Congregation," *The Reconstructionist*, July–August 1985, pp. 21–26.

27. M. M. Kaplan, "Affiliation with the Synagogue," *Jewish Communal Register of New York City, 1917–1918* (New York, 1918), pp. 121–22; "Table Showing the Distribution of Synagogues in the Various Kehillah Districts and also the Salient Features of those Synagogues," *Jewish Communal Register*, p. 123.

28. Ibid.

29. Quoted in *AH*, December 9, 1904.

30. Mordecai M. Kaplan Diaries, October 25, 1914.

31. Bernard Shientag, "Rabbi Joseph H. Lookstein: A Character Study by a Congregant," in *Congregation Kehilath Jeshurun Diamond Jubilee Yearbook*, 1946, p. 55.

32. Joseph H. Lookstein, "God Owes Me Nothing," typescript, p. 288.

33. Alexander Altmann, "The New Style of Preaching in Nineteenth-Century German Jewry," *Studies in Nineteenth-Century Jewish Intellectual History* (Cambridge, 1964), p. 101; Leo Jung, "Preaching and Teaching," in *Foundations of Judaism* (New York, 1923), p. 93.

34. Roundtable Discussion with KJ Congregants, November 10, 1987; interview with Rabbi and Mrs. Louis Engelberg, December 21, 1986.

35. Mordecai M. Kaplan Diaries, January 6, 1930; interview with Mr. Maurice Spanbock.

36. Jung, "Preaching and Teaching," p. 94.

37. H. Pereira Mendes quoted in Joseph H. Lookstein, "Dr. Revel and Homiletics: A Page of Yeshiva Memoirs," in *Hedenu, Jubilee Publication of the Students' Organization of RIETS* (New York, 1936), p. 62.

38. Rev. Dr. Louis A. Alexander to Moses Davis, November 1, 1903, KJ Archives. See also the author's "Of Manners, Morals and Orthodox Judaism: Decorum within the Orthodox Synagogue," in *Ramaz: School, Community, Scholarship, and Orthodoxy*, ed. Jeffrey Gurock (Hoboken, 1989).

39. "Remarks of Harry Fischel on the Fortieth Anniversary of His Membership in Congregation Kehilath Jeshurun," KJ Minutes, April 25, 1944. For parallels with German Jewish history, see Robert Liberles, *Religious Conflict in Social Context: The Resurgence of Orthodox Judaism in Frankfurt Am Main, 1838–1877* (Westport, Conn., 1985), especially pp. 141–46.

40. Solomon, "Downtown Synagogues," p. 3.

41. H. Pereira Mendes, "Current Problems of Orthodox Jewry," *OU* 1, no. 10 (June 1934): 1.

42. Solomon, "Downtown Synagogues," p. 10; *American Israelite* 34, no. 12 (September 1887): 4. I would like to thank the Eldridge Street Synagogue Restoration Project for sharing this document with me.

43. Solomon, "Downtown Synagogues," pp. 6–7.

44. Ibid., p. 11.

45. Irwin Edman, "Reuben Cohen Goes to Temple," *Menorah Journal* 14, no. 6 (June 1928): 528.

46. *HS*, December 29, 1905.

47. Solomon, "Downtown Synagogues," p. 10.

48. "Trustees Meeting," May 5, 1915, Minutes of the Eldridge Street Synagogue, p. 655.

49. See, for example, Stephen Brumberg, *Going to America, Going to School* (New York, 1986) for material on the incorporation of manners and morals into the New York public-school system curriculum. Anzia Yeserskia's semiautobiographical writings on immigrant life in New York colorfully reveal the importance attached to the proper use of knife and fork. Yezerskia's *Salome of the Tenements* (New York, 1922) is a vivid case in point.

50. A similar critique a century earlier led to the formation of the Reform movement in Western Europe. See, for example, David Philipson, *The Reform Movement in Judaism* (New York, 1931); Steven M. Lowenstein, "The 1840's and the Creation of the German-Jewish Reform Movement," in *Revolution and Evolution: 1848 in German-Jewish History* (Tübingen, 1981).

51. Moses Hoenig, "In Retrospect: Twenty Years of Young Israel," in *Young Israel Twentieth Anniversary Convention Annual*, 1932.

52. Leo Jung, "Jews and Jewishness in America," *JF* 9, no. 3 (May 1926): 132.

53. Joseph H. Lookstein, "Digest of Rabbi Lookstein's Address on Practical Rabbinics," typescript n.d., p. 1, KJ Archives.

54. Moishe Krumbein, quoted in *Twentieth Anniversary Convention Annual*, p. 17; see also Moses Hoenig, "Young Israel in the Community," *JF* 9, no. 10 (December 1926): 526, 528.

55. In one respect, though, the Young Israel was somewhat atypical: it lacked a rabbi. This was not so much a matter of anticlericalism as a reflection of the scarcity of suitable English-speaking, college-educated Orthodox rabbis.

56. Transcript of an Oral History Interview with Mr. Harold C. Wilkenfeld, November 29, 1973, pp. 11, 12, 13.

57. Harry G. Fromberg, "The Tremendous Triumph of East Side Young Jewry in Religious Revival," *HS*, January 18, 1918, p. 9.

58. Quoted in *Jewish Center Bulletin*, October 1935.

59. *HS*, August 14, 1914, p. 8.

60. See, for example KJ Minutes, December 7, 1942; September 27, 1943; *Jewish Center Bulletin*, November 17, 1951; *West Side Institutional Review*, September 20, 1940, p. 4; September 21, 1945, p. 4; Schack, "O'Leary's Shul," p. 464. Invariably, interviews with congregants of KJ or the Jewish Center touched on the centrality of proper dress. Interviews with Mrs. Gertrude Lookstein, Dr. Nathalie Friedman, Rabbi Haskel Lookstein, Mrs. Lillian Jacobs, Mrs. Lillian Leifert, and Mrs. Sylvia Kramer.

61. Joseph H. Lookstein to Mr. M. Most, March 12, 1946, KJ Archives.

62. "Notes on our Synagogue Service," *Jewish Center Bulletin*, November 17, 1951, p. 5; "For Dignity and Decorum at Religious Services," *OU* 7, no. 3 (December–January 1939/1940): 2. Some synagogues even extended the practice by maintaining a stock of jackets and ties to avoid potentially embarrassing situations of a more secular nature.

63. KJ Roundtable.

64. KJ Minutes, May 2, 1904; October 30, 1906.

65. Fischel, "Fortieth Anniversary."

66. *American Israelite* 34, no. 12 (September 1887): 4.

67. *Proceedings of the Rabbinical Association, Thirty-second Annual Convention*, 1932, p. 329.

68. KJ Minutes, December 4, 1930. See also David J. Putterman, "Congregational Singing," *Journal of Sacred Music* 1, no. 4 (September 1968): 23–26; Max Wohlberg, "Shiru Lo: Aspects of Congregational Singing," *Journal of Sacred Music* 13, no. 2 (January 1984): 35–43.

69. Joseph H. Lookstein, "Problems of the Orthodox Rabbinate," typescript, n.d., pp. 4–5. See also "New Features in the Sabbath Service," *KJ Bulletin*, November 18, 1938.

70. KJ Minutes, November 19, 1912; November 20, 1913; April 11, 1918. For parallels with English Jewry, see the *Jewish Chronicle*, February 19, 1904, pp. 6, 22; February 26, 1904.

"I wish to state that I was against the present method of abolishing the offerings at the beginning . . . [for] in my opinion it is a step toward Reform," Harry Fischel wrote to KJ's president, Jacob Hecht, in 1909. Apparently, Rabbi Margolies was able to persuade Fischel of the proposal's merits, for the philanthropist went on to note that "I am now thoroughly satisfied being that Rabbi Margolies has assured me that it is a benefit to Orthodoxy, instead of a step to Reform." Harry Fischel to Jacob Hecht, June 2, 1909, Harry Fischel Papers, Agudath Israel Archives.

71. "President's Report," KJ Minutes, 1943, p. 2; October 8, 1942.

72. Interview with Judith Gottesman Friedman, December 30, 1987.

73. See, for example, KJ Minutes, October 3, 1927; January 10, 1928.

74. Joseph H. Lookstein, "Digest of Rabbi Lookstein's Address on Practical Rabbinics," typescript, n.d., p. 2, KJ Archives.

75. Fischel, "Fortieth Anniversary."

76. KJ Minutes, December 3, 1906.

77. In his unpublished autobiography, Lookstein relates, in passing, that some of his older congregants referred to his innovations as "gimmicks." "God Owes Me Nothing," p. 258.

78. *KJ Bulletin*, October 1, 1937.

79. "President's Report," November 27, 1945, KJ Minutes.

80. So much so that former bastions of synagogue etiquette were forced publicly to spell out what constituted appropriate synagogue behavior and dress. "There is," observed the *Jewish Center Bulletin* in 1976, "a flagrant violation of etiquette," as it proceeded to define normative Center conduct: tie and jacket for the men, a scarf or hat for women ("A yarmulke," the bulletin explained, "is ludicrous"), and absolutely no sandals.

Talking during the service or exiting before its conclusion was also censured. An elaboration of institutional norms as well as a gentle rebuke, this kind of statement would have been thoroughly unnecessary a generation earlier. "Sanctuary Decorum," *Jewish Center Bulletin*, November 17, 1967, p. 4; "Proper Dress," *Jewish Center Bulletin*, April 2, 1976, p. 12.

81. Cynthia Ozick, "Toward a New Yiddish," in *Art and Ardor: Essays* (New York, 1983), p. 161.

82. "Kehilath Jeshurun—A Congregational Portrait," in *Diamond Jubilee Yearbook*, pp. 93–96.

83. Mordecai M. Kaplan Diaries, March 19, 1957.

84. "The Significance of the Jewish Center," typescript draft of what appears to have been a promotional brochure, n.d., p. 6, Jewish Center Archives. See also "Jewish Center Activities Membership," *Jewish Center Bulletin*, January 24, 1947, p. 5.

85. "Significance of the Jewish Center," p. 8.

86. "Congregational Portrait," p. 94.

87. Ibid.

88. Ibid.

89. Ibid., p. 93. See also Leo Jung, "America and the Jew," Shearith Israel Thanksgiving Day Services, 1922, in Jung, *Foundations of Judaism*, p. 101.

90. Transcript of interview with Mr. Lawrence Kobrin, October 29, 1986, p. 6, Ramaz Oral History Project. I would like to thank Dr. Noam Shudofsky for sharing this material with me.

91. "Dedication of the Jewish Center," *HS*, March 15, 1918, p. 10A; "Significance of the Jewish Center," p. 5.

92. "Something New in Your Neighborhood," West Side Institutional Synagogue, ca. 1936, collection of Rabbi Moshe Morduchowitz. See also Aaron Reichel, *The Maverick Rabbi* (Norfolk, 1986), pp. 170–71.

93. "Vestry Rooms Being Remodelled," *KJ Bulletin*, January–February 1932, p. 2.

94. KJ Minutes, December 28, 1939.

95. Text reprinted in its entirety in Reichel, *Maverick Rabbi*, p. 198.

96. "Significance of the Jewish Center," p. 7.

97. KJ Minutes, May 22, 1947. For a recent study of the afternoon Hebrew school, see Barry Chazan, "Education in the Synagogue: The Transformation of the Supplementary School," in *The American Synagogue: A Sanctuary Transformed*, ed. Jack Wertheimer (Cambridge, Eng., 1987), pp. 170–84.

98. Interview with Mrs. Ami Texon, Roundtable Discussion with KJ Congregants, November 10, 1987. On the history of the American synagogue sisterhood, see the author's "The Special Sphere of the Middle-Class American Jewish Woman: The Synagogue Sisterhood," in Wertheimer, *The American Synagogue*, pp. 206–30.

99. Quoted in Mrs. Harry Etra, "Jewish Womanhood in Action—A History of the Kehilath Jeshurun Sisterhood," in *Diamond Jubilee Yearbook*, p. 40.

100. "The Kehilath Jeshurun Men's Club: What It Is and What It Does," reproduced in full in *OU* 13, no. 3 (March 1946): 2, 27.

101. Ibid.; interviews with Mr. Hy Bucher, a former men's club president, and Mrs. Gertrude Lookstein, for years president of the sisterhood. See also Ira F. Weisman, "The Kehilath Jeshurun Men's Club—History and Evaluation," in *Diamond Jubilee Yearbook*, pp. 44–46.

102. "Kehilath Jeshurun Men's Club," pp. 2, 27. As "dispensers of benevolence," the men's club and sisterhood often donated the proceeds from some of their events to extra-synagogal charitable causes such as a neighborhood clothing drive and war bonds. One former men's club president even intimated that in 1948 his organization contributed funds toward the purchase of arms for Israel.

103. Abraham Karp, "Overview: The Synagogue in America—A Historical Typology," in Wertheimer, *The American Synagogue*, p. 19.

104. Ibid., p. 20. For insight into the workings of the Conservative synagogue-center, see Deborah Dash Moore's study of the Brooklyn Jewish Center, "A Synagogue Grows in Brooklyn," in Wertheimer, *The American Synagogue*, pp. 297–326.

105. Wertheimer, *The American Synagogue*, p. 122.

106. Joseph H. Lookstein, "Problems of the Orthodox Rabbinate," typescript, n.d., pp. 9–10, KJ Archives.

107. "Annual Meeting, May 10, 1923. Order of Business," p. 2, Jewish Center Archives.

108. "Report of Rabbi Joseph H. Lookstein," KJ Minutes, January 20, 1944.

109. "Judaism in Practice: High Holy Days," *Jewish Center Bulletin*, September 11, 1947, pp. 6–7.

110. These entries were culled from the "Getting Personal" column of the *West Side Institutional Review* from September through December 1945.

111. Abraham N. AvRutnick, "The Synagogue Bulletin," *OU* 13, no. 4 (April 1946): 9.

112. Arthur Hertzberg, "The Changing American Rabbinate," *Midstream* 12, no. 1 (January 1966): 19.

113. Joseph H. Lookstein quoted in KJ Minutes, December 11, 1947.

114. KJ Minutes, April 3, 1929.

115. Mordecai M. Kaplan Diaries, July 27, 1920.

116. "Verbatim Report of Annual Meeting," The Jewish Center, May 10, 1923, p. 21, Jewish Center Archives.

117. Mordecai M. Kaplan Diaries, July 28, 1919.

118. Committee names were culled from the KJ Minutes, 1903–1950, and "Minutes of the Board of Trustees of the Jewish Center," September 16, 1931, Jewish Center Archives.

119. See, for example, Minutes of the Eldridge Street Synagogue, 1890–1916.

120. Minutes of the Eldridge Street Synagogue, February 8, 1891.

121. KJ Minutes, March 7, 1946.

122. See, for example, "Quarterly Members Meeting," KJ Minutes, June 21, 1927.

123. Strict rules, however, governed the collection of money generated through *shnuddering*. KJ Minutes in 1913 record the following: "No member is entitled to a refund or credit should his aggregate shnuddering during the year be less than his annual subscription." KJ Minutes, November 20, 1913.

124. See, for example, KJ Minutes, December 7, 1942; "President's Report," 1943, KJ Minutes. Concern over the possibility of diminished income animated, in part, Harry Fischel's opposition to the abolition of *shnuddering*. "It reduces the income of the 'Mashorshei Kehila' [congregational employees] to such an extent that it is impossible for them to make a living," he explained. See Harry Fischel to Jacob Hecht, June 2, 1909, Harry Fischel Papers, Agudath Israel of America Archives.

125. KJ Minutes, May 1, 1928.

126. "Features of the Memorial Tablet," *KJ Bulletin*, January–February 1932, p. 4.

127. "Samuel M. Kaplan Donates $3500.00 For Memorial Tablet," *KJ Bulletin*, January–February 1932, p. 1.

128. KJ Minutes, March 5, 1929; "President's Report, 1943," KJ Minutes.

129. KJ Minutes, November 27, 1945.

130. Joseph H. Lookstein, "Talk Delivered Before the New York Board of Rabbis," typescript, n.d., p. 13, KJ Archives.

3. "AN UTTERLY NOVEL PHENOMENON"

1. *JF* 2, no. 4 (April 1919): 827.

2. "The Rabbi Isaac Elchanan Yeshibah," *JF* 2, no. 4 (April 1919): 863.

3. Jeffrey Gurock, "Resisters and Accommodators: Varieties of Orthodox Rabbis in America," *American Jewish Archives* 35, no. 2 (November 1983): 100.

4. *JF* 2, no. 4 (April 1919): 827-28.

5. Joseph Hartstein, "Yeshiva University," *American Jewish Yearbook* 48 (1946-47): 74.

6. Gilbert Klaperman, *The Story of Yeshiva University* (New York, 1969), p. 53.

7. "Excerpts from an Address Delivered by Joseph H. Lookstein at a Rabbinic Alumni Convention of Yeshiva University," October 10, 1961, KJ Archives.

8. The definitive biography of Dr. Revel is written by Aaron Rakeffet-Rothkoff, *Bernard Revel: Builder of American Jewish Orthodoxy* (New York, 1981, revised edition).

9. Occasionally, Revel's ambivalence toward a modern rabbinical seminary would surface. See Rakeffet-Rothkoff, *Bernard Revel*, especially pp. 268-75.

10. Quoted in Herbert Goldstein, ed., *Forty Years of Struggle for a Principle: The Biography of Harry Fischel* (New York, 1928), p. 163.

11. H. Pereira Mendes, "Orthodox Judaism: The Past and the Future of the Orthodox Congregations of America," *JF* 2, no. 9 (September 1919): 1171.

12. Klaperman, *Story of Yeshiva University*, p. 140.

13. Joseph H. Lookstein, "Dr. Revel and Homiletics: A Page of Yeshiva Memoirs," in *Hedenu: Jubilee Publication of the Students' Organization of RIETS and Yeshiva College* (New York, 1936), pp. 61-62.

14. Ibid., p. 63.

15. Despite the belief that JTS and RIETS were, in effect, different sides of the same coin and despite frequent talk of merger between the two institutions, talk that surfaced periodically throughout the twenties and early thirties, the boundaries and denominational divisions between the two institutions began to harden during Revel's prewar tenure.

16. Mordecai M. Kaplan Diaries, December 31, 1944.

17. Mendes, "Orthodox Judaism," pp. 1166, 1171.

18. Mordecai M. Kaplan Diaries, July 16, 1917.

19. *JF* 2, no. 4 (April 1919): 827.

20. Arthur Hertzberg, "The Changing American Rabbinate," *Midstream* 12, no. 1 (January 1966): 29.

21. Quoted in Klaperman, *Story of Yeshiva University*, p. 208.

22. See Marsha Rozenblit, "The Ideology of the Modern Rabbi," manuscript; Ismar Schorsch, "Emancipation and the Crisis of Religious Authority—The Emergence of the Modern Rabbinate," in *Revolution and Evolution: 1848 in German-Jewish History*, ed. Werner E. Mosse, Arnold Paucker, and Reinhold Rurup (Tübingen, 1981), pp. 205-47.

23. *American Israelite* 34, no. 12 (September 1887): 4.

24. Quoted in Joseph H. Lookstein, "God Owes Me Nothing," manuscript, p. 254.

25. Mordecai M. Kaplan Diaries, October 13, 1961.

26. Lookstein, "God Owes Me Nothing," p. 46. Interviews with Rabbis Leo Jung, Herschel Schacter, Louis Engelberg, and Haskel Lookstein.

27. Leo Jung, *The Path of a Pioneer: The Autobiography of Leo Jung* (London and New York, 1980), p. 47; Israel Goldstein, "The Rabbinical Assembly—An Appraisal," in *Proceedings of the Rabbinical Assembly* (1927), p. 35.

28. Aaron I. Reichel, *The Maverick Rabbi* (Norfolk, 1984), p. 44.

29. Herbert S. Goldstein, "The Younger Orthodox Rabbis in America," *HS*, June 18,

1915, p. 1. See also Reichel, *Maverick Rabbi*, a full-length and highly partisan biography of one of the architects of the modernized Orthodox rabbinate in New York.

30. Goldstein, *Forty Years*, p. 1. (My emphasis.)

31. Interview with Rabbi Louis Engelberg, December 21, 1986.

32. Quoted in Reichel, *Maverick Rabbi*, p. 28.

33. Mordecai M. Kaplan Diaries, July 2, 1955.

34. Hertzberg, "Changing American Rabbinate," p. 29.

35. Quoted in Lookstein, "God Owes Me Nothing," p. 44.

36. *The Jewish Communal Register of New York City* (New York, 1918), pp. 1187–88.

37. Lookstein, "God Owes Me Nothing," p. 43.

38. Mordecai M. Kaplan Diaries, September 17, 1950.

39. Rabbis M. S. Margolies, "The Union of Orthodox Rabbis of the United States and Canada," in *Jewish Communal Register*, p. 1180.

40. Mordecai M. Kaplan Diaries, October 29, 1914.

41. Margolies, "Union of Orthodox Rabbis," p. 1180.

42. The classic account of Rabbi Jacob Joseph's encounter with America can be found in Abraham Karp, "New York Chooses a Chief Rabbi," *American Jewish Historical Society Quarterly* 64 (March 1955): 129–98.

43. Irving Howe, *World of Our Fathers* (New York, 1976), p. 194.

44. *New York Times*, August 26, 1936, p. 21.

45. S. N. Behrman, "Daughter of the Ramaz," in *The Worcester Account* (New York, 1946), p. 105.

46. Robert A. Woods, *Americans in Progress: A Settlement Study* (Boston, 1902), p. 276. See also Aaron Pinkney, "Pioneer Congregations of the North End," *Boston Jewish Advocate*, April 14, 1949, p. 9B.

47. Behrman, "Daughter," p. 108.

48. Ibid., p. 103.

49. Ibid., p. 123; interviews with Rabbi Haskel Lookstein and Mrs. Gertrude Lookstein.

50. Quoted in *New York Times*, August 27, 1936, p. 21; Joseph H. Lookstein, "Rabbi Moses Zebulun Margolies—High Priest of Kehilath Jeshurun," in *Congregation Kehilath Jeshurun, Diamond Jubilee Yearbook, 1946*, pp. 48–51.

51. Behrman, "Daughter," p. 106.

52. Mordecai M. Kaplan, "The Influences that Have Shaped My Life," *The Reconstructionist* 8, no. 10 (June 26, 1942): 30; *HS*, January 12, 1906, p. 9.

53. Quoted in Aaron Rakeffet-Rothkoff, *The Silver Era: Rabbi Eliezer Silver and His Generation* (New York, 1981), pp. 106–107.

54. Kaplan, "Influences," p. 30.

55. Lookstein, "God Owes Me Nothing," p. 257.

56. Joseph H. Lookstein, "Seventy-Five Yesteryears," in *KJ Diamond Jubilee Yearbook*, p. 29.

57. Lookstein, "God Owes Me Nothing," p. 38; interview with Mrs. Sylvia Shatzman, December 9, 1982.

58. Lookstein, "God Owes Me Nothing," p. 45.

59. Interview with Rabbi Lookstein conducted by Professor Elmer Offenbacher, 1975.

60. Interview with Rabbi Haskel Lookstein, July 6, 1987.

61. Roundtable Discussion with KJ Congregants, November 10, 1987.

62. Joseph H. Lookstein, "Problems of the Orthodox Rabbinate," typescript, n.d., p. 3, KJ Archives.

63. Interviews with Rabbi Haskel Lookstein, August 4, 1981; Mrs. Gertrude Lookstein, May 26, 1981, and August 17, 1987; Roundtable Discussion.

64. Offenbacher interview.

65. Roundtable Discussion; interview with Rabbi Haskel Lookstein, June 2, 1982.
66. Roundtable Discussion.
67. Interview with Mrs. Lillian Leifert, April 29, 1982.
68. Interviews with Rabbi Haskel Lookstein, August 4, 1981; Mrs. Gertrude Lookstein, May 26, 1981; Dr. Nathalie L. Friedman, September 18, 1981; Rabbi Herschel Schacter, June 10, 1983; Roundtable Discussion.
69. The slightly more senior Goldsteins also enjoyed such gatherings. The latter, confided Mrs. Goldstein in her diary, "are working very well." Quoted in Reichel, *Maverick Rabbi*, p. 59.
70. Interview with Mrs. Sadie Wohl and Mrs. Selma Roeder, September 1, 1987; interview with Mr. Jack Weiler, June 30, 1981.
71. Interview with Rabbi Jack Bieler, July 27, 1982.
72. Interview with Rabbi Shlomo Riskin, October 16, 1981; Lookstein, "Problems," pp. 11–12.
73. Lookstein, "Problems," p. 13.
74. Interview with Mrs. Lillian Leifert.
75. Cited in Introduction to Jung, *The Path*, p. xii.
76. Interview with Rabbi Leo Jung, February 3, 1987.
77. Interview with Rabbi Shubert Spiro, October 21, 1987.
78. Jung, *The Path*, p. 126.
79. Leo Jung, *What is Orthodox Judaism?* (New York, 1929), p. 7.
80. Jung, *The Path*, p. 126.
81. Ibid., p. 48. See also "Verbatim Report of Annual Meeting," The Jewish Center, May 10, 1923, pp. 9–17, Jewish Center Archives.
82. Jung, *The Path*, p. 52. Interviews with Mrs. Judith Gottesman Friedman, December 30, 1987; Mr. and Mrs. Clarence Horwitz, January 15, 1987; Nechama and Maurice Courland, August 25, 1986.
83. Quoted in Jung, *The Path*, p. xiii.
84. See, for example, "Verbatim Report," pp. 14–15.
85. Interview with Mrs. Samuel Kramer, December 25, 1986. Sermon topics were culled from back issues of the *Jewish Center Bulletin*.
86. Quoted in *The Path*, p. ix.
87. Ibid., p. 77; interview with Rabbi Jung, February 3, 1987.
88. Jung, *The Path*, p. 85; interview with Jung; interview with Judith Friedman.
89. Quoted in Jung, *The Path*, p. x.
90. Joseph H. Lookstein quoted in *KJ Diamond Jubilee Yearbook*, p. 29.
91. Mordecai M. Kaplan Diaries, October 25, 1914. It was no wonder, then, that KJ decided, in an inventive compromise, to appoint Kaplan as its "minister" until he received a traditional European *smicha*. At that time, he would be accorded the title of rabbi. See Kaplan, "Influences," p. 30.
92. Quoted in *KJ Diamond Jubilee Yearbook*, p. 28. (My emphasis.)
93. Lookstein, "God Owes Me Nothing," p. 256.
94. Hertzberg, "Changing American Rabbinate," p. 19.
95. Mordecai M. Kaplan Diaries, October 25, 1914.
96. Margolies, "Union of Orthodox Rabbis," p. 1183; Uri Miller, "The Orthodox Rabbinate: Burden and Challenge," *Jewish Life* 14, no. 1 (October 1946): 39–42; see also Max Etra, "The Rabbi and the Layman," *Jewish Life* 20, no. 1 (September/October 1952): 52–55.
97. Mordecai M. Kaplan Diaries, October 3, 1918.
98. Lookstein, "God Owes Me Nothing," p. 259.
99. Ibid., p. 257.
100. Etra, "Rabbi and the Layman," p. 54.

101. Mordecai M. Kaplan Diaries, April 10, 1915.

102. Ibid., August 29, 1917.

103. Ibid., April 27, 1918.

104. Ibid., May 11, 1921.

105. Ibid., March 3, 1918.

106. Ibid., July 28, 1919.

107. Ibid., January 7, 1919.

108. Ibid., May 9, 1921.

109. Ibid., May 6, 1921.

110. Ibid., May 11, 1921.

111. Ibid., May 9, 1921.

112. Ibid., May 16, 1921.

113. Ibid., May 27, 1921.

114. Ibid.

115. Ibid., September 21, 1921; interview with Mr. Clarence Horwitz, January 15, 1987.

116. Mordecai M. Kaplan Diaries, January 17, 1922. Interestingly enough, in commenting on the history of the Center prior to his becoming its rabbi, Jung attributed the ongoing tension between Kaplan and the board to the latter's inability to understand the young rabbi. "The founders and trustees of the Center," Jung writes, "were not adept enough in the English language and the heavy style in which Dr. Kaplan indulged, to apprehend the real tendency of his direction." Jung, *The Path*, p. 75.

117. Introduction to *Proceedings of the Seventh Annual Convention of the Rabbinical Council of America* (1942), p. 3.

118. Goldstein, *Forty Years*, p. 35.

119. For a full history of the RCA, see Louis Bernstein, *Challenge and Mission: The Emergence of the English-Speaking Rabbinate* (New York, 1982) Morris Max, "When Orthodox Rabbis Meet," *Jewish Life* 14, no. 5 (June 1947): 27–33.

120. Samuel Belkin, "Orthodox Judaism in America," in *Proceedings, Seventh Annual Convention*, p. 11.

121. Rabbi Mendel Lewittes, "Principle and Practice in American Orthodoxy," *OU* 12, no. 6, October 1944, p. 7; Rakeffet-Rothkoff, *Silver Era*, chap. 4.

122. Bernstein, *Challenge and Mission*, pp. 16–23.

123. Ibid., p. 20.

124. Aaron Lichtenstein, "Rabbi Joseph Soloveitchik," in *Great Jewish Thinkers of the Twentieth Century*, ed. Simon Noveck (Clinton, Mass., 1963); Gurock, "Resisters and Accommodators," pp. 144–46.

125. Gurock, "Resisters and Accommodators," p. 145; interview with Rabbi Moshe Morduchowitz, November 8, 1988.

126. Lewittes, "Principle and Practice," p. 7.

127. Lookstein, "Problems," p. 5.

128. Harold Gastwirt, *Fraud, Corruption and Holiness: The Controversy over the Supervision of the Jewish Dietary Practice in New York* (Port Washington, 1974); Bernstein, *Challenge and Mission*, chap. 4.

129. Bernstein, *Challenge and Mission*, p. 94.

130. Ibid., p. 100.

131. Rakeffet-Rothkoff, *Silver Era*, p. 145.

132. Today there are several rival and competing organizations—the OK Laboratories, the *KUF KAY*—each of which is patterned after the OU system. A reflection of the competing ritual requirements among the Orthodox of the postwar era, the existence of these communal forms of Kashruth supervision also attests to the proliferation in available kosher food products.

133. Interview with Rabbis Herschel Schacter, June 10, 1983, and Shubert Spiro, October 21, 1987.

134. Schacter interview.

135. The following section is derived from Marshall Sklare's classic work on the phenomenon, *Conservative Judaism: An American Religious Movement*, 2d ed. (New York, 1972). For a reevaluation of this volume some twenty years after its publication in 1955, see "A Reexamination of a Classic Work in American Jewish History: Marshall Sklare's *Conservative Judaism* Thirty Years Later," *American Jewish History* 74, no. 2 (December 1984), especially Jenna Weissman Joselit, "Modern Orthodox Jews and the Ordeal of Civility," pp. 133–42.

136. Sklare, *Conservative Judaism*, p. 256.

137. Ibid., p. 208.

138. *Proceedings of the Rabbinical Assembly* (1950), vol. 14, pp. 112–35; (1951), vol. 15, pp. 106–12.

139. Asher Siev, "The Distortion of Conservative Judaism," *Jewish Life* 14, no. 2 (December 1946): 20.

140. See, for example, Morris Max, "The 'Traditional' Prayerbook that Violates Tradition," *Jewish Life* 15, no. 3 (February 1948): 30–36; Morris Max, "Mixed Pews," *Jewish Life* 17, no. 1 (October 1949): 16–24; Victor Geller, "Basement Ghettos," *Jewish Life* 19, no. 1 (September–October 1951): 34–36.

141. "Letters to the Editor," *Jewish Life* 16, no. 1 (October 1948): 70. (My emphasis.)

142. Jeffrey Gurock, *The Men and Women of Yeshiva* (New York, 1988), chap. 7.

143. Max Routtenberg quoted in Sklare, *Conservative Judaism*, p. 263. See also Abraham Karp, "The Conservative Rabbi—'Dissatisfied But Not Unhappy,'" *American Jewish Archives* 35, no. 2 (November 1983): 188–262.

144. Quoted in *Proceedings of the Twelfth Annual Convention of the RCA* (1948), p. 7; Isaac Trainin, "Address Before the RCA," in *Proceedings of the Twelfth Annual Convention*, pp. 42–45.

145. Charles Liebman, "Orthodoxy in American Jewish Life," in *Aspects of the Religious Behavior of American Jews* (New York, 1974), p. 157; William Helmreich, *The World of the Yeshiva: An Intimate Portrait of Orthodox Jewry* (New York, 1982).

146. George Kranzler, *Williamsburg: A Jewish Community in Transition* (New York, 1961), p. 103; interview with Rabbi Moshe Morduchowitz.

147. Interviews with Rabbis Engelberg, Schacter, Spiro, Riskin.

148. Riskin interview; personal communication with Dr. Jeffrey Gurock.

149. Norman Lamm, "Modern Orthodoxy's Identity Crisis," *Jewish Life* 36, no. 5 (May–June 1969): 8. See also Shlomo Riskin, "Where Modern Orthodoxy Is At—And Where It Is Going," *Jewish Life* (Spring 1976): 27–31.

150. Riskin interview.

4. THE JEWISH PRIESTESS AND RITUAL

1. Emil Hirsch, "The Modern Jewess," *The American Jewess* 1, no. 1 (April 1895): 11; Betty F. Goldstein, "The Women's Branch of the UOJCA," in *The Jewish Library*, Third Series (New York, 1934), p. 108.

2. See, for example, "Save the Sabbath," *The American Jewess* 7, no. 2 (May 1898): 97.

3. David Philipson, "Woman and the Congregation," in *Proceedings, National Federation of Temple Sisterhoods* (1913), p. 22.

4. Irene Wolff, "The Jewish Woman in the Home, in *The Jewish Library*, pp. 100, 103.

5. See, for example, Betty Greenberg and Althea O. Silverman, *The Jewish Home Beautiful* (New York, 1941), p. 17; David Philipson, "The Ideal Jewess," *The American Jewess* 4, no. 6 (March 1897): 257; David Goldberg, "Woman's Part in Religion's Decline," *JF* 4, no. 4 (May 1921): 871.

6. Wolff, "The Jewish Woman," pp. 93–94.

7. Mathilde (Mrs. Solomon) Schechter, "Aims and Ideals of the Women's League," typescript address, May 1918, pp. 1, 4, Women's League Archives.

8. Goldberg, "Woman's Part in Religion's Decline," p. 874.

9. Wolff, "The Jewish Woman," p. 103.

10. Mrs. Abram Simon, "The President's Message," in *Proceedings of the National Federation of Temple Sisterhoods* (1915), p. 46.

11. Joseph Leiser, *American Judaism* (New York, 1925), p. 180.

12. Ibid., pp. 179, 198.

13. Ibid., p. 198.

14. Mrs. Stella Freiberg, "Report of the President," in *Proceedings of the National Federation of Temple Sisterhoods*, January 4, 1924, p. 14.

15. Jenna Weissman Joselit, "The Special Sphere of the Middle-Class American Jewish Woman: The Synagogue Sisterhood, 1890–1940," in *The American Synagogue: A Sanctuary Transformed*, ed. Jack Wertheimer (New York, 1987), pp. 206–30.

16. *AH*, January 6, 1928; Leiser, *American Judaism*, p. 191.

17. Leiser, *American Judaism*, p. 193.

18. Joseph H. Lookstein, "The Jewish Woman," *OU* 2, no. 11 (August 1935): 3.

19. See, for example, Joseph H. Lookstein, "A New Deal for the Forgotten Jewish Woman," *OU* 5, no. 7 (April–May 1938): 2.

20. Ibid.

21. Mrs. Herbert S. Goldstein, "A Rosh Hashonah Message," *OU* 3, no. 1 (September 1935): 2. See also Mrs. Moses Hyamson, "The Rabbi's Wife," *JF* 8, no. 10 (December 1925): 584.

22. Goldstein, "Rosh Hashonah Message," p. 2.

23. *KJ Bulletin*, October 28, 1938; Minutes of the Jewish Center, May 10, 1923, p. 2, Jewish Center Archives; "New Features in Sabbath Services," *KJ Bulletin*, November 18, 1938; "Mrs. Freedman Again Heads Women's Branch of UOJCA," *OU* 12, no. 2 (December 1944): 24; Ina Israelite, "The Woman and Her Part in Young Israel," *JF* 9, no. 10 (December 1926): 547.

24. Barbara Welter, "The Feminization of American Religion: 1800–1860," in *Clio's Consciousness Raised*, ed. Mary Hartman and Lois Banner (New York, 1973), p. 138; Richard Stiels, "The Feminization of American Congregationalism, 1730–1835," *American Quarterly* 33, no. 1 (Spring 1981): 52.

25. Chava Weissler, "Issues in the Study of Women's Religion: An Eighteenth-Century Example," paper, 1986. Quoted with permission of the author.

26. The presence of a significant number of attentive, well-clad and eager women worshipers occasioned considerable comment. Somewhat tongue in cheek, Israel Zangwill allegedly remarked that "when women in the gallery were admitted to the main floor of the synagogue, the men disappeared from the services," while another observer, somewhat less humorously, noted that women were the most frequent and "enthusiastic" of worshipers. While this may have been the case in Reform and Conservative circles, where the men often worked on the Sabbath, the proportion of women in the Orthodox sanctuary never exceeded that of the men. At KJ, for example, it has been estimated that during the forties, women worshipers numbered approximately 100 and male worshipers 150. (Israel Zangwill quoted in *Proceedings of the First Convention of the National Federa-*

tion of Temple Sisterhoods [1913], p. 27.) See also Alter Landesman, "Synagogue Attendance: A Statistical Survey," *Proceedings of the Rabbinical Assembly* (1928), vol. 2, p. 50; Benjamin Kline Hunnicutt, "The Jewish Sabbath Movement in the Early 20th Century," *American Jewish History* 69, no. 2 (December 1979): 196–215; Rabbi Lookstein's handwritten comments on the Sabbath service, KJ Archives; interview with Rabbi Haskel Lookstein, August 4, 1981.

27. Lookstein, "The Jewish Woman."

28. Interview with Mrs. Gertrude Engelberg, December 21, 1986.

29. Interviews with Mrs. Gertrude Lookstein and Dr. Nathalie Friedman, August 17, 1987.

30. Interview with Mrs. Elizabeth Gilbert, August 18, 1987.

31. Interview with Mrs. Gertrude Lookstein, August 17, 1987. In virtually every interview conducted with modern Orthodox women of this period, the importance of dressing up for services was stressed.

32. Interviews with Mrs. Sylvia Kramer, December 25, 1986; Mrs. Sadie Wohl and Mrs. Selma Roeder, September 1, 1987.

33. Ray Stannard Baker, *The Spiritual Unrest* (New York, 1909), p. 115.

34. Sarah Schack, "O'Leary's Shul—and Others," *Menorah Journal* 16, no. 5 (May 1929): 463.

35. Ibid., p. 464.

36. Jonathan Sarna, "The Debate over Mixed Seating in the American Synagogue," in Wertheimer, *American Synagogue*, p. 369.

37. Personal communication with Rabbi Jacob J. Schacter, September 7, 1987.

38. "Solutions and Resolutions," *OU* 1, no. 8 (April 1934): 2.

39. Rabbi Norman Lamm, "Separate Pews in the Synagogue: A Social and Psychological Approach," in *The Sanctity of the Synagogue*, ed. Baruch Litvin (New York, 1962), p. 323.

40. Ibid., p. 318. See also Morris Max, "Mixed Pews," *OU* 17, no. 1 (October 1949): 16–24.

41. *KJ Bulletin*, November 18, 1938.

42. In fact, women congregants were often among the first to protest the introduction of a new prayer book. Even if they did not fully understand every prayer or interpolation, women worshipers were accustomed to the text and knew their way around it. The introduction of a new and different version of the *siddur* confused and dislocated them; the comfort of the familiar, even if somewhat outdated, was much preferred.

43. David de Sola Pool, "Congregational Singing," *HS*, November 18, 1910, p. 1.

44. Ibid. See also Israel Goldfarb, "Congregational Singing," *United Synagogue Recorder* 1, no. 1 (January 1921): 12, 13.

45. De Sola Pool, "Congregational Singing," p. 1.

46. *Reform Advocate* 13, no. 1 (February)1897: 17, and 13, no. 4 (March 1897): 60.

47. *KJ Yearbook*, 1945, p. 12.

48. *KJ Yearbook*, 1948–49, n.p.

49. Quoted in Joselit, "Special Sphere," p. 211.

50. Material in this section is derived from interviews with former Women's Branch presidents, most notably Mrs. Elizabeth Gilbert, and from the *Orthodox Union*, which carried news of the organization's activities. See especially Selma Freedman, "The Women's Branch—Twenty-five Years of Achievement," *Jewish Life* 15, no. 5 (June 1948): 51–56; and Goldstein, "The Women's Branch," pp. 107–11.

51. "The Efficient Sisterhood," Women's Page, *OU* 12, no. 4 (April 1945): 12; Stella Burstein, *Manual for Sisterhoods* (New York, 1947).

52. Burstein, *Manual*, p. 19.

53. "Women's Branch Calls for the Study of Jewish History," *OU* 3, no. 8 (May 1936): 7.

54. Ibid.

55. Mrs. Herbert S. Goldstein, "The Jewish Woman—A Force for Jewishness," *JF* 8, no. 10 (December 1925): 571–73. On the religious nature of pre–World War II sisterhoods, see Joselit, "Special Sphere," passim.

56. "UOJCA Publications," *Jewish Life* 21, no. 1 (September/October 1953): 85.

57. Goldstein, "The Jewish Woman," p. 572.

58. *OU* 12, no. 2 (December 1944): 17.

59. Eva Schechter, *Symbols and Ceremonies of the Jewish Home* (New York, 1930).

60. Interview with Mrs. Elizabeth Gilbert.

61. Beatrice S. Genn, "The Religious Training of the Adolescent Girl," *JF* 9, no. 10 (December 1926): 543. See also "The Wall of Difference," *JF* 8, no. 5 (June 1925): 234, in which Bernard Revel was taken to task for failing to provide Jewish education for American-born Orthodox girls.

62. Lookstein, "A New Deal," p. 2.

63. Ibid.

64. "Hebrew Teachers Training School for Girls," *OU* 1, no. 2 (September 1933): 6; "The American Orthodox Scene: Torah-Training for Women," *OU* 4, no. 9 (June 1937): 3; interviews with Mrs. Elizabeth Gilbert and Mrs. Gertrude Lookstein.

65. Lookstein, "A New Deal"; "Mrs. Freedman," p. 24.

66. Wolff, "The Jewish Woman," p. 100.

67. "Women's Branch Holds Successful Convention," Women's Page, *OU* 5, no. 8 (June 1938): 12.

68. Greenberg and Silverman, *Jewish Home Beautiful*, pp. 40–41. An extremely popular guide to Jewish observance, as well as a compilation of recipes, *The Jewish Home Beautiful*, in its own words, "offered a few suggestions . . . [to] inspire Jewish women to a deeper search of their own treasure house." It attempted to wean middle-class Jewish women away from "the attractive settings offered by our large department stores and women's magazines for Valentine's Day, Halloween, Christmas and other non-Jewish festive days" (p. 14) and direct them toward the richness of Jewish tradition.

69. Deborah Melamed, *The Three Pillars of Wisdom: A Book for Jewish Women* (New York, 1927), p. 40. See also "Yes, I Keep Kosher," *Jewish Life* 21, no. 1 (September/October 1953): 85.

70. Melamed, *Three Pillars*, p. 39.

71. "Cookery, *Jewish Encyclopedia*, 1903, p. 254.

72. Greenberg and Silverman, *Jewish Home Beautiful*, p. 13.

73. Morris Freedman, "Orthodox Sweets for Heterodox New York: The Story of Barton's," *Commentary*, May 1952, p. 478.

74. The *Orthodox Union* inaugurated a "Kashruth Column" in August 1933 to respond to inquiries of this sort. See, for example, *OU* 1, no. 1 (August 1933): 5; 1, no. 6 (January/February 1934): 7; 2, no. 5 (March 1935): 4; 4, no. 3 (December 1936): 7.

75. *OU* 3, no. 11 (July/August 1936): 7. (My emphasis.)

76. *OU* 1, no. 3 (October 1933): 7.

77. *JF* 10, no. 3 (March 1927): 167. The advertisements of kosher caterers can be found in the pages of the *Orthodox Union* and in synagogue bulletins like that of Manhattan's Jewish Center.

78. "The Social Life of the Orthodox Jew," *JF* 10, no. 12 (December 1927): 596. See also advertisement for "Gottlieb's Kosher Restaurant—Eating Place of Refinement," *OU* 3, no. 3 (November 1935): 4.

79. The following section is derived from an examination of dozens of kosher cookbooks, some of them printed publications and others informal, mimeographed texts, and

from personal communications with anthropologist and folklorist Barbara Kirshenblatt-Gimblett. For a survey of the Jewish cookbook as a literary genre, see Barbara Kirshen-blatt-Gimblett, "The Kosher Gourmet in the Nineteenth-Century Kitchen: Three Jewish Cookbooks in Historical Perspective," *Journal of Gastronomy* 2, no. 4 (1986/7): 51–89, and Barbara Kirshenblatt-Gimblett, "Jewish Charity Cookbooks in the United States and Canada: A Bibliography of 201 Recent Publications," *Jewish Folklore and Ethnology Review* 9, no. 1 (1987): 13–18.

80. One of the most popular and representative kosher cookbooks was Florence K. Greenbaum's *Jewish Cookbook* (New York, 1918). By the time of its twelfth printing in 1938, it was said to have sold more than 100,000 copies. Interestingly enough, the publishers of this volume touted the author's scientific credentials as a way of highlighting the modernity of the dietary laws. Mrs. Greenbaum, Bloch Publishers noted in a "Publisher's Note" to the 1931 edition, "is a household efficiency woman, an expert Jewish cook and thoroughly understands the scientific combining of foods."

81. Greenberg and Silverman, *Jewish Home Beautiful*, p. 88.

82. Ibid., p. 72.

83. Ibid., p. 40.

84. Goldstein, "The Jewish Woman," p. 571.

85. Interviews with Mrs. Elizabeth Gilbert and Mrs. Sylvia Kramer. See also Gella Block, "Passover Meals—For Today," *Jewish Life* 17, no. 4 (April 1950): 65–79.

86. Full-page advertisement in the *Orthodox Union* 3, no. 4 (December 1935). See also, "Dinner Celebrates Endorsement of Loft Candies," *OU* 3, no. 5 (January 1936): 2.

87. "Dinner Celebrates."

88. "Kashruth Directory," *OU* 4, no. 10 (July/August 1937): 10; *OU* 3, no. 3 (November 1935): last page.

89. Henry Keller, "Mizrachism—The Cornerstone of Zionism," in *Mizrachi, Jubilee Publication of the Mizrachi Organization of America (1911–36)*, ed. Pinchos Churgin and Leon Gellman (New York, 1936), p. 11.

90. "Presidential Message at Convention Delivered by Acting President Mrs. Jesse Ginsberg," *Mizrachi Women's News* 5, no. 2 (Convention Issue 1937): 4.

91. See, for example, *Mizrachi Women's News* 5, no. 1 (Spring 1937): 1.

92. "Mrs. Simcha Rabinowitz: Excerpts from an Address," *The Mizrachi Woman* 20, no. 2 (December 1947): 4.

93. Rabbi Manuel Laderman, "American Orthodoxy and Mizrachi," in Churgin and Gellman, *Jubilee Volume*, p. 28.

94. Mrs. Abraham Shapiro, "Message to the Mizrachi Woman," *Mizrachi Women's News* 4, no. 2 (Fall 1936): 2.

95. "Our President, Mrs. Abraham Shapiro, Brought Greetings to Hadassah's Recent Convention in Atlantic City," *Mizrachi Women's News* 5, no. 4 (Fall 1937): 2.

96. Laderman, "American Orthodoxy," p. 28.

97. Quoted in *Mizrachi Women's News* 5, no. 1 (Spring 1937): 1.

98. Benjamin Koenigsberg, "The Newest Mikvah in New York City," *OU* 8, no. 4 (March/April 1941): 16.

99. Quoted in Lis Harris, *Holy Days: The World of a Hasidic Family* (New York, 1985), p. 113.

100. Quoted in Mrs. Moses Hyamson, "Ritual Baths," *JF*, January 1, 1927, p. 23.

101. Quoted in *Sefer Ha-Yovel Shel Agudat Ha-Rabbanim Ha-Orthodoksim De-Artzot Ha-Brit Ve-Canada* (New York, 1928), in section entitled "Agudat ha-Rabbanim and Taharas Hamispocha."

102. Rabbi Morris Max, "Taharas Hamispocha: Organization and Maintenance," *OU* 11, no. 1 (October 1943): 6.

103. "Committee on Traditional Observances," *Proceedings, Seventh Annual Conven-*

tion of the Rabbinical Council of America (1942), p. 60; see also Eleazar M. Preil, *A hantbukh far der yidishe froy* (New York, 1920), Introduction.

104. Hyamson, "Ritual Baths," p. 23.

105. Interviews with Rabbi Jung, January 11 and February 3, 1987, and with Jewish Center congregants, including Mrs. Irma Horowitz, Judy Gottesman Friedman, January 15, 1987, and December 30, 1987. Though prenuptial meetings with the rabbi were common enough, explicit discussions of the family-purity laws were not. For some Orthodox rabbis, mikvah was "not a big issue." Interview with Rabbi Haskel Lookstein, July 8, 1987.

106. Interviews with Mrs. Irma Horwitz, Mrs. Gertrude Engelberg.

107. One of the most enduring of mikvah manuals was compiled by Sidney B. Hoenig and entitled *Jewish Family Life: The Duty of the Woman*. First published in New York in 1942, the text went through eleven editions, the most recent of which was published in 1969. Other examples of this genre include: Hyman E. Goldin, *The Jewish Woman and Her Home* (New York, 1941); Harris Lazarus, *The Ways of Her Household: A Practical Handbook for Jewish Women on Traditional Customs and Observances* (London, 1923); Deborah Melamed, *The Three Pillars*, pp. 37–38; The Rabbinical Alliance of America, *A Marriage Guide for Jewish Women: Especially Prepared for the American Jewish Woman* (New York, 1953); Rabbi Morris Max and the Rabbinical Council of America, "The Jewish Concept of Marriage," ca. 1940; and Eleazar M. Preil, *Hantbukh*.

108. Preil, *Hantbukh*, p. 5.

109. Hoenig, *Jewish Family Life*, 1942 ed., p. 39. The Preil guidebook similarly addressed itself to this apparently common practice and contained an entire section, "A bath is not a mikvah," on this point. See Preil, *Hantbukh*, pp. 13–19.

110. Hoenig, *Jewish Family Life*, 1942 ed., pp. 92–93.

111. Hoenig, 1969 ed., p. 18. See also "Five Reasons Why Every Jewish Woman Should Adhere to Taharas Hamispocha," *OU* 9, no. 2 (November/December 1941): 13; Hyamson, "Ritual Baths," p. 24.

112. Hoenig, *Jewish Family Life*, 1969 ed., p. 29.

113. See, for example, "Scientific Views on the Laws of Menstruation," in Hoenig, *Jewish Family Life*, 1942 ed., and pp. 20–22 in the 1969 edition; Preil, *Hantbukh*, pp. 15–16. Jacob Smithline, *Scientific Aspects of Sexual Hygiene: The Bath of Immersion (Mikvah)* (New York, 1930) was the most commonly quoted authority for this view. Popular folk wisdom, or in this case, wives' tales, espoused a similar view. Sexual abstinence, interviewees regularly informed me, was "good for the body," or, as one woman put it, "the family-purity laws enabled the organs of the body to rest."

114. Melamed, *Three Pillars*, p. 37.

115. Hoenig, *Jewish Family Life*, 1969 ed., p. 27.

116. Koenigsberg, "Newest Mikvah," p. 16.

117. Rabbi Leo Jung, *The Path of a Pioneer: The Autobiography of Leo Jung* (London and New York, 1980), pp. 48–49.

118. H. F. J. Porter, "The Menace of the Bathing Pool," *Survey* 28, no. 17 (July 27, 1912): 588–89.

119. Ibid., p. 588; W. A. Manheimer, "Mikveh Baths of New York City," *Survey* 32, no. 3 (April 18, 1914): 77; Wallace A. Manheimer, "The Sanitary Condition of Mikvehs and Turkish Baths," in *Collected Studies*, vol. 9, Bureau of Laboratories, New York City Department of Health, 1916–19, pp. 407–15.

120. "Sanctioned Mikvah Bath Owners Organize," *Survey* 34, no. 22 (August 28, 1915): 482.

121. Builders of the modern ritual bath consciously used the term "model mikvah" to invoke comparisons between it and "model homes." Koenigsberg, "Newest Mikvah," p. 16; advertisement in the *Morgen Zhurnal*, May 30, 1941; Hyamson, "Ritual Baths," p. 24.

Though the wholesale construction of "model mikvahs" began in earnest on the eve of World War II, evidence of a similar consciousness can be found as early as 1910. Thus, the *Hebrew Standard* in September of that year carried a tiny ad for a Harlem mikvah that was reputedly "first class in every detail." A month later a slightly reworked advertisement for the same facility appeared: "Kosher Mickwah (plunge) with all modern improvements." *HS*, September 2, 1910, p. 9; October 21, 1910, p. 13. I would like to thank Shulamith Berger for directing me to these advertisements.

For years, the Harlem mikvah remained the most modern of New York's ritual baths, but by the end of the 1930s it had become, as several former users recalled, "somewhat unpleasant." Interviews with Mrs. Gertrude Engelberg, Mrs. Irma Horwitz.

122. Koenigsberg, "Newest Mikvah."

123. Abba Hillel Silver quoted in Jung, *The Path*, p. 50.

124. Interview with Mr. Raphael Courland, August 25, 1986; "Certificate of Occupancy," 311 East Broadway, May 15, 1941, No. 27677, New York City Department of Housing and Buildings, New York City Municipal Archives.

125. Advertisement in the *Morgen Zhurnal*; Hoenig, *Jewish Family Life*, 1969 ed., pp. 36–37.

126. Koenigsberg, "Newest Mikvah," p. 16; "Orthodox Women Stimulate Religion," *OU* 2, no. 7 (April 1935): 8.

127. Max, "Taharas Hamispocha," p. 7; Hoenig, *Jewish Family Life*, p. 19; Koenigsberg, "Newest Mikvah," p. 16; *Jewish Center Bulletin*, November 15, 1940.

128. Quoted in Hoenig, *Jewish Family Life*, 1942 ed., p. 39.

129. Max, "Taharas Hamispocha," p. 7; Koenigsberg, "Newest Mikvah," p. 16.

130. Koenigsberg, ibid., (My emphasis.)

131. Interviews with Mrs. Gertrude Engelberg and Mrs. Irma Horwitz.

132. Max, "Taharas Hamispocha," p. 6.

133. Hyamson, "Ritual Baths," pp. 23–24.

134. Leiser, *American Judaism*, p. 178.

5. "THE SCHOOL OF TODAY AND TOMORROW"

1. Harold U. Ribalow, "My Child Goes to Jewish Parochial School: A Parent's Report Card," *Commentary*, January 1954, pp. 64, 67.

2. Joseph Kaminetsky, "The Yeshiva Ketanah," *Jewish Life* 15, no. 4 (April 1948); Jacob Hartstein, "Jewish Community Elementary Parochial Schools," *Jewish Education* 9, no. 3 (October–December 1937); Ribalow, "My Child," p. 67.

3. *OU* 12, no. 3 (February 1945): 4.

4. Samuel Hurwitz, "Orthodox Judaism in American Life," *Hebrew Union College Monthly* 4, no. 3 (December 1917): 86.

5. Samson Benderly quoted in Alexander Dushkin, *Jewish Education in New York City* (New York, 1918), p. 138.

6. Isaac Berkson, *Theories of Americanization: A Critical Study* (New York, 1920), p. 103.

7. Alexander Dushkin, "The Next Decade of Jewish Education in New York City," *Jewish Education* 12, no. 2 (September 1940): 71.

8. *Judisches Tageblatt*, February 24, 1908.

9. Dushkin, *Jewish Education*, pp. 156–59; Uriah Z. Engelman, "The Strength of Hebrew in America," *The Menorah Journal* 16, no. 3 (March 1929): 233; Dushkin, "Next Decade," p. 71.

10. Robert Gordis, "Jewish Education in New York City—Its Chaos and A Possible Remedy," *The Menorah Journal* 17, no. 2 (November 1929): 133.

11. Samson Benderly, "The Present Status of Jewish Religious Education in New York City," *Jewish Communal Register* (New York, 1918), p. 350.

12. Dushkin, *Jewish Education*, p. 168.

13. Benderly, "The Present Status," p. 351. In an earlier report on the same subject, Benderly had made the point that talmud torah students were apt to pick up germs from the lamentable physical conditions of most talmud torahs. Having spent a long day in public school, students arrived at the Hebrew school physically spent: "the power of resistance being then greatly reduced, we must avoid every chance of infection." S. Benderly, "Aims and Activities of the Bureau of Education of the Jewish Community (Kehillah) of New York," 1912, Publication no. 5, p. 96. In 1915 the New York City Department of Health, acting on a complaint about the "objectionable conditions" in many local Hebrew schools, looked into the matter, and in a subsequent study excoriated the environment characteristic of most talmud torahs. Noting the potential for the "aerial transmission of diseases," the study went on to record that the hygienic state of the toilets was such that they "would not bear very favorable comparison with the Southern school privy, against which sanitarians hold up their hands in horror." "Health Conditions in Certain Private Schools," *Annual Report, The New York City Department of Health* (1915), pp. 128–29.

14. Meyer Waxman, "American Orthodoxy—The Fifth Unknowable," *JF* 7, no. 10 (October 1924): 656.

15. Quoted in Samuel Joseph, "Israel Konovitz: Pioneer Jewish Educator in America," unpublished manuscript, p. 4.

16. Transcript of interview with George Jacobs, ca. 1986, Ramaz Oral History Project, p. 2.

17. Joseph H. Lookstein quoted in KJ Minutes, December 11, 1947.

18. Jacob H. Rubin, "Report of the Talmud Torah Committee," March 2, 1921, p. 1, CJI Archives.

19. Irving Howe, *World of Our Fathers* (New York, 1976), p. 201.

20. Dushkin, *Jewish Education*, p. 103.

21. Isaac Rosengarten, "Order Out of Chaos in Jewish Education," *JF* 3, no. 9 (November 1920): 520.

22. Ben Rosen, "Survey of Jewish Education in New York City," *Jewish Education* 1, no. 2 (May 1929): 85.

23. See, for example, *American Israelite*, January 24, 1924; "The Wall of Difference," *JF* 8, no. 5 (June 1925): 233–35.

24. Dushkin, *Jewish Education*, pp. 137–38.

25. Jacob Goldberg, "Health Problems of Children in Yeshivahs," *JF* 7, no. 12 (December 1924): 770–74, especially p. 774.

26. Rosengarten, "Order," p. 522; transcript of interview with Mrs. Hortense Kobrin, 1986, p. 4, Ramaz Oral History Project.

27. Report of the President, "Meeting of the Board of Directors, CJI," February 24, 1918, CJI Archives.

28. On the history of the Uptown Talmud Torah, see Jeffrey Gurock, *When Harlem Was Jewish, 1870–1930* (New York, 1979), pp. 103–109; Herbert S. Goldstein, ed., *Forty Years of Struggle for a Principle: The Biography of Harry Fischel* (New York, 1928), chaps. 17 and 18. See especially p. 93.

29. Mordecai M. Kaplan Diaries, August 14, 1918; see also July 14, 1944, for Kaplan's personal eulogy of the Jewish educator.

30. Harry Fischel quoted in Gurock, *When Harlem Was Jewish*, p. 109.

31. Louis Marshall quoted in "Report of the President," CJI, November 12, 1925, p. 2, CJI Archives; "The CJI," *HS*, May 26, 1916, p. 8.

32. Built in 1903 as the religious school of Congregation Kehilath Jeshurun, the facility later became an autonomous community-wide institution known first as the Yorkville Talmud Torah and then, in 1916, as the Central Jewish Institute. Though many KJ congregants served on its board, there were no formal ties between the synagogue and the school. On the early years of the CJI, see Joseph Epstein, "The Early History of the CJI: The Emergence of a Jewish Community School Center" (Master's Thesis, Yeshiva University, 1978).

33. "Report of the President, Jacob H. Rubin," Meeting of the Board of Directors, CJI, February 24, 1918, p. 1, CJI Archives; "Report of the Talmud Torah Committee," March 2, 1921, p. 3., CJI Archives.

34. Transcript of Stenographic Minutes of the Board of Directors Meeting, October 30, 1924, p. 12; December 4, 1924, p. 3, CJI Archives.

35. Alexander Dushkin, *Living Bridges: Memoirs of an Educator* (Jerusalem, 1975), p. 12.

36. Engelman, "The Strength of Hebrew," p. 237.

37. Benderly, "Aims and Activities of the Bureau of Education," pp. 102–106, especially p. 105.

38. It has even been suggested that to Dr. Benderly goes the credit for the earliest Hebrew typewriter. According to Rebecca A. Brickner, Benderly "devised the first Hebrew typewriter, and the Remington Co. had it made up for him. I believe it was the first Hebrew typewriter in the world. With it, we began to publish our own textbooks." Rebecca A. Brickner, "As I Remember Dr. Benderly," *Jewish Education* 20, no. 3 (Summer 1949): 57.

39. Israel Friedlander quoted in Arthur Goren, *New York Jews and The Quest for Community* (New York, 1970), p. 114.

40. Rabbi Jacob Levinson, "On the Twenty-Fifth Anniversary of the Teachers Institute," *The Teachers Institute of Yeshiva College, Twenty-Fifth Anniversary* (New York, 1944), p. 100.

41. Alexander Dushkin, "Two Decades of Progress in Jewish Education—A Survey," *Jewish Education* 4, no. 1 (January–March 1932): p. 3.

42. Joseph Lookstein quoted in KJ Minutes, April 25, 1944.

43. "Let Us Talk It Out," *Jewish Education* 6, no. 1 (January–March 1934): 4. See also *Jewish Education* 20, no. 3 (Summer 1949), for reminiscences of the former Benderly boys, as well as Isidor Margolis, *Jewish Training Schools in the United States* (New York, 1964).

44. Benderly, "Aims and Activities," p. 102.

45. Ibid.

46. Israel Chipkin, "The Jewish Teacher in New York City and the Remuneration for his Services," *Jewish Education* 2, no. 3 (October 1930): 166. See also Freda Fine, "The Place of Women in Jewish Education," *JF* 13, no. 2 (February 1930): 45–48.

47. Midge Decter, "The Fruits of Modern Jewish Education," *Commentary*, October 1951, p. 326.

48. Ibid., p. 327.

49. Interview with Mrs. Elizabeth Isaacs Gilbert, August 18, 1987.

50. *OU* 3, no. 8 (May 1936): 8; "Hebrew Teachers Training School for Girls," *OU* 1, no. 2 (September 1933): 6; interviews with Mrs. Elizabeth Isaacs Gilbert and Mrs. Gertrude Lookstein, August 17, 1987.

51. Though not without engendering some amount of controversy within non-Orthodox educational circles. Kaplan relates in his diary that several members of the Jewish Board of License held a meeting in April 1943 to protest that board's decision to grant

automatic licenses to the graduates of the Hebrew Teachers Training School; the pro-
testers felt that the school's standards were far too low. See Mordecai M. Kaplan Diaries,
April 22, 1943.

52. Herzliah Hebrew Academy, *Educational Survey, 1921–1941*, (New York, 1942), p. 4.

53. "The American Orthodox Scene: Torah-Training for Women," *OU* 4, no. 9 (June 1937): 3.

54. Transcript of Stenographic Minutes of Board of Directors Meeting, March 6, 1927, p. 2, CJI Archives; Report of the Talmud Torah Committee, March 2, 1921, January 7, 1926, CJI Archives.

55. Transcript of Stenographic Minutes of Board of Directors Meeting, November 8, 1923, p. 5, CJI Archives.

56. Quoted in Goren, *New York Jews*, p. 128.

57. Ibid., p. 131.

58. Ibid., p. 132.

59. Text of letter quoted in Goldstein, *Forty Years of Struggle*, p. 110.

60. Dushkin, *Living Bridges*, p. 12.

61. Mordecai M. Kaplan Diaries, June 18, 1952.

62. Barry Chazan, "Education in the Synagogue: The Transformation of the Supplementary School," in *The American Synagogue: A Sanctuary Transformed* ed. Jack Wertheimer (Cambridge, Eng., 1987) pp. 170–84. To some Jewish educators, the congregational school was cause for great alarm. A "retrogressive step," it threatened to de-professionalize their status and to lower educational standards. Jacob S. Golub, "Transition in Jewish Education," *Jewish Education* 3, no. 2 (April–June 1931): 67–68. For others, housing the afternoon Hebrew school in the quarters of the modernized synagogue was an encouraging sign. See Gordis, "Jewish Education in New York City," pp. 136–37.

63. Gordis, "Jewish Education in New York City," p. 136. On the history of the American Jewish day school, see Alvin Schiff, *The Jewish Day School in America* (New York, 1966).

64. Joseph H. Lookstein, "The Modern American Yeshivah," reprint of an article in the "Symposium on the Jewish Day School," *Jewish Education* 16, no. 3 (May 1945): 2.
The Brooklyn Jewish Center School was perhaps the most notable exception to the prevailing Orthodoxy of the modern day schools formed during this period. "The single spirit dominating the school," writes Deborah Dash Moore, "was Hebraic and Zionist, rather than Judaic." Deborah Dash Moore, "A Synagogue Center Grows in Brooklyn," in Wertheimer, *American Synagogue*, p. 317.

65. Joseph H. Lookstein, "God Owes Me Nothing," typescript, p. 68; interviews with Mrs. Gertrude Lookstein, May 26, 1981, and Rabbi Haskel Lookstein, June 2, 1982.

66. Fannie Neumann, "A Modern Jewish Experimental School—In Quest of A Synthesis," *Jewish Education* 4, no. 1 (January–March 1932): 26–27.

67. Ibid., p. 26. See also Elaine Pohl Moore, "An Answer to Jewish Apathy: Thirty Years of the Yeshivah of Flatbush," *JF* 40, no. 2 (February 1957): 18–24.

68. Lookstein, "God Owes Me Nothing," p. 56.

69. The formation of Yeshiva College in 1928 provides further proof that the notion of a modern Jewish parochial school system, from kindergarten on through college, was "in the air." The establishment of a liberal arts college under the aegis of Bernard Revel was enthusiastically received, hailed as "the forerunner of a healthy Judaism walking hand in hand with a sound Americanism. A new era," commented the *JF* excitedly, "has begun ... " "A New Era in American Jewish Life," *JF* 11, no. 5 (May 1928): 237–38.

70. Joseph H. Lookstein to Jonah Wise, March 21, 1947, KJ Archives.

71. Neumann, "Modern Jewish Experimental School," p. 26.

72. Lookstein, "God Owes Me Nothing," p. 85.

73. Neumann, "Modern Jewish Experimental School," p. 34.

74. Ibid., p. 35.

75. "A Model School for the American Jewish Child," *AH*, September 6, 1940, p. 14.

76. Naomi W. Cohen, *American Jews and the Zionist Idea* (New York, 1975), pp. 11, 32–33.

77. "Vision in Zionist Ranks," *JF* 23, no. 4 (May 1940): 72.

78. See, for example, Philip Raskin, "Palestine As I Saw It: Impressions of Present Jewish Life in the Land of Israel," *JF* 8, nos. 5–10 (June–December 1925); Samuel Tenenbaum, "The New Woman in Palestine," *JF* 13, no. 1 (January 1930): 24–27; Harris Pine, "The Palestinian Song," *JF* 18, no. 2 (February 1935): 25–26; "The 'New' Agreement in Zionist Ranks," *JF* 18, no. 10 (November 1935): 241.

79. Jessie E. Sampter, *A Course in Zionism* (New York, 1915), p. 67.

80. Meyer Waxman, *The Mizrachi: Its Aims and Purposes* (New York, 1917); Samuel Rosenblatt, *The Mizrachi Movement: Its Philosophy, Achievements and Prospects* (New York, 1940); Hyman Grinstein, "History of the Teachers Institute of Yeshiva University," in *Samuel Belkin Memorial Volume* (in Hebrew), ed. Moshe Carmilly and Hayim Leaf (New York, 1981), pp. 257–64; Joseph H. Lookstein to Zacharia M. Kirstein, October 14, 1942, Ramaz School Archives.

81. See, for example, Joseph Heimowitz, "A Study of the Graduates of the Yeshivah of Flatbush High School" (Master's thesis, Yeshiva University, 1979).

82. Dushkin, *Jewish Education*, p. 331. See also Bernard Revel, "Jewish Education," *JF* 9, no. 1 (March 1926): 9–10, in which the dean of American Jewish educators maintained that the day school was appropriate for a small group of specially chosen children, or what was elsewhere dubbed "the saving remnant." " 'Hofjuden' and Jewish Education," *JF* 7, no. 2 (February 1924): 75.

83. Lookstein, "God Owes Me Nothing," p. 58.

84. Milton Himmelfarb, "Reflections on the Jewish Day School," *Commentary*, July 1960, p. 31.

85. Lookstein, "The Modern American Yeshivah," p. 2; "Character of the Institution," Petition to the Board of Regents, The Ramaz School, December 1947, p. 4, KJ Archives; Neumann, "Modern Jewish Experimental School," passim; Elaine Pohl Moore, "An Answer," p. 18.

86. *JF* 3, no. 10 (December 1920): 582. When pressed, a few advocates of the Jewish school drew parallels between their institution and the American Catholic parochial-school system, hoping the latter would legitimate the former. Hardly the quintessential American institution misguided Jewish day-school advocates made it out to be, the Catholic school was ultimately dropped as a model. "The designation parochial," Lookstein related, "was also abhorrent to me. It was a borrowed name; it was alien to the Jewish tradition; and it was used pejoratively, never flatteringly." Lookstein, "God Owes Me Nothing," p. 59.

87. Lookstein, "God Owes Me Nothing," p. 59.

88. "The Significance of the Jewish Center," typescript, p. 3, *Jewish Center Archives*.

89. Kobrin interview, p. 4.

90. Lookstein, "God Owes Me Nothing," p. 59.

91. Interview with Mrs. Irma Horwitz, January 15, 1987.

92. See, for example, "Education Number," *JF* 9, no. 1 (March 1926): 4–6.

93. Ibid.

94. "Harvard, Yale, Princeton Accept Ramazites," *The Ramaz Mirror* 1, no. 6 (June 22, 1951): 1.

95. Lookstein, "God Owes Me Nothing," p. 61. Fortunately for the historian, the very self-consciousness of Ramaz's founder about the novelty of his school has led to the preservation of a substantial body of material, thus allowing Ramaz's early years to be

reconstructed. This material can be found both at the Ramaz School and in the archives of Congregation Kehilath Jeshurun.

96. Joseph H. Lookstein, "The Ramaz Academy—Our Newest Venture," *Journal of the KJ "Dinner Dance,"* December 12, 1937, p. 4.

97. Transcript of interview with Mr. Max Etra, 1986, p. 1, Ramaz Oral History Project.

98. KJ Minutes, January 20, 1944.

99. On the early years of the school, see KJ Minutes, September 22, 1937; January 5, 1938; March 7, 1940; May 9, 1940.

100. Joseph H. Lookstein, "A New Deal for the Forgotten Jewish Woman," *OU* 5, no. 7 (April–May 1938): 2.

101. Joseph H. Lookstein to S. Erdberg, June 8, 1937, p. 1, Ramaz School Archives.

102. Interview with Rabbi Haskel Lookstein, July 8, 1987.

103. "Dr. Rafsky Report," KJ Minutes, May 9, 1939, p. 1.

104. "Regents Petition," p. 6.

105. "A Model School for the American Jewish Child," p. 14.

106. Lookstein to Zacharia Kirstein, p. 1.

107. Joseph H. Lookstein to David Wertheim, October 19, 1945, p. 1, KJ Archives; "Report of the Advisory Committee on Instructional Matters," January 1944, Ramaz School Minutes.

108. Lookstein, "God Owes Me Nothing," p. 58.

109. Ibid., p. 59.

110. Lookstein, "The Modern American Yeshivah," p. 3.

111. "Regents Petition," pp. 6–7.

112. Ibid., p. 7.

113. "Principal's Report," October 12, 1950, p. 4, KJ Archives.

114. Ibid.

115. "Rafsky Report," p. 1.

116. Abraham G. Duker, "The Jewish All Day School," typescript draft, October 1949, p. 20, Ramaz School Archives.

117. "Rafsky Report," p. 1.

118. Joseph H. Lookstein to Nat Holman, March 23, 1950, KJ Archives.

119. Transcript of interview with Rabbi Haskel Lookstein, 1986, p. 20, Ramaz Oral History Project. Interestingly enough, female high school students studied Gemara through their sophomore year, after which it was replaced by courses in typing and cooking.

120. "Memorandum from Rabbi Lookstein to Mr. Rosenblum Re: Building Mainte-nance," February 20, 1950, KJ Archives.

121. "Regents Petition," pp. 11–12.

122. "A Picture Feature—Ramaz: School of Today and Tomorrow," *Jewish Life* 15, no. 2 (December 1947): 29–34.

123. Saul J. Lance, "A Layman's Evaluation of Ramaz School," *Kehilath Jeshurun Year Book*, 1951–52, p. 31.

124. Transcript of interview with George Jacobs, p. 4. And yet, Lookstein worried, on occasion, that his school would develop into a "school of social snobs." To that end, scholarships were made available to approximately 20 percent of the student body. Lookstein to Erdberg, p. 2.

125. "The Ramaz Academy—Our Newest Venture," p. 4. The minutes of both KJ and the Ramaz School are replete with references to the upstanding caliber of the student body. See, for example, KJ Minutes, September 25, 1941.

126. "Principal's Report," 1950, p. 5.

127. Report of the Talmud Torah Committee, December 4, 1924, p. 1; transcript of

the Stenographic Minutes of the Board of Directors Meeting, December 4, 1924, p. 7, CJI Archives; interview with Professor Nathalie S. Friedman, September 18, 1981.

128. Interview with Mrs. Gertrude Lookstein, May 26, 1981.

129. Interview with Mrs. Lillian Leifert, February 16, 1982.

130. Joseph H. Lookstein, *Three Decades of Ramaz School: A Review and a Forecast* (New York, 1968), p. 22.

131. Waxman, *The Mizrachi*, p. 23.

132. Kobrin interview, p. 4.

133. Transcript of interview with Mrs. Gertrude Lookstein, 1986, p. 4, Ramaz Oral History Project.

134. Interview with Mrs. Gertrude Herlands Engelberg, December 21, 1986.

135. Lance, "Layman's Evaluation," p. 29.

136. Duker, "Jewish All Day School," p. 2.

137. Quoted in *Jewish Life* 23, no. 3 (January–February 1956): 3.

138. Horwitz interview; Joseph Kaminetsky, "Torah Umesorah: A Pioneering Educational Agency," *Jewish Education* 20, no. 2 (February 1949): 21–23.

139. "Too Much Experimentation," *OU* 12, no. 3 (February 1945): 4.

140. Mordecai M. Kaplan Diaries, October 21, 1956.

141. Emanuel Rackman, "From Synagogue to Yeshiva," *Commentary*, April 1956, p. 356.

6. POSTSCRIPT

1. *Hapardes*, January 1956, quoted in Israel Levinthal, *Point of View: An Analysis of American Judaism* (London and New York, 1958), p. 55.

2. Interview with Dr. Marvin Schick, August 17, 1981; Marvin Schick, "The New Style of American Orthodox Jewry," *Jewish Life* 34, no. 3 (January/February 1967): 29–36.

3. Charles Liebman, "Orthodoxy in American Jewish Life," in *Aspects of the Religious Behavior of American Jews* (New York, 1974), pp. 157–162; William Helmreich, *The World of the Yeshiva: An Intimate Portrait of America's Orthodox Jewry* (New York, 1982); Egon Mayer, *From Suburb to Shtetl: The Jews of Boro Park* (Philadelphia, 1979); Lis Harris, *Holy Days* (New York, 1986).

4. Quoted in George Kranzler, *Williamsburg: A Jewish Community in Transition* (New York, 1961), p. 219. A sociological study of Williamsburg, Kranzler's work was the first to document the changing nature of American Orthodoxy in the years following World War II.

5. Interview with Mrs. Elizabeth Gilbert, August 18, 1987; her view was corroborated by Rabbi Louis Engleberg and Mrs. Gertrude Herlands Engelberg, among others, in an interview on December 21, 1986. See also Joseph Weiss, "Why Wear A Yarmulke," *Jewish Life* 20, no. 4 (March/April 1953): 20–26.

6. Joseph H. Lookstein, "Talk Delivered before New York Board of Rabbis," typescript, ca. 1950, pp. 16–17, KJ Archives.

7. Norman Lamm, "Modern Orthodoxy's Identity Crisis," *Jewish Life* 36 no. 5 (May/June 1969): 5, 8.

8. Interview with Mr. Clarence Horwitz, January 15, 1987.

9. Interview with Mrs. Irma Horwitz, January 15, 1987: interview with Mrs. Gertrude Lookstein, August 17, 1987.

10. Interview with Rabbi Louis Engelberg, December 21, 1986; interview with Rabbi Herschel Schacter, June 10, 1983; interview with Rabbi Shubert Spiro, October 21, 1987.